Mary Chesnut

THE PUBLICATIONS OF THE
SOUTHERN TEXTS SOCIETY

Michael O'Brien, Editor

TWO NOVELS BY

Mary Chesnut

EDITED BY
Elisabeth Muhlenfeld

WITH AN INTRODUCTION BY
Elizabeth Hanson

UNIVERSITY PRESS OF VIRGINIA
Charlottesville and London

#4722499

The University Press of Virginia

First published 2002

1 3 5 7 9 8 6 4 2

LIBRARY OF CONGRESS CATALOGING-IN-PUBLICATION DATA

Chesnut, Mary Boykin Miller, 1823–1886.
[Captain and the colonel]
Two novels / by Mary Chesnut ; edited by Elisabeth Muhlenfeld,
with an introduction by Elizabeth Hanson.
p.   cm.—(The publications of the Southern Texts Society)
Includes bibliographical references
ISBN 0-8139-2058-2 (acid-free paper)
1. United States—History—Civil War, 1861–1865—Fiction.
2. Charleston (S.C.)—Fiction.   3. Mississippi—Fiction.
I. Muhlenfeld, Elisabeth, 1944– II. Chesnut, Mary Boykin Miller, 1823–1886.
Two years. III. Title. IV. Series.
PS1292. C59 C36 2002
813'.4—dc21
2001003 52

CONTENTS

ABBREVIATIONS

MBC   Mary Boykin Chesnut

MBC   Elisabeth Muhlenfeld, *Mary Boykin Chesnut: A Biography* (Baton Rouge: Louisiana State University Press, 1981)

MCCW   *Mary Chesnut's Civil War,* ed. C. Vann Woodward (New Haven: Yale University Press, 1981)

TPMC   *The Private Mary Chesnut: The Unpublished Civil War Diaries,* ed. C. Vann Woodward and Elisabeth Muhlenfeld (New York: Oxford University Press, 1984)

INTRODUCTION

The Fiction of Mary Boykin Chesnut

ELIZABETH HANSON

If the choice were given me to be a cat or a tiger, I should choose
the tiger life, if I died for it.

Mary Boykin Chesnut, *Two Years—or The Way We Lived Then*

Mary Boykin Chesnut (1823–86) created one of the nineteenth century's most significant texts about the Confederate South and the Civil War: her famous "diaries," the result of more than twenty-five years of quiet concentration and revision of her Civil War writings. An abridged version of the diaries was printed in 1905, but a complete edition was not available until the publication, nearly a century after her death, of C. Vann Woodward's magisterial *Mary Chesnut's Civil War*.[1] Almost unknown, because unpublished until now, are her novels, *The Captain and the Colonel* and *Two Years—or The Way We Lived Then*, two intensely autobiographical fictions that explore the world of women in the American South.

Mary Boykin Miller was born in 1823 into an elite antebellum South Carolina family, the daughter of governor and then United States senator Stephen Decatur Miller, who was a leader among those southerners who sought to nullify federal law in the 1830s.[2] Her childhood was marked by loss as well as privilege: her father died suddenly in 1838, when she was just fifteen. The family had moved back and forth between South Carolina and

This essay was written by Elizabeth Hanson before her early death from cancer in 1999 and is here published little changed. The idea of publishing Mary Chesnut's novels was, from the first, Elizabeth's project, which first drew me in as the editor of the Southern Texts Society, and then attracted the indispensable expertise of Elisabeth Muhlenfeld. During the mid-1990s many sunny conversations in Charleston, in gardens and in restaurants, refined the venture, which was sustained by Elizabeth's passion for Chesnut, especially that side of Chesnut which offered a meditation on the complicated experience of being a Southern woman. Now this introduction, by giving such marked evidence of her intelligence and acumen as a literary critic, must also serve as a posthumous tribute to Elizabeth as a scholar. —MICHAEL O'BRIEN

Mississippi, where Stephen Miller, like many of his contemporaries, had invested in new lands and slaves. Mary received an excellent education at Madame Talvande's School in Charleston, where she studied literature, history, French—she was occasionally taken for a native speaker—German, and rhetoric as well as the proper behavior and social skills required by "a society where the role of women was carefully delineated and women were, by both law and custom, dominated by men."[3] While there, she had met James Chesnut, the scion of one of the wealthiest plantation families in South Carolina, a lawyer and politician-to-be. The story of her schooldays and their courtship forms the essence of *Two Years.*

On 23 April 1840, at the age of seventeen, Chesnut married and moved to live with her husband's family on Mulberry Plantation near Camden, South Carolina. There she entered the complex world of marriage and morals that she would fictionalize in *The Captain and the Colonel.* Childless and bored, Chesnut would scrutinize Camden stolidity in her Civil War narrative journals.[4] Feeling trapped and useless, Chesnut came to perceive the paradoxes of her life. She was deeply loved by her husband, yet he was a notably cool and reserved man. She enjoyed freedom to pursue interests and friendships so long as her husband's comfort was not neglected. Still, the wide-ranging reading she had time for in the 1840s and '50s would prove a stimulus to creativity; her fiction reflects thorough familiarity with William Makepeace Thackeray especially, but also with Jane Austen, Alfred Lord Tennyson, Madame de Staël, Goethe, and Honoré de Balzac. She traveled, to Europe in 1845 and to spas in the North during the summers. Always among the South's brightest intellects, Chesnut shone in drawing rooms where ideas and politics were dissected and flirtations and gossip flourished.

The Civil War became the focus of her creative work. From late 1860, when James Chesnut became the first United States senator from the seceding states to resign his seat, until mid-1865, when the Chesnuts retired in poverty and despair to the family estate in South Carolina, she lived what would become the essential basis for most of her later writing. She was in Charleston when Fort Sumter was bombarded and in Montgomery when the Confederacy was established. She lived in Richmond for extended periods because James Chesnut was an aide-de-camp to Jefferson Davis, and here she became close to Varina Howell Davis, the President's wife. During these years, she kept diaries that episodically chronicled the birth, ambition, vicissitudes, and defeat of the Confederacy.[5] As Woodward and Elisabeth Muhlenfeld have documented, between 1875 and her death in 1886, Chesnut took the fragmentary raw material of these diaries, expanded it from memory and by invention, and rewrote it in the form of narrative journals, which she left as a mass of manuscripts.[6] But somewhat earlier, between about 1874 and 1877 (see the textual introduction to this volume for a chronology), she also wrote fiction, likewise unfinished.

Given the fame of *Mary Chesnut's Civil War,* significant previously unpublished material that reflects on or enhances our understanding of that book deserves our consideration. Both of her novels explore ideas relevant to the diaries and expand our knowledge of the characters and milieu Chesnut described there. For example, John Chesnut, James's nephew, twenty-four at the outbreak of the war, was a special favorite of his aunt; he figures in the narrative journals and is transformed into Dr. Charles Johannis ("Johnny") in *The Captain and the Colonel,* where he is a complex character whose masculine persona embodies the slave owner and Civil War survivor. In the same novel, characters reflect upon the meaning of war and emancipation much as in *Mary Chesnut's Civil War,* but from many differing angles of perception. Similarly, *Two Years* illuminates Chesnut's antebellum life. It contains, for example, not only self-portraits and a romance that recalls Chesnut's own with her husband, but also sketches of Charlestonians of the 1830s like Bishop John England, Madame Talvande, and the slaves who helped to run the school on Legare Street. Although many schoolgirls' diaries and commonplace books survive from this period, *Two Years* is one of the few extant autobiographical studies of a woman's education in the antebellum South.

Chesnut's novels bear comparison with pre–Civil War meditations on women in the South by writers such as Chesnut's friend from Madame Talvande's School, Susan Petigru King, as well as Augusta Jane Evans Wilson, Caroline Gilman, and Caroline Lee Hentz. She differs from postbellum southern writers like Elizabeth Alston Pringle, Grace King, Ellen Glasgow, and Kate Chopin in her lack of interest in local color tale-telling, however.[7] As with her northern contemporary, Emily Dickinson, the results of Chesnut's incessant creativity would go unpublished in her own lifetime. Chesnut also shares with Dickinson an experimental bent, a quest for language able to reflect a complex life within, a vastly sophisticated literary education, and an abiding and ironic ambivalence.

As a chronicler of war, Chesnut refined and then redefined its meaning for women who suffer its losses while savoring few of its triumphs. Her Civil War novel, *The Captain and the Colonel,* is a kind of novelistic war on the war, waged by means of women's responses to the suffering and chaos surrounding them.[8] A novel of considerable chronological scope, it spans the antebellum period, wartime, and Reconstruction. It follows the career of Joanna Hardhead, the daughter of a New York merchant whose death leaves her with little money. To escape the fate of becoming a governess, she cynically seizes a husband in Frank Effingham, a wealthy South Carolina planter "utterly weak-willed and . . . almost a caricature of those qualities in James Chesnut, Jr., which Mary both admired and was most annoyed by."[9] When at length Frank dies, he leaves her with three daughters, Margaret, Susan, and Emily, as well as control of the family fortune in land and slaves. A young neighboring planter, Charles (Johnny) Johannis, has long been in love with Emily, although she doesn't care for him: her feelings are attached to a friend of Johnny's, a Kentuckian named Robert Collingwood. Collingwood reciprocates Emily's love, but Mrs. Effingham autocratically forbids the match. Meanwhile, Margaret has also fallen in love with Collingwood; when she realizes that Collingwood prefers her sister, she takes revenge by waylaying a crucial letter between the lovers, making it appear that each has betrayed the other. In despair, Collingwood goes off to war, as does Johannis. Later the two men meet, quarrel about the women and the purloined letter, and fight a duel. The wounded Johnny is nursed by Margaret; they grow closer and are married when he has recovered. After the war, Margaret confesses her guilt in seeking to destroy the relationship between Emily and Collingwood, and Johnny grows coldly distant on learning of her treachery. Collingwood and Emily finally reunite and marry. By chance, the two couples sail on the same ship. Despairing at the fact she must face her guilt, Margaret attempts suicide and Collingwood rescues her. The novel ends with Johnny promising "to be a more understanding husband in the future."[10]

Two Years—or The Way We Lived Then is closer to a memoir and its plot is more linear than *The Captain and the Colonel.* Its autobiographical content is signaled by the fact that Chesnut's school and its inhabitants are described without fictional disguise and by its first-person narration. *Two Years* is also fragmentary, both because Chesnut had difficulty in sustaining narrative structures and because there are two chapters missing from the manuscripts. The novel that we have follows the central character, young Helen, from her dismay at her forced departure from her school in Charleston to her adventures with her family as they travel to Mississippi. Helen recovers her good humor and the novel becomes a treasure of tales about a young woman's experience in the wild west that was Mississippi in the 1830s. Eventually, Helen is allowed to return to her precious Charleston and resume her highly sophisticated schooling in Southern Ladyhood. The novel relates details of this schooling and of the relations among the young students, their teachers, and the slaves who care for them all. In Charleston, too, Helen resumes her relationship with her admirer—walking with him in the moonlight along the Battery had precipitated her exile to Mississippi in the first place. Finally, after her father's death, Helen marries her lover, and the novel closes with Helen's sense of excitement and anxiety at the beginning of her marriage.[11]

Chesnut's fiction evaluates notions of gender from a range of perspectives offered by her experience as a white woman of the planter class in the American South. *The Captain and the Colonel* explores the contrast between the secure if ambiguous southern women's world before the war and the chaotic, yet emotionally more clearly defined, experience of a widow and her three daughters during and after the war. Men, whether captains or colonels or merely gentlemen, are important objects of power, but women are much in control. *Two Years* examines the elegance and inadequacy of a young girl's education for marriage in antebellum Charleston and pioneer Mississippi. It opens with Helen's protest against being "dragged" away from school and courtship in Charleston: "I don't want to be buried in a Mississippi swamp." Even Helen's mother objects to her husband's decision to remove the young girl from Charleston, not because her daughter will be buried, but because "there are men every where" and they are "nicer in town" than any Helen is "likely to meet in the wilderness" (117). And "in town" Helen had the benefit of the "very beau ideal of a 'select school for young ladies'" where planters' daughters, like Helen, "were models of propriety in dress and in conduct" and, unlike Helen, "absolutely blameless in every respect" (167).

The most important lesson a southern woman learns is articulated on the first page of *Two Years:* "You will find," Helen's mother reminds her daughter, "this world does not arrange itself exactly to suit you" (112). Divided within and without, the heroines of Chesnut's novels marry men who claim to love them, but the questions raised by women's own inner struggles to know themselves remain unanswered. Chesnut articulates a paradoxical vision of a world of slavery and noblesse oblige, romance and manipulation, triumph and defeat, power and loss. A woman's life in that world is seen as a matter of choosing between bad and worse, between imperfect consciousness and moral complicity on the one hand and failure and self-abnegation on the other. Her journey was complicated by a fundamental paradox: The harder her head, the more power she attained. Yet the more power she held, the more she stood to lose. At the same time that our "Explainer General" (as Chesnut once self-mockingly called her authorial presence)[12] explicates this world, she also asks us to reject it. Offering versions and counter-versions of the role of "woman," Chesnut unpacks its meanings, interprets its value system, and explores its images. So what in other hands might be a story of completion and of stability through marriage becomes something quite different. Because Chesnut embodies herself in the novels, her interpretive effort defines and redefines her own identity. At the end of *Two Years,* "Helen Newtown" has ceased to be an individual. In the concluding wedding scene, she has become a type, "The Bride," whose story becomes one of interpretation and confusion, knowledge and bewilderment:

> Stranded [outside the house] the bride leaned upon the railing which surrounded this first landing. . . .
>
> The Bride left alone looked down, utterly without interest, subdued by the numbness, and deadness of mind and body which always overtook her at the supreme moments of her life. She seemed to hear a roar, as of the sound of many waters, and the echoes of faint far away cries; nearer and nearer they were coming.
>
> A man standing near the gay party below, caught sight of this slim figure in white; he gently pushed aside the crowd who were blocking the stair way.
>
> He sprang up three steps at a time.
>
> She saw him coming, as in a dream, for the sound was still in her ear of that far away voice on the Florida shore. She was calmly watching the white gloved hand, as at each upward bound it grasped the railing. (216)

Here the experience of the beginning of a marriage is conceived through a series of images of comprehension and incomprehension. The uncertainties of coming of age, of marriage, of knowledge, of "him coming" are reflected in the visionary moment of sounds and emotions that ends the fictional text. But the story itself has not ended, because the vision is chilling. The husband coming up the stairs is as much like Bram Stoker's Dracula as Jane Austen's Mr. Darcy. Reading the denouement, it is hard not to suspect that it will be followed by less radiant moments. The dream will end or transform itself. "The Bride" might become another Margaret, leaning over a ship's rail, looking at the sea, thinking about damage and death.

In such a vision of marriage, women become the tools of conflict. Duels, skirmishes, battles, machinations, feuds, arguments, triumphs, and defeats all mark the troop movements within the confines of the "Confederate Drawing Rooms" of Chesnut's text. Every relationship—between parents and their children, husbands and wives, lovers, siblings, friends, slaves and mistresses—becomes a battleground. Marriage, the most intimate and important of relationships, becomes the most impossible to harmonize. And the most fraught with danger, especially for women.

At times, it seems that the risks on the field of battle at the home are larger, the stakes higher, than at the front. Colonels outrank captains in these struggles, and potential mothers-in-law outrank everyone. The dynamics of gender operate within precisely such paradoxes. The worse the husband, the happier the wife—and vice versa. Margaret coerces her way into marriage by means of a letter as her mother had done before her. She then wins a wonderful husband who makes her so miserable that she attempts suicide. In this frightening pairing of a mother's and daughter's histories of manipulation, Chesnut demonstrates that women who win husbands through machination, as their mothers had done and instructed, ensure consequent lives of misery.

It is Margaret who explains how women in the South come to create such marriages for themselves, and how bad husbands manage to provide the most happiness for their wives. As a "consequence of [the] escapades" of their adulterous husbands, southern women come to regard such men "as a dark background to bring out" a woman's virtues: "in that light her beautiful life shines brightly. And she has had all this world can give. And means to have the best of Heaven too." What is the source of such power and happiness? "She does not look for the impossible" (103).

There is less bitterness in *Two Years,* and positive warmth in the chapters about Madame Talvande's school, yet the skepticism that informs *The Captain and the Colonel* persists. Chesnut was acutely conscious that the young girl of her memory and the old woman who held the pen of the narrator were not the same person, though they were related. This tension helps to explain the multiple narratives she conceived and articulated, the swarms of stories imagined by Chesnut's "self." The "I" of Chesnut's own mature voice, remembering her coming of age in the South, tells us, "I considered myself 'a grown up' young lady and a possible heroine" (113). She has Helen Newtown describe her own constant story-making in similar terms: "Some times I went in for love in a cottage; but that was before I had seen or lived in the three room log house on the plantation. Some times I left for Europe in a coach and six, where I had innumerable adventures with every body I had ever read of and equally thrilling ones, with purely imaginary characters. I rescued every body from suffering; and by my astounding sweetness and my persuasive tongue alone, I turned all wrong doers from their evil ways" (122). Caught up in her tales, Helen is brought to reality when she manages "to get into trouble, and to be disgraced in the eyes of all, by a good scolding" from her mother (113). So Chesnut topples Helen's image of herself as an astoundingly sweet heroine and reveals her to be simply a young girl in love with "Sydney Howard," the novel's version of James Chesnut, the Princeton graduate "studying Law" whom young Helen imagines standing beside her at the altar, "fumbling in his pocket for a wedding ring" (122). To the extent that the novel is a bildungsroman, our "possible heroine" Helen is educated through the task of deciphering the tales that surround her. In this way, in her latter-day form as narrator of *Two Years,*

Chesnut tried to make sense of the fictions of her life through the creation of the text she had before her and we have before us.

In *The Captain and the Colonel,* the most dominant character, Joanna Hardhead, also seeks to understand herself, initially via genealogy. She tells her future husband, Frank Effingham, "You did not know 'who we were.' You know you did not! Neither do I. But then I have been trying to find out." Joanna's family cannot provide knowledge of a genuine, stable identity, a history: "Papa knows less than I do." Indeed, Joanna's father suggests to her that "if we tell any story . . . we must invent it" (4). This both clarifies and undermines the relation between the invention of identity and the invention of selfhood. To some extent, individual identity, for Chesnut, is a function of the expression of power, some of which is social and material. Even as Frank affirms Joanna's power, despite her uncertain identity, he asserts his own power; he knows *his* "real history." He is Francis Effingham, Esquire, of Effhall, a man whose very name sounds out the consonants of a "First Family" of the South in Chesnut's satirical play on southern obsession with the power of lineage. She could, after all, afford not to take such anxieties too seriously: as a Boykin and a Chesnut, daughter of a governor and wife of a senator, she was connected to many powerful family lines in South Carolina and elsewhere.

In Chesnut's vision, identity is variously clung to and rejected, sought after and denied. The contingency of knowledge—"Nobody knows"—pervades *The Captain and the Colonel.* The novel's very structure depends upon constant shifts and divisions within character roles as well as abrupt alterations and disruptions in style and language. These shiftings point to the lack of clear lines of reconciliation and connection between human beings: "In a state of civil war one's ideas grow confused. Right and wrong seem to change places according to circumstances" (69). The story itself is not directed by some final goal or one central character; indeed, even Joanna, the "Regina" who queens over her world, fails utterly to control her private civil war. Rather, the text explores significant moments of recognition and confusion regarding all the "circumstances" of war within the family of women who, in the text, express Chesnut's vision of the South.

When Chesnut writes of the response of Joanna Effingham to the reality of war, the whole world of the South is embodied as it is doomed. Joanna describes "the strain on heart, mind, and body" of men's war and of women's pain (80). It is a military funeral that stimulates Joanna's epiphany, and in the text the language subtly shifts into hysterical gasps separated by dashes: "The hearse—and the music—and the empty saddle—I meet them every day, and supposed I was callous." Just as Joanna feels she "must be breaking down," the words of the text break down into fragments.

The structured reality of Joanna's speech ceases to express her meaning. "With a pale smile," Joanna regains a measure of control: "I did not grow hysterical." Yet the necessary lapse in control has generated insight: "I can understand now the women who do" (81).

Signaled in language and embodied in structure, disruption pervades the text. More questions are posed than answered. In part, Chesnut's narratives acquiesce in the notion of fixed, coherent structures, but at the very point of acquiescence, a discordant theme will be reinforced through fragmentary language and structural ruptures. Chesnut's thematic focus is on disruption itself. So it is no wonder that her texts, whether they explore the breakage inevitable during war or the self-disintegration demanded by a woman's education for marriage, replicate fragmentation on every level. Theme, character, language, narrative voice, and structure form an intricate demonstration of Chesnut's commitment to a fiction of disordered order.

Unlike the traditional nineteenth-century literary plot that moved progressively toward the resolution of conflict between the individual and the family or the social world, the structure and themes of Chesnut's vision make traditional resolutions impossible: "In this silly adventure—however—*one* cannot be a monster—a murderer or a suicide—and the *other* a martyr and a victim" (69). In the "Confederate Drawing Rooms" of Chesnut's fiction, Joanna Effingham insists that "the Christian religion ought to eliminate duelling," and her most intelligent daughter, Emily, adds, "And War" (68). But women's demands signify nothing. Within and without the drawing room are disorder and defeat, monsters, murderers, suicides, martyrs, and victims. This "silly adventure" called war renders all clarity, all knowledge, all order, meaningless.

So marriage becomes in Chesnut's vision a source of intense confusion and constant uncertainty. Marriage, the incessant object of all the female characters in *The Captain and the Colonel,* becomes more "impossible" than it usually is through the shifting patterns of triumph and defeat that the war creates, even after the surrender of the South. As Emily thinks, "In all that dreadful time I had hope—hope was my life. Now—why should I expect to be happy—who is?" And the narrator says, "All the weary grief and desolation she had witnessed in these latter days came surging up before her" (102). Why should a woman expect to be happy in her marriage? "Who is?"

There is no resolution. Instead there are only paradoxical changes in role for every character in the text. Whether monster or martyr, suicide or victim, murderer or hero, each character exists in the world of the novel as a variable. Even when characters think they know the answer—as Joanna so frequently believes before her epiphany—the plot reasserts itself to expose how traditional resolutions are impossible. At such a moment in the text, Chesnut has the voice of a character poignantly paraphrase Goethe, "There is something in the heart of man the devil himself can not satisfy" (78).

Chesnut certainly did not write fully formed conventional novels of southern manners and morals. Her fictions are far more interesting than that. Instead of resolving and fixing meanings by offering the "correct" interpretation of, for example, a woman's response to "the strain on heart, mind, and body" amid the trauma of war, Chesnut's novels pose more questions than they settle. Chesnut devises fictional narratives to explore women's official, even "callous," externally demanded facade and the ambiguities within the structured reality that enfolds them.

This is true of both her "fiction" and her "history," the narrative journals. In the latter, Chesnut designs dialogues to express the complexity of her creative perspective. As "two young women look over" the manuscript of what will become *Mary Chesnut's Civil War,* the authorial "self" responds. The young women inquire: "'Why do you write such contradictory statements? It is all contradiction and counterstatements.'" And the "self" answers, "'I write what I hear, not what I know.'"[13] Women's experience of war offers epistemological challenges to the "characters" in the text. Both text and characters are sources of meaning. And both are resistant to certainty: to write what one "hears" is not the same thing as writing what one "knows." For Chesnut, to create is to write what she hears, not what she knows, because knowledge itself is so tentative as to be almost meaningless. This narrative strategy, which is defined and redefined in the journals, is also part of the meaning of Chesnut's fiction.

It is no wonder, then, that Chesnut's fiction lacks a shaping unity—or even coherence, as Elisabeth Muhlenfeld has argued. With the publication of these novels, readers will be able to judge for themselves whether these characteristics are weaknesses. My own sense is that Chesnut saw but rejected the option of imposing a conventional structure on her fiction. Muhlenfeld has observed, for example, that at times Chesnut makes little or no effort to identify speakers when she is portraying general discussion.[14] Although this complicates the dialogue, these deluges of argument replicate the conflicts and confusions of the characters involved. The reader of *The Captain and The Colonel* is swept up within the characters' violence and chaos through Chesnut's experiments in dialogue.

The harrowing turmoil of gender and war helps to explain why Chesnut's fiction was unconventional. Literary experimentation drew her beyond social observation and ideology to a fictional form that located meaning in the levels of story, language, and the interpretive acts of both characters and her readers. But who is her audience? Who would listen to her side of things, to her story, to her South? As one of Joanna's daughters explains, "We continue to be on the wrong side of every thing. Mamma declaims to empty benches" (86). Chesnut herself has declaimed her fiction to empty benches for more than a century.

If her southern world was doomed at the outset of the Civil War and if she, like her fictional selves, "continues to be on the wrong side of everything," Chesnut comes, however, to make a triumph out of failure. Because of Chesnut, we begin to see how little we know about southern women's real experience of loss. Of one thing we can be certain: Chesnut herself broke away from the constraints of her culture to create texts incorporating real knowledge of her self and her society. They remain to teach us that we ignore lessons of paradox and texts of obscurity at our own peril.

NOTES

1. The first version was published as Isabella D. Martin and Myrta Lockett Avary, eds., *A Diary from Dixie, as Written by Mary Boykin Chesnut, Wife of James Chesnut, Jr., United States Senator from South Carolina, 1859–1861, and Afterward an Aide to Jefferson Davis and a Brigadier-General in the Confederate Army* (New York: D. Appleton, 1905). It was revised and extended in Ben Ames Williams, ed., *A Diary from Dixie by Mary Boykin Chesnut* (Boston: Houghton Mifflin, 1949). The modern era of Chesnut studies begins with C. Vann Woodward, ed., *Mary Chesnut's Civil War* (New Haven: Yale University Press, 1981).

2. The definitive life is Elisabeth Muhlenfeld, *Mary Boykin Chesnut: A Biography* (Baton Rouge: Louisiana State University Press, 1981).

3. *MBC*, 27.

4. I adopt the term used by Michael O'Brien, "The Flight Down the Middle Walk: Mary Chesnut and the Forms of Observance," in Anne Goodwyn Jones and Susan V. Donaldson, eds., *Haunted Bodies: Gender and Southern Texts* (Charlottesville: University Press of Virginia, 1997), who asks, "What do we call this book, these manuscripts, this jumble? . . . My own preference is, simply, to call it a narrative journal, which conflates her own terms" (111–12). O'Brien's conflation is based on a diary entry by MBC from 23 September 1863: "Bloomsbury. So this is no longer a journal but a narrative of all I cannot bear in mind which has occurred since August 1862" (*MCCW,* 425).

5. Published as C. Vann Woodward and Elisabeth Muhlenfeld, eds., *The Private Mary Chesnut: The Unpublished Civil War Diaries* (New York: Oxford University Press, 1984).

6. An account of the complicated history of the texts can be found in *MCCW,* xv–xxix; see also *MBC*, 7–9, 136–37, 158–59, 196, and Woodward's meditation on her literary experimentation in "Mary Chesnut in Search of Her Genre," *The Future of the Past* (New York: Oxford University Press, 1989), 250–62.

7. For recent scholarship, see Emily Toth, *Kate Chopin* (New York: William Morrow, 1990); Lynda S. Boren and Sara DeSaussure Davis, eds., *Kate Chopin Reconsidered: Beyond the Bayou* (Baton Rouge: Louisiana State University Press, 1992); Robert Bush, *Grace King: A Southern Destiny* (Baton Rouge: Louisiana State University Press, 1983); Dorothy Scura, ed., *Ellen Glasgow: New Perspectives* (Knoxville: University of Tennessee Press, 1995); Helen Taylor, *Gender, Race, and Region in the Writings of Grace King, Ruth McEnery Stuart, and Kate Chopin* (Baton Rouge: Louisiana State University Press, 1989). General perspectives are established

in Anne Goodwyn Jones, *Tomorrow Is Another Day: The Woman Writer in the South, 1859–1936* (Baton Rouge: Louisiana State University Press, 1981); Lucinda H. MacKethan, *Daughters of Time: Creating Woman's Voice in Southern Story* (Athens: University of Georgia Press, 1990); and Carol S. Manning, ed., *The Female Tradition in Southern Literature* (Urbana: University of Illinois Press, 1993). On sectionalism and gender, see Nina Silber, *The Romance of Reunion: Northerners and the South, 1865–1900* (Chapel Hill: University of North Carolina Press, 1993) and Catherine Clinton and Nina Silber, eds., *Divided Houses: Gender and the Civil War* (New York: Oxford University Press, 1992).

8. *MCCW,* 63, 377.

9. *MBC,* 143.

10. *MBC,* 148–49.

11. *MBC,* 172.

12. *MCCW,* 172.

13. *MCCW,* 740.

14. *MBC,* 197–98; see also Muhlenfeld, "Literary Elements in Mary Chesnut's Journal," in James B. Meriwether, ed., *South Carolina Women Writers* (Spartanburg, S.C.: Southern Studies Program, University of South Carolina, 1979), 245–61.

TEXTUAL INTRODUCTION

ELISABETH MUHLENFELD

When the Civil War ended, Mary Boykin Chesnut returned to Camden, South Carolina, with a treasure: twelve or more journals she had kept throughout the war, volumes that had accompanied their author throughout her many moves over the course of four years. Chesnut reread them in 1866, fully aware of the importance of the material she had amassed, but aware as well of the extent to which her journals were private documents, personal, exceedingly candid and at many points confusing in their brevity.[1] As the postwar years rolled by, and as she watched the publication of the first romanticized histories and memoirs of the war, she must have thought more than once of ways to prepare her own extensive diaries for publication. But she was distracted and absorbed by the poverty and dislocation of family members, by her husband James's political disenfranchisement and legal wranglings over his properties, by the day-to-day challenges of life in a war-torn country, and by her own loneliness. Much of the hard work of keeping her extended family fed, clothed, and educated fell to her, and so the Confederate journals were set aside for the next several years.

In 1873, Mary and James built a new home in Camden using the bricks from the outbuildings at Mulberry, the family seat. In the process of unpacking books and papers, Chesnut focused again on her private journals, and on the possibility of earning some money by writing. Her first efforts in this regard seem to have been attempts at translations of French tales, in hopes of selling them to the newspapers for a bit of extra income.[2] Shortly, however, she who was an inveterate lover of novels decided to try her hand at fiction.

This was not the first time she had thought of such a thing. She had written in an 1861 diary entry, "The scribbling mania is strong upon me—have an insane idea in my brain to write a *tale* for Dr. Gibbes's weekly literary paper."[3] And on New Year's Eve, 1863, she had amused herself by developing the story line for a novel about the war.

The last night of the old year, Gloria Mundi [Chesnut's landlady, identified elsewhere as a Mrs. Grundy] sent me a cup of strong, *good* coffee. I drank
two cups, and so I did not sleep a wink.

Like a fool I passed my whole life in review—and bitter memories mad-
dened me quite. Then came a happy thought. I mapped out a story of the war.
The plot came to hand, for it was true. Johnny is the hero—light dragoon and
heavy swell. I will call it F.F.'s [First Families], for it is F.F.'s both of South Carolina and Virginia. It is to be a war story, and the filling out of the skeleton is
the pleasantest way to put myself to sleep.[4]

In the mid-1870s, finally settled in the new house, in her "splendid library"
with its "bay window—filled with Confed tropheys [and] books,"[5] Mary
Chesnut completed drafts of at least three novels. The first, *The Captain and
the Colonel,* grown out of her midnight New Year's Eve musings more than
a decade before, constituted Chesnut's first sustained effort to use her Civil
War material.

THE TEXT OF *The Captain and the Colonel*
Copy-text for *The Captain and the Colonel* is a complete manuscript draft of
388 pages on deposit in the South Caroliniana Library.[6] Written in ink about
1874 or 1875 and revised in pencil, the copy-text is not a fair copy of a
single draft, but rather a patchwork consisting of at least four distinct levels of revision.

We cannot be certain of the exact order of the novel's composition. The
usual clues for determining such matters do not afford the editor much insight in this case. Chesnut did not use up one stock of paper before she
began another, for example, nor did she habitually number her pages as she
was writing, preferring instead to paginate only after she had finished revising a draft. Nevertheless, we can draw some conclusions about the general way in which she went about constructing *The Captain and the Colonel.*

When she began her first novel, Chesnut had been thinking about its
characters and plot for a decade, and she had the story line complete in her
mind. Evidence suggests she wrote an abbreviated or outline draft of the
entire novel, from which she could go back and fill in certain scenes and incidents. A few pages in the surviving manuscript appear to be portions of
this original draft. The first page of chapter 11, which introduces Mrs. Jefferson Davis's reception and the "military magpie" who speaks to Emily, for
example, is probably original, as is MS page 180 (page 57 of this edition)
which begins "Laudari a viro laudato" and describes Emily's shock at seeing
Collingwood. Other examples of original draft material include the first
few pages of chapter 12, informing the reader of the impending duel, and

the two letters at the novel's end. The opening of chapter 19 (from the second epigraph through "A case to disgrace any" in the second paragraph), which may be original, suggests that chapter 18 was at one time devoted to explaining a scandal involving Joanna's sister and brother-in-law, the Von Endens—an intriguing episode that frustrates the reader because it is alluded to only vaguely in the final draft

The manuscript seems to be, in the main, at least a second draft. Approximately the first third is heavily revised in pencil, full of cancellations and interlinear and marginal insertions. There are two points in the first five chapters where Chesnut has rewritten whole scenes and substituted them for their counterparts in the main draft: the scene at the end of chapter 2 in which Frank Effingham dies, and the conversation at the beginning of chapter 5 where Susan, Emily, Johnny, and Collingwood are waiting for Margaret and decide to row on the river. Penciled revisions for these two scenes had become so complicated that Chesnut decided to recopy them completely, but the new versions themselves contain many interlinear revisions.

In the last two-thirds of the novel, revisions are far less extensive, in part because Chesnut appears to have handled troublesome scenes as she had handled the two described above, by writing another version and patching it into the main draft. Most patches occur in scenes filled with dialogue: several pages of Johnny's confrontation with Collingwood at Varina Davis's reception, for example, and several from the scene between Emily and Johnny following the duel have been revised, recopied, and inserted into the main draft. This kind of wholesale patching has often been used to expand discussions about themes or events unrelated to the plot of the novel, but nevertheless of interest to Chesnut. In these additions, the author drew upon her Civil War journals. One such passage is Joanna's monologue in chapter 14 about young Paul and Lennox and the condition of wounded soldiers. The general discussions about slavery and the plight of newly freed slaves in chapters 15 and 16 also appear to have been thoroughly overhauled.

Several additions expand the portraits of individual blacks in the novel. These are usually humorous, stereotyped, and heavily reliant on dialect: Sambo's gossip in chapter 12 about the cause of the duel; Binky Anne's speech about "playing ladies and gentlemen and talking dictionary" in chapter 13, and the description in chapter 16 of Binky Anne's departure in her stolen finery. Still other additions—the comic story of Miss Emily Eyebright (chapter 15) and the recounting of a Yankee raid (chapter 16), which Chesnut based on a similar raid experienced by her sister Kate and her nieces Mary and Serena—concern the hardships suffered by whites after the war.

Having completed these revisions, Chesnut apparently put her novel aside for some time. When she returned to it she must have concluded that Emily had received less attention than the author intended, for a number of hastily scrawled revisions occur at the end of the novel concerning Emily's thoughts and feelings. If (as biographical evidence suggests) Chesnut had been rereading her war journals,[7] she may also have decided that the tone of the 1865 scenes in the novel was too comic to portray accurately the despair that she and so many other white southerners had felt at the end of the war. Accordingly, Chesnut now added the description of Blockington's funeral that closes chapter 17, and that ends with Joanna's statement, "It was too much for me. I cried like a baby" and Emily's reply, "Did you Mamma? . . . I stood there like stone."

The last two chapters have been rewritten in a tone that becomes, at times, bitter. Material in earlier drafts for which these last two chapters were now substituted must have referred to a number of incidents that no longer appear in the surviving draft, for the letters that end the novel allude to a trip Margaret has taken to New York, the birth and death of her baby, and Susan's departure for Europe—matters which are not mentioned in the surviving manuscript and which suggest that in Chesnut's original concept, Margaret's attempted suicide took place months after the events of chapter 19 rather than only a few days later.

Chesnut returned to *The Captain and the Colonel* once more several years later, when she decided to recopy the novel, changing the names of her central characters.[8] True to form, in the process of recopying she began to revise chapter 1 yet again. Of this new effort at revision, forty-four manuscript pages survive; parts of the last twelve have crumbled away. This new revision has a very different tone from the earlier work, far more formal and wordy (these forty-four pages cover the same materials as MS pages 1–19 of the main draft, corresponding to pages 1–8 of the edited text). In it, the author addresses the reader in the mildly cynical, worldly-wise way of much nineteenth-century fiction:

> As Mrs. Effmost is the Mother of our heroine, these are not unnecessary details; and it may not be amiss to trespass further on your time and patience, by giving even a slight sketch of the Parent Stock of Hardheads. In this day of faith in evolution, it may cast a stern light upon the characters whose fate we are about to record.

Joanna is "Mrs. Effmost" for two pages, and then becomes "Mrs. Effmore."

Because this draft fragment was obviously written at considerable remove from the main draft, because it represents only about 5 percent of the whole novel, and most importantly, because the tone of this latest draft is quite different from the main draft, it has not been incorporated into the edited text. Nevertheless, by studying selected passages from both versions we can see the ways in which the author might have polished *The Captain and the Colonel* (a title given to the novel as late as 1885)[9] had she completed this late rewrite. A comparison of the two opening passages will serve to suggest the extent to which the last version expands earlier material.

Copy-text	Late Revision
Mrs. Effingham, widow of Francis Effingham Esq. of Effhall, was before her marriage Miss Joanna Hardhead, the daughter of a wealthy merchant of New York.	In 1860 Mrs. Effmost ruled at Effhall—she may be said to have ruled there with a rod of Iron.
	She was the widow of Francis Effmost Esq. And had been a noted personage before her marriage in New York. There her father in his time was conspicuous, in a way—as one of the rich city's Merchant Princes.
Mr. Hardhead, when he found himself alone with two motherless daughters, had taken a sensible, business like view of the situation. He obtained a highly recommended English governess and when she had proved herself competent and judicious, he gave her carte blanche to secure the best masters the city afforded.	To go back to the time when Mr. Hardhead pere ~~had~~ found himself a desolate widower with two small children. He calmly surveyed his surroundings and took a business like view of this situation as he did of all others.
	He sought dilligently for a trust worthy governess—and he discovered such a person, who came with satisfactory recommendations.
	An English woman, who had seen better days, of course. For awhile he absolutely neglected his business, to keep a watchful eye upon this unknown inmates proceedings. He found her not only an accomplished woman, but a good one—and in her management of his children, judicious, kind and effective. So he put more power in her hands —ended by giving her carte blanche.

In all such narrative passages, the new version lacks the pith and compression of the earlier manuscript. Some of the dialogue passages in chapter 1 that had proved so troublesome for the author are straightened out considerably in the later version, but in the process she has lost the informal and realistic diction and rhythm of her characters' conversations.

It is unlikely that Chesnut completed any more of this last revision than has survived; she did not even go back over it to punctuate her dialogue clearly. More likely this was the task of a few afternoons several years after completion of the main draft, an experiment to see if the novel was worth reworking. The verdict seems to have been "no." The fact that Chesnut preserved the complete patched draft of *The Captain and the Colonel* with her papers suggests that she did not work further with it. She apparently made no provision for the novel at the time she entrusted her journal manuscripts to her friend Isabella Martin, who was to oversee their publication. No reference to her attempts at fiction appear in her extant correspondence of the late 1870s and 1880s.

Two incomplete drafts have survived of a second novel, *Two Years—or The Way We Lived Then,* also written in the mid-1870s.[10] Both are fairly late drafts, written close in time to one another, probably about 1877. The earlier of the two, entitled *Two Years of My Life,* was bound with brads by the author into six segments of varying numbers of pages. Unfortunately, only five of these sections survive: section 1 of 67 pages comprises chapters 1–3; section 3 of 79 pages, chapters 6–8; section 4 of 59 pages, chapters 9–10; section 5 of 61 pages, chapters 11 and 12; and section 6 of 85 pages, chapters 13–16.[11] Missing is section 2 of approximately 45 pages, comprising chapters 4 and 5.[12]

The later draft of the novel is entitled *Two Years—or The Way We Lived Then,* a title she adapted from an Anthony Trollope novel she had read in 1875.[13] Of this later draft, two sections survive: one of 46 pages numbered 1–50 (pages 44–47 are missing) corresponds to pages 1–30 of the earlier draft and comprises all of chapter 1 and part of chapter 2; the second segment of 89 pages intended to be numbered 267–359 corresponds to pages 200–263 of the earlier draft and comprises chapters 10 and 11.[14] Where the later draft exists (for chapter 1, part of chapter 2, chapters 10 and 11), it serves as copy-text; for the rest of the novel, copy-text is the earlier draft.

Like those of *The Captain and the Colonel,* the manuscript drafts of *Two Years* contain various stages and kinds of revision, but in general, the *Two Years* manuscripts are revised far less heavily than *The Captain and the Colonel.* Chesnut seems to have considered *Two Years,* like its predecessor, a private endeavor; no evidence exists that she regarded this second novel as any more worthy of publication than the first, at the point at which she set it aside. It was, nevertheless, an important exercise in writing and in dramatizing her experience, and as such it also served as apprentice work in preparation for the revision of her Civil War journals. About 1878, Ches-

nut laid aside *Two Years* and turned to work on another novel with the working title *Manassas,* of which only a few pages toward the end survive;[15] by
1881 she had abandoned all efforts to write fiction and concentrated on the
huge task of reworking the war journals.

We can tell far less about the composition of *Two Years* than about *The
Captain and the Colonel.* We know that both of the surviving drafts of *Two
Years* are late ones, for the earlier of the two contains a description of Miss
Stella's school in Camden, and a note on the verso of the cover page for one
section of manuscript reads, in part, "My sister when she read this MSS—
asked—Why not discribe Miss Stella's school also. That prepared us for the
hard lines at Madame Talvande. You see I have taken her advice."[16] Clearly,
then, the earliest draft or drafts of the novel, written before 1876 when
Chesnut's sister Kate died, did not contain any reference to Miss Stella. Although these early drafts may have been as riddled with revisions as those
of *The Captain and the Colonel,* the surviving *Two Years* drafts are neatly written, and show little evidence of the involved patching and reworking that
Chesnut's first novel had received.[17]

Both surviving drafts, the earlier one missing two chapters (MS-A) and
the later one that includes only chapters 1, 2, 10 and 11 (MS-B), provide
insight into Chesnut's revision practices, which she would soon exercise on
a grand scale to produce the book first published as *A Diary from Dixie,* and
that we have now come to know as *Mary Chesnut's Civil War.* For much of
chapter 1, the earlier version of *Two Years* contains extensive penciled revisions and additions which are then incorporated into Version B. The opening lines of chapter 1, for example, appear first in Version A, thus (angle
brackets indicate an insertion):

> —"Why am I to be dragged away when I want so much to stay? Why am I to
> be taken into the heart of a Mississippi swamp?" said I in a mournful <dis-
> contented> voice to my mother. (MS-A, 1)[18]

On the verso of the preceding page containing the chapter's epigraphs,
Chesnut then penciled a revision:

> Why am I to be buried alive in a Miss Swamp—Why drag me away—when I
> want so very much to stay? ~~Inquired a discon asked~~ a disconted voice was heard
> to say—

In the late manuscript, the passage reads:

> —"Why are you dragging me away? I don't want to be buried in a Mis-
> sissippi swamp. I do want so very much to stay <here>. (MS-B, 1)

For many passages in chapter 1, these three versions may be compared: early draft, penciled revision, late draft—a pattern Chesnut would later use in revising her Civil War journals, for which she made an interim draft in purple pencil of large portions—perhaps all—of *Mary Chesnut's Civil War.*

In several instances, the late draft of *Two Years* expands the earlier one without any intervening penciled revision. On the other hand, one sentence that occurs only in the earlier draft is interesting in light of the almost complete lack of description in *The Captain and the Colonel.* It follows Helen's mention of her dislike of the boring scenery, so unlike that pictured in Sir Walter Scott's "The Lady of the Lake": "To tell the truth I was given to skipping discriptive chapters in prose or verse" (MS-A, 22).

Chesnut has made a real improvement in the arrangement of her material in the later draft, particularly in chapters 10 and 11. In the earlier version, for example, the description of the different groups of girls at Madame Talvande's is broken up, with the daughters of Santo Domingo refugees and Sea Island planters mentioned early in chapter 10 and the portrait of girls of Huguenot and English descent ending chapter 11. In MS-B, all these descriptions are provided early in chapter 10. Chesnut's rearrangement in these two chapters has as its goal (and its effect) to place logical groups of subjects together.

MS-A	MS-B
St. Domingo refugees	St. Domingo refugees
Sea Island planters' daughters	Huguenots
The Misses Bannister	Essay on Boston [only in MS-B]
Madame in her dressing room	English girls
Madame in the school room	Sea Island planters' daughters
Madame's niece Heloise	The Misses Bannister
The Idle bench	Madame in her dressing room
The mantlepiece	Madame in the school room
Piece day	The Idle bench
Harriet who can't read	Madame's niece Heloise
[end of chapter 10]	The mantlepiece
Madame in the drawing room	Piece day
Monkey's history	Today's boarding schools
Today's boarding schools	Harriet who can't read
The first class	Essay on Charleston
The male teachers	[end of chapter 10]
Dancing	Madame in the drawing room
Dédé and servants	Monkey's history
The Bishop's turkeys	The first class

Maum Jute's midnight suppers

Illness, contraband books

Small and Earlies

Huguenots

English girls

Essay on Charleston

[end of chapter 11]

The male teachers

Dancing

Dédé and servants

The Bishop's turkeys

Maum Jute's midnight suppers

Illness, contraband books

Small and Earlies

[end of chapter 11]

Chesnut's ability to rearrange material proved valuable when she finally began a full-scale revision of her Civil War journals, where one can see this same pattern of consolidation and regrouping.

The earliest draft of *Two Years* (MS-A), the draft that is complete except for chapters 4 and 5, contains hundreds of revisions, some in black pencil, some in purple, and a few in red. Numerous interlinear and marginal revisions, usually of a trivial nature, are penciled in: "longed" becomes "sighed," "Horror and terror" becomes "horror and dismay," and so on. Even the last draft (MS-B) shows that Chesnut was still tinkering with her text when she put the novel aside.

These editions of *The Captain and the Colonel* and *Two Years—or The Way We Lived Then* represent publication of two rough and unpolished manuscripts rife with inconsistencies, confusions, and awkward patches; both were set aside by their author in favor of a far more important and promising project: rewriting the Civil War journals. Certainly, the techniques of revision Mary Chesnut developed in her fiction would prove to be essential to her Civil War journal material, finally allowing her to shape and expand those materials toward their full potential. Just as certainly, Chesnut never perfected the art of revision. She never finished her major work. In a letter to Varina Davis in 1883, she wrote, "How I wish you could read over—my journal—I have been two years over looking it—copying—leaving my self out. You must see it—before it goes to print—but that may not be just now. I mean the printing—for I must over haul it again—and again." At her death, she had not decided how to end the book, nor precisely how to begin it. She had not given it a title, and continued to play with wording every time she picked up the manuscript. Chesnut's conscious need to "overhaul" the journal "again and again" suggests that no amount of time would have sufficed to finish her novels, either. These editions, then, arrest on the printed page abandoned works-in-progress.

Chesnut's apprentice novels have been edited conservatively. Because the manuscripts reflect various stages of revision, and because their author's punctuation practices were erratic, emendations have been made when necessary to fit authorial revisions smoothly into the text, to make some sense of the original punctuation, and to correct the slips of the pen that most manuscripts contain. In the footnotes to these texts, the editor has commented on the most important inconsistencies as well as other matters of textual interest.

Chesnut's unceasing revisions give rise to inevitable problems. In many instances, she failed to fit changes smoothly into the text. Sometimes, a revision has been substituted for an original phrase or sentence without cancellation of all or part of the original. Often there is no indication where an interlined word or phrase should go. Not infrequently, she signals a change in sentence order by placing Arabic numerals over parts of the sentence or sentences she intends to rearrange. An early, and complicated, example of this kind appears as follows (angle brackets indicate insertions above the line):

> Then <2> Mr. Hardhead allowed ~~his mind~~<himself> once more to be ~~engrossed~~<thoroughly absorbed> by his business; <2> <from> his domestic cares <1> <, his mind> ~~were~~as thenceforth <entirely> relieved, <and> his home trials over; ~~and~~ <1> ~~h~~<H>e felt he had done his duty.

This is probably meant to read: "His mind was thenceforth entirely relieved from domestic cares, and his home trials over. He felt he had done his duty. Then Mr. Hardhead allowed himself once more to be thoroughly absorbed by his business." But as is often the case, the intended order is not clear, so here the editor has had to disregard Chesnut's numerals.

Chesnut's punctuation practice—or lack thereof—further complicates matters because attempting to determine her "usual" practice is, finally, impossible. She seems to have regarded proper punctuation as desirable, but perhaps because she was unsure of the rules, she left punctuation to be attended to in the "tidying up" stages of composition. Chesnut usually ignored punctuation when she was in the process of revising, and she frequently followed interlinear insertions with a dash. Sometimes she went back over a passage and inserted an exclamation point or a question mark without canceling the punctuation she wished to replace. And apparently, whenever she paused—to get up or shift her seat, to get more ink or to think of a word—she inserted a dash.

In very rough drafts few punctuation marks other than dashes appear. She often went back over a draft and inserted punctuation sporadically, correcting one or two sentences but ignoring others equally in need of attention. Occasionally when she went back to punctuate dialogue after the fact, she lost track of the conversation, producing some very muddled moments. Emendation has most often been necessary in dialogue passages. Chesnut was especially casual about quotation marks, often leaving out half of a pair. She rarely used single quotes for interior quotations (though they do appear occasionally); end punctuation sometimes appears inside the quote, sometimes outside; and so on. These inconsistencies have been regularized.

Where they occur, superscript letters have been lowered and followed by a period (Mr., Mrs., Gnl.). Dashes of various lengths have been regularized, and long dashes occasionally used to separate epigraphs or sections of a chapter from each other have been eliminated. Finally, it is Chesnut's usual (though by no means consistent) practice in the 1870s and 1880s to precede quotation marks beginning dialogue with a dash (—"), probably an adaptation of the French practice of using a dash to precede dialogue. Because the pre–quotation mark dash is not used consistently, and because it serves no function that the quotation mark alone does not serve equally well, it has been silently eliminated wherever it occurs.

Chesnut's handwriting is clear enough for most words to be read with certainty by someone familiar with the hand. But minor problems abound. For nearly two-thirds of the alphabet, Chesnut's capital and lower case letters are indistinguishable, so it is sometimes hard to determine the beginning of a sentence. This problem is compounded by her habit of using dashes for dots, so that a lower case "i" may be dotted with a dash, the dots at the base of question marks and exclamation points may be dashes, a colon may resemble an equal sign (=). It is hard to tell whether or not a sentence ends with a period; in carefully copied passages, periods are clear, but in drafts they are not.

Familiar proper names have been given their standard forms, and obvious misspellings have been corrected. (A frequent misspelling is "dis" for "des" as in "discribe" for "describe.") As with most manuscript material, misspellings sometimes occur as a result of haste in writing. Chesnut often used two acceptable forms of the same word ("color" and "colour," for example, or "everybody" and "every body"); no attempt has been made to impose consistency. Accents have been supplied for French words where Chesnut omitted them.

These two manuscripts offer scholars a special kind of documentary evidence. Mary Boykin Chesnut was not a professional writer; she had no editor to point out inconsistency or error in spelling, capitalization, and punctuation. But she was notably observant and widely read. Her fiction and the revised Civil War journal, therefore, represent writing by an intelligent woman who had been unschooled in the more mechanical aspects of grammar. The variants that appear in these unpublished novels offer the scholar an opportunity to judge the extent to which many forms had not yet become standardized among the general public in the mid-nineteenth century.

Explanatory footnotes briefly identify references to historical persons and events, foreign words and phrases, published books, quotations, and literary allusions. Chesnut has often drawn upon material in her original Civil War diaries, published as *The Private Mary Chesnut: The Unpublished Civil War Diaries* (edited by C. Vann Woodward and Elisabeth Muhlenfeld in 1984), and from other material that would eventually appear in *Mary Chesnut's Civil War*. Where appropriate, these borrowings or analogues have been noted.

In most instances when Chesnut quotes or refers to a literary work, it has been impossible to determine the specific edition she used. After her marriage, she had access to books in the library of James Chesnut Sr., and she and her husband amassed a large library, buying books regularly in Columbia, Charleston, New York, and Philadelphia, and ordering books from England and France. In addition, she used the library of the South Carolina College (now the University of South Carolina) in Columbia, the Library of Congress in Washington, the Senate library in Confederate Richmond, and the private libraries of many friends. Particularly after the war, she frequently borrowed or traded books. Chesnut was fond of clipping poems from newspapers; several of the unidentified poems quoted in these novels may well be by minor or anonymous writers whose work she read in newspapers or periodicals. Other quotations may be her own work; she occasionally tried her hand at poetry. Some quotations from major writers may have come from reprints in newspapers (a newsprint clipping of Edmund Waller's "On a Girdle," for example, is preserved in one of her daybooks). Chesnut often quotes from memory; no attempt has been made to correct quotations. Chesnut frequently included French quotations, and occasionally quotations in other languages. Except where noted, translations are the editor's. If no note appears, the person, allusion, poem fragment, quotation, or other reference remains unidentified.

The reader who wishes to study all revisions may consult complete transcriptions of these manuscripts available for interlibrary loan at the South Caroliniana Library of the University of South Carolina. Microfilm or photocopies of the manuscripts themselves are also available. Finally, editorial changes made from manuscript readings are recorded in a list of Emendations and Textual Notes for each novel, on deposit at the South Caroliniana Library, University of South Carolina, and at the Southern Historical Collection of the University of North Carolina, Chapel Hill.

The editor wishes to express her gratitude to the descendents of Mary Boykin Chesnut and the proprietors of her papers, who have allowed me access to her manuscripts and permission to publish these novels. In the preparation of this edition, I have received gracious and enthusiastic assistance from everyone to whom I turned for help. Martha Williams Daniels has provided so many tidbits of information that I've lost count. Dominique Leveau assisted with French translations, as did my editor, David Sewell, who has done an exemplary job on every aspect of the editing of a challenging text. The reference staffs of several libraries, particularly the Thomas Cooper and South Caroliniana libraries at the University of South Carolina, the Robert Manning Strozier Library at Florida State University, and the Mary Helen Cochran Library at Sweet Briar College have helped me track down myriad references and allusions. For his knowledge, wisdom and judicious shepherding, I must thank Michael O'Brien.

Two people of great importance to this volume died during its preparation. C. Vann Woodward's work on Mary Chesnut brought her vividly to the forefront of southern studies; this edition profited greatly from his reading of it. And as series editor Michael O'Brien points out, the idea to include Chesnut in the Southern Text Society series was Elizabeth Hanson's. I am thus in her debt not only for her astute introduction, but for the very genesis of this volume. I hope it may stand *in memoriam* for her.

NOTES

1. See *TPMC*, xxv. Chesnut wrote on 23 February 1865 of her "*10* volumes of memoirs of the times I have written" (emphasis MBC's) and at least two subsequent volumes were written. The following year, commenting on her entry of February 20, 1861, she noted, "what a fool I was 1866."

2. See *MBC*, 141, 242 for discussion of Chesnut's attempts in the early 1870s to translate French fiction.

3. 3 October 1861, *TPMC*, 169. The "literary paper" referred to is the Columbia *Banner* (the weekly edition of the *South Carolinian*), published by Dr. Robert Wilson Gibbes (1809–66).

4. *MCCW*, 1 January 1864, 523–24.

5. Letters to Varina Davis, dated 18 June 1883, and Virginia Clay, dated September 1866, quoted in *MBC*, 141.

6. The manuscript is bound by brads into six segments of varying numbers of pages. On the cover sheets of several of the sections the words "*The Effs*" or "*The Effinghams*" had been written in pencil and erased, replaced by the title "*The Captain and the Colonel.*" Section 1 of 82 pages comprises chapters 1–4; section 2 of 78 pages, chapters 5–8; section 3 of 45 pages, chapters 9–11; section 4 of 63 pages, chapters 12–13; section 5 of 78 pages, chapters 14–17; and section 6 of 42 pages, chapters 18–19. The six sections seem to represent convenient bundles for fastening together rather than significant units of the novel.

7. Chesnut clearly spent considerable time recopying and revising her Civil War journals in the mid-1870s. By spring 1876, she had recopied, on legal-sized paper, entries through at

least November 1864. She bound these together in a manner similar to the manuscript of *The Captain and the Colonel,* in segments of approximately fifty pages. Segments numbered 10, 11, 21, and 22 survive. In the upper left-hand corner of several cover sheets are the symbols "X75," probably her notation that the segments were completed in 1875. See *MBC,* 158, 244–45.

8. The working title of the novel had been *The Effinghams,* which Chesnut usually shortened to *The Effs.* The title, taken from the surname of her main characters, was a play on the term "FF's" or First Families (see above, p. xxii). The title, and the name, had several literary predecessors, a fact that Chesnut may at some point have discovered (or remembered). James Fenimore Cooper used the name in the Leatherstocking Tales as well as in *Homeward Bound* and *Home as Found* (Philadelphia, 1838), and John Esten Cooke had named his focal family Effingham in the two-volume work *The Virginia Comedians* (New York, 1854) and had called his Effingham family estate Effhall. Chesnut had very likely read some or all of these works; if so, she may have forgotten their use of the name Effingham and, when she realized the duplication, determined to rename her characters.

9. Even the late draft fragment was originally titled, in pencil, *The Effinghams.* At some point after dividing the manuscript of the main draft into six sections and fastening each section together, she systematically erased all references to "The Effinghams" as a title and substituted "The Captain and the Colonel." This may have been done in 1885 when, following the death of her husband, she spent a great deal of time getting her papers in order.

10. Like the MS of *The Captain and the Colonel,* both *Two Years* MSS are on deposit at the South Caroliniana Library. Both are written in ink on the recto of each page.

11. The four chapters in section 6 are designated chapters 13, 13, 16, and 17 in the MS, though pages are numbered consecutively and none of this sequence is missing. The last three chapters have been renumbered 14, 15, and 16 in this edition.

12. Two of six sections of *Two Years of My Life* became separated from the rest of the manuscript at some point. Section 2 has never been found. Section 3 of eighty pages, chapters 6–8, was found in the possession of a descendant of Katherine Miller Williams (Mary's sister Kate), Mary Ames Alfriend, and has been deposited with the rest of the manuscript in the South Caroliniana Library.

13. Anthony Trollope, *The Way We Live Now* (London, 1875). Apart from the title, the book seems to have no connection with Chesnut's novel. Chesnut mentions reading Trollope's book in a letter to her sister Kate of 25 September 1875.

14. MBC actually numbered this segment 267–309, skipping numbers 278, 302, and 303, and losing track of her numbering toward the end of the manuscript. She also inadvertently numbered chapter 10 as 9, and chapter 11 as 12, though the pages are consecutively numbered.

15. The ten-page fragment from Chesnut's third novel, numbered from 411 to 419, includes two pages numbered 415. On the cover sheet appears the crossed-out identification "Manassas—rough copy" and beneath it the title "Susie Effingh." Although ten pages toward the end of this third major effort at fiction provide few clues to the novel's plot, it seems to combine elements of both *The Captain and the Colonel* and *Two Years—or The Way We Lived Then.* The characters in this fragment include members of the Newtown family of *Two Years* (Kitty, Tatty, and Mrs. Newtown), but the situation resembles more closely the repartee between Johannis, Collingwood, and the three Effingham sisters in *The Captain and the Colonel.* Certainly the working title of "Manassas" suggests the war years. The surviving fragment is a dialogue passage recounting a humorous courting story.

16. On verso of cover sheet for section 5 of earlier MS draft.

17. A few pages (MS 232, 286, 330) show evidence of patching, where a portion of a page from one draft is pasted onto another draft. The handwriting of the patched portions, however, is identical to that of the unpatched portions, indicating that the work on both these late (post-1876) drafts was done at about the same time.

18. Over each of the first two sentences, MBC wrote the number "2" to indicate that she wanted to rearrange the phrases, but inasmuch as it is not clear what her intentions were, the numerals have been omitted here.

TWO NOVELS BY

Mary Chesnut

The Captain and the Colonel

Spider! thou need'st not run in fear about
　　To shun my curious eyes:
I won't humanely crush thy bowels out,
　　Lest thou should eat the flies;
Nor will I toast thee with a damned delight
　　Thy strange instructive fortitude to see;
For there is one who might
　　One day roast me.

1

The tide of time flows back with me,
The forward flowing tide of time.[1]

Mrs. Effingham, widow of Francis Effingham Esq. of Effhall, was before her marriage Miss Joanna Hardhead, the daughter of a wealthy merchant of New York.[2]

Mr. Hardhead, when he found himself alone with two motherless daughters, had taken a sensible, business like view of the situation. He obtained

---

1. Alfred, Lord Tennyson, "Recollections of the Arabian Nights," lines 3–4, in *Poems, Chiefly Lyrical* (London, 1830).

2. MBC uses aspects of her own personality in her characterization of Mrs. Francis Effingham (née Joanna Hardhead). See *MBC,* 143. MBC's mother-in-law Mary Cox Chesnut was of Dutch descent, according to a letter from Horace Binney, her brother-in-law, to James Chesnut Sr., dated Philadelphia, 6 February 1852, copied in MBC's hand, in the Williams-Chesnut-Manning Collection, South Caroliniana Library, University of South Carolina. Joanna's maiden name, Hardhead, anglicized from the Dutch Hartkopf, reflects what MBC seems to have regarded as a national trait of the Dutch. Peter Stuyvesant, General Director of New Amsterdam (New York), 1647–64, was nicknamed "Hardkoppige Piet" (Hardheaded Pete).

a highly recommended English governess and when she had proved herself competent and judicious, he gave her carte blanche to secure the best masters the city afforded. Aided by so powerful a staff, Mrs. Blythe soon had cause to be proud of her pupils.

Then Mr. Hardhead allowed himself once more to be thoroughly absorbed by business; from his domestic cares, his mind was thenceforth entirely relieved, and his home trials over. He felt he had done his duty.

His confidence in Mrs. Blythe became so perfect that he persuaded her to take his daughters across the Atlantic for two years. They returned vastly improved, everyone said, in French, in dress, in manners and complexion.

Even the friends of feu Madame Hardhead,[3] who had been hitherto inclined to captious criticism, now conceded, that the veteran trader had behaved handsomely. "He has given those dear girls every advantage."

No one knew when Queen Joanna's reign began. She was the autocrat of the establishment, her right there was none to dispute. Her elder sister, Annie, called her "Joanna Regina" in jest; the governess soon joined her in this harmless pleasantry; and in sober certainty they yielded to her, as a power too strong to be resisted. All this happened in the prescientific period, before the days of "sweet girl graduates" or Science Primers.[4] So Joanna was satisfied with her absolute sway over the minds and bodies of her subjects; and in her practice did not crave License or Diploma.

She took rank however as a superior person because of her proficiency in Music, and her excellent painting in water colors. Then she spoke French fluently, she read Italian and Spanish with ease. She had always a new language on the stocks. Before they had been a week at home, she discovered a German Professor, and arranged a class for him, of which she was *facile princeps.*[5] He pathetically inquired why her sister, the "beautiful lady mit de blue eye, and mit de fair hair" did not join them?

Annie firmly declined to do this. She thought her education completed;

3. The late Mrs. Hardhead.

4. "Sweet girl graduates" is from Tennyson, *The Princess* (London, 1847), Prologue, line 142. In alluding to the "prescientific period" and "Science Primers," MBC refers to the changes that had come to the education of women in the first half of the nineteenth century. Schools for girls were rare in the colonial period, limited to "French schools" that taught "polite" subjects, primarily French and needlework, and which incidentally were more prevalent in the South (particularly Charleston) than the North. By the 1830s, girls were being taught as much science as boys. In fact, according to Christie Anne Farnham, "it was in the sciences that female institutions were most notably advanced," in many cases surpassing the science instruction in academies for boys (*The Education of the Southern Belle* [New York: New York University Press, 1994], 80).

5. A common phrase in Cicero meaning "certainly (or easily) the best," in this context, "easily the star pupil." See, e.g., the *Oratio Pro Cluentio,* 5, 11.

she had so much more English at her command than she ever used. Her rosebud mouth and her violet eyes, spoke for her with a thousand tongues. She was mutely aware of that; even when those eyes were shaded by their long tangled lashes, they cast a spell no words of hers were likely to heighten and she knew it.

Joanna had absorbed the intellect and the strength of the family. Annie was only lovely and good; to the last she was a mere baby in her sister's hands. The governess when consulted always counselled abject submission to the inevitable, and Mr. Hardhead the nominal head of the house was never at home.

Annie without being clever had a soft, sweet, feminine way of accomplishing her purposes, at least when they did not conflict with the tyrant's will.

And she could make herself loved to a degree that astounded her more highly informed sister; she was only gracious and graceful, appreciative and sympathetic.

Among the friends they had made abroad, highly approved of by Mrs. Blythe, were two men, who continued their intimacy at the home in New York. The younger sister they always found busy; nay worse she was inclined to find fault with their idleness; so they gradually fell into a habit of loitering around the fascinating *désoeuvrée*[6]—Annie.

It was only after they moved into their fine house in the then fashionable quarter of the City,[7] that the Hh's, as Mr. Hardhead jocularly styled them, undertook the difficult task of moulding refractory Dutchmen, into a shape and form befitting forefathers worthy of their descendants' prosperous position.

The parental Hardhead cared for none of these things; and Annie was even more shamefully indifferent. This want of sympathy on the part of her family, in no wise daunted the resolute Joanna.

In Europe the want of a pedigree had not inconvenienced them; no one required it of them there—they were simply citizens of the U S A. At home it had begun to be the one thing needful.

Joanna ferreted out an old Dutchman, that suited her purposes admirably. He was an undoubted Ancestor; and though still in the Singular Number, with this bird in the hand she felt safe and forebore any further to beat about the bush.

6. Fr., idle girl.

7. MBC first visited New York City in 1845. There is no indication that she had any particular "then fashionable quarter" in mind. During the mid-1830s the city was expanding rapidly; perhaps the most fashionable area was on the Hudson River side of Manhattan, from the Battery to the Barclay Street area.

Still she determined to consult with Francis Effingham, one of the above mentioned loiterers around Annie, before she went deeper into the matter, or spread abroad her discoveries.

"You remember," she said to him, "Mrs. Blythe's annoyance on the steamer. Those insolent tosses of the head! and 'who are the Hardheads after all!' You see Annie is so beautiful—" (he smiled acquiescence), "she has that rare distinction, a thoroughbred air—Mrs. Blythe had dressed us so well—we owe her that. Papa you know *is* liberal. Well! No wonder they disliked us! Mrs. Blythe poses as grande dame, splendidly: How utterly she sunk the governess[8] aboard. I was the only black sheep of the flock. Von Enden and you, though you rarely left us, still, it was long enough to confess your ignorance. Behind our backs they all knew you, and questioned you.

"You did not know 'who we were.' You know you did not! Neither do I. But then I have been trying to find out."

"Let it alone. Do not be a mole. I have no curiosity. I am satisfied with the face of things." Annie's, at least, he thought.

"Papa knows less than I do. Nobody seems to know anything about our ancestors."

"Lucky people."

"Our Ancestors or ourselves?"

"*You.*"

"He says his father and grandfather were agents in a small way for some house in Holland; they made no figure in the world and are forgotten. If we tell any story about them he says we must invent it."

"Let it alone—let sleeping dogs lie. You have no idea, how powerful your position is—'Nobody knows.'"

"Our real history seems to date from the building of this house."

"Are you sure, obscure as you deem them, that neither your thread of life, nor your forefathers were ever entangled, at any time, with that of an incipient celebrity—a rudimentary 'distinguished American citizen,' Ambassador, Senator, President, then only Smith or Jones, whose scanty early Annals are the despair of his present biographers?"

"Do not laugh at me!—this is business."

"Did they ever employ an errand boy since celebrated, or odd jobber, who impertinently got ahead of you hundreds of years ago, in the race for wealth and honors, and so in spite of you, casts back a lurid stern light on your shop?"[9]

8. Dispensed with her role as governess.

9. This passage reflects the fact that after the Civil War, Chesnut was resentful of what she perceived as slights against her husband's family. She was particularly insulted by a series of articles in the local paper written by Colonel William M. Shannon, entitled "Old Times in

"We had no shop. How could we have a shop boy?"

"I was only making a preliminary investigation. There is always that fearful biographer of other people, lacking materials for the life of his famous hero, who did or said nothing; at any moment he may impale you on the walls of some primeval grocery or shanty. But you seem delightfully free from that apprehension. How came you, by so purely an English name?"

"My father was educated in England; and his outlandish patronymic was made a torture to him by the boys at school. So he translated his name."

"Keep the change of name to yourself! Indeed I should say—tell people nothing. Spare yourselves a Pedigree *pour rire*.[10] If the world is not contented with you, as you are, it must be hard to please. I have a theory on that subject. If you have not had a name made for you in your country's history, do not trouble your friends with oral traditions. They never believe a word you say, though you pay a fortune to the Herald's office."

"A Seal? You remember we, alone on the steamer, had none."

"And a good thing it was too—What does your father suggest as the family coat of arms?"

"Oh something with his eternal small joke of the Hh's."

"Let us see what profit the owners of those seals derived from them on the steamer. To begin with the bird of the Browns[11]—[as] unostentatious and modest a bird as one would care to see—with a twig between its eyes. A titter went round; it recalled the Münchausen legend;[12] the stag with the

---

Camden," in which credit is heaped on Joseph Kershaw and his family for the founding of the town. In her papers are several attempts at a response—some of which are quite bitter (see *MBC*, 163 ff.). Cf. *MCCW,* 816:

> The first comer of that name [Chesnut] to this state was but ten when he got here. Leaving his land in Virginia, being penniless otherwise, he went into Mr. Joseph Kershaw's grocery shop as a clerk. And the Kershaws, I think, have that fact on their coat of arms. Our Johnny, as he was driving me down to Mulberry yesterday, declared himself delighted with the fact that the present Joseph Kershaw had so distinguished himself in our war that they would let the shop of a hundred years ago rest for a while. "Upon my soul," cried the cool Captain, "I have a desire to go in there and look at the Kershaw tombstones. I am sure they have put it on their marble tablets that we had an ancestor one day a hundred years ago who was a clerk in their shop."

10. Fr., a joke of a pedigree. Frank Effingham objects to the idea of producing a pedigree that would be laughed at.

11. The ensuing passage is often unclear; extensive revisions made by MBC suggest that she recognized the problem, but did not solve it.

12. In chapter 4 of Rudolph Erich Raspe's *The Travels of Baron Munchausen,* Munchausen, out of ammunition, shoots a stag with a handful of cherry stones; in a year or two, he sees a cherry tree growing from the stag's head. Chesnut may have read this work, first published in 1786, in its original English or in one of many editions of the German translation by Gottfried August Burger.

cherry tree growing from the stone shot into its head. A year before as all well know—Jones was contented with only the head of a bird, unpretending enough as to disarm criticism one might hope: but no—a supercilious Englishman murmured:

> 'Little Tom Noddy
> All head and nobody.'[13]

Then young Robinson came to the front with his two robin red breasts, clawing up the leaves—babes in the wood understood.[14] Miss R held her brother's ring up to me with a simper—the Legend was—'Ah don't leave me.' She called for my seal ring. And my skylark responsively came soaring, head up and wings spread, apparently with an eye to the uppermost plains of the air. And I had to say for him, 'I aspire higher.'"

"Ah," said Joanna laughing. "I can never forget that hideous malapropos encounter of rings. Those birds did not pair. I admit that."

"But the Irishman trumped the bird trick, with his American 'aigle that no king could envaigle, or put salt on its magnificent tail,' which flapped from the Atlantic to the Pacific. But we have had enough of the feathered tribe. Please, don't let us go into the beasts.

"Many men like Chantrey would point with pride, to the table, which they had made, in their early Carpentering days; aye! even at Roger's festive board[15]—surrounded by the high born and the high bred of the Earth. Few men can bring themselves to brag of a Carpenter father. Why is that? I know one pious old dame who falls down and worships Carpenters—because our Savior was one she says. Instinctively all men go in for fine ancestry. I acknowledge the Irishman has my sympathy. He said, you know, 'I am none of your self made fellows. I had a Mother and a father.'

"But you have handsomely disposed of your forefathers. And now we have the 'Coat of Arms' on our hands. I set my face like flint against birds of the air—and beasts of the field."

13. Tom Noddy was a common epithet in the nineteenth century, and the name appeared in several poems, including "My Lord Tomnoddy" by Robert Barnabas Brough (1828–60). These lines are unidentified, and are probably MBC's own.

14. Reference to "The Children in the Woods," an old English ballad recorded in Thomas Percy's *Reliques of Ancient English Poetry* (1765, hereafter referred to as Percy's *Reliques*) in which two children, victims of a wicked uncle, are abandoned in the woods. After their death, "Robin-red-breast piously / Did cover them with leaves," lines 121–28.

15. Sir Francis Legatt Chantrey (1781–1841), sculptor. As noted in the *Dictionary of National Biography* (London, 1921–22; reprint London, 1973) 4:45, "Samuel Rogers, the banker and poet, had a table which Chantrey in after years, when dining with him, recognised as his work."

This man Frank Effingham was from the South. He really owned a magnificent Estate there—which being and lying so far away, rumor magnified forty fold. Von Enden, his constant companion (since the days of the steamer), belonged to a Knickerbocker family,[16] who retained their old Colonial country house, with its lordly name; but the lordly lands which had for so long a time constituted their wealth and fortified their high position were fast slipping through their fingers. No mortal had aught to bring forward against either of Annie's suitors. Neither of these men need quail before the father's eye, could he secure the daughter's good will.

They were both heels over head in love with Annie—and every body knew it—*so they thought.*

The Knickerbocker had decidedly the advantage in personal appearance. So far the family were as friendly with one as with the other; but with Frank Effingham their manner had all the ease of intimacy. With the other there was a shade of stiffness.

"I wonder why you like Von Enden so much better than Frank?" said Joanna to Annie.

Annie was never so positive as her sister in any of her conclusions; but she had long ceased to argue or contend with her about any thing what ever. At this attack she flushed scarlet—and silently turned away. She uttered no word of contradiction—although her air was one of indignant surprise. And so the case went by default.

Joanna persisted in her view of the subject; and as usual she had her own way.

Quietly with Joanna's help Von Enden won the inside track; and every opportunity was given him to urge his suit.

One day while talking with her good friend Mr. Effingham, Joanna asked his advice as to some of her future plans. "As you see Annie will soon leave me."

"Where is she going?"

"The fact is *en évidence,*[17] and this man is blind!"

"All the world can see what is the matter with Von Enden. Surely you are too hasty in your assertions with regard to her."

"My previsions are not premature," said Queen Joanna with a glance of sovereign contempt, cast at this bewildered man. "I have insight and foresight. If you doubt me—ask her yourself. Rest assured my friend it is all right."

16. A descendant of one of the original Dutch settlers of Manhattan Island during the period New York was a colonial settlement of the Dutch, 1624–64.

17. Fr., evident or obvious.

Now to poor Frank it was all wrong; but he took her advice; he did ask
Annie. In that enterprise he ran off the main track awkwardly.

"Is it true? Will you marry Von Enden?"

"Did he send you to propose for him?"

"No—certainly not."

"Then I will not answer that question until he asks it himself."

So blundering and blind, the impatient fellow handsomely helped to pave
the way for his rival. Ever after that fatal interview he felt it was all over
with him—his hopes were crushed and he prepared to abandon the field.

Now was Joanna radiant with delight. She, fairly hilarious with success,
claimed his admiration for herself, in the character of a prophetess. Poor
Frank scowled—dumb and despairing. Von Enden with a fair field and so
much favor came up to the winning post in gallant style.

Mr. Effingham was midway of the ocean when the wedding took place.
He sent back as his bridal present a splendid parure of Pearls. And then he
wandered in an aimless way for a year or two on the Continent; then came
to him tidings of Mr. Hardhead's sudden death.[18]

Joanna was amazed to find her father's affairs in confusion; clever business woman as she was, she soon had things in order; and for her pains,
found herself well nigh penniless.

One of two alternatives stared her in the face: to accept the Von Endens'
invitation, and live henceforth with her sister; or go out as a governess.
Annie's handsome dowry had been consistent with the general idea of her
father's wealth. And her husband had always a vague feeling rather than
thought which he kept to himself that he owed much to Joanna's timely
aid and assistance. He accounted for her zeal in his behalf by a natural, if
modest reflection, that it was not personal preference after all—for she evidently liked his rival best; but she was prejudiced against the South—she
did not wish her sister to go there.

The impoverished lady leaned toward the governess alternative. Her accomplishments and her art of governing were so well known; the world had
seen her father and Annie meekly submit to her instruction and her discipline—with a laugh indeed—but acknowledging it was good for them.

But she remembered how anxiously Frank Effingham had sought her
friendship, and tried, poor fellow, to propitiate her in every way. She persuaded herself that, if she had had time to give him, from her music, her
German, or even had been without the burden of a "demoiselle à marier"[19]

18. MBC's own father, Stephen Decatur Miller, died in 1838, when she was fifteen. Like Mr.
Hardhead, he left his affairs in confusion, and when his widow and eldest daughter had straightened them out to the best of their ability, they discovered that their inheritance was small.

19. Fr., young woman of marriageable age.

on her hands—how different things might have been. How was he to speak when she had never a moment to listen to him!

In all that followed, she was cool and deliberate, intending in any case not to compromise herself. Her own personal dignity—she said to herself, came first—but she would give Frank a chance. In her letter she candidly stated, "If he ever meant to come forward, now was the time. She had to choose between charity from the Von Endens and the position of a governess. She would not put her 'notice to the public' in the printer's hands until she heard from him."

One day she was packing away some of the few remaining relics of the happy past—and with a heart like lead in her bosom, not the least heavy weight upon it, that hazardous letter, when without a word of warning, Frank Effingham walked into the room. He was valiantly forcing a smile; his face was pale, and his expression rather wild. He held out his hand.

"What brought you home?" she cried—the brave Joanna blushing like a school girl the while.

"I came to your wedding!"

"All right Frank!"—and now she took his hand—which he held out.

She boasted there was not a word of foolish sentimentality in their courtship, and that they were sensibly married at once, after things were settled in that way, without nonsense or childish frivolity.

The Von Endens' amazement was excessive. Annie's husband in a moment of conjugal confidence whispered, "And so after all it was Joanna! Do you know at one time I felt that fellow most damnably in my way."

In those early days of this century men had not ceased to use that form of speech[20] when much moved.

Under Joanna's iron rule, Annie had learned to keep her own counsel. But she thought of the day Frank Effingham had offended her with his maladroit question—and indeed of many other days; she said nothing however. Neither of them ever dreamed of *that letter,* "confiding in his honor," which had been a snare unto the feet of the lonely wanderer.

---

20. I.e., "damnably." Chesnut is alluding here to the heightened sense of propriety, especially with respect to "improper" language, that characterized the late nineteenth century.

2

"I bring two powerful Gods—Persuasion, and Force."
They answered—"On our side are deities not less powerful—Patience—
Poverty and Despair."[1]

You seize the flow'r, the bloom is shed.
Or like the snow falls in the river,
A moment white—then melts forever.[2]

Frank Effingham was not so handsome as his brother in law; but he was as pleasant a fellow as one would care to meet, in person tall and spare; with a dead white complexion and regular features, a thorough bred air his chief attraction.[3]

Henceforth he was contented at home; or to be strictly correct in his library.

Queen Joanna did not abdicate; she had conquered new realms. She took possession of her house promptly, but she relieved her husband of the care of his plantation by degrees; and her management was perfect.

He thought her a trifle too stout, and too loud, and at times he fancied she was too clever; but he smiled as persistently when she was wrong as when she was right. He rarely spoke ill of any one; and even after a domestic storm that might have shaken the serenity of an angel, he was as unruffled, as calm, and as benign as ever, a true philosopher, self complete and brave, never taking the world into his confidence. That slight smile of his might be caused by his own blunders, or by the noise and folly of others. No one knew. After years of a life in which he stood aside, a mere looker on, he grew inert; even given to self indulgence at table.

He was a literary glutton, devouring all that came in his way, good or bad. If the new book, so anxiously looked for, failed him, so much the better, for had he not the old, in his library, to fall back upon, he said—cheerfully.

In season and out of it, he spoke of Regina always in terms of loftiest

1. Themistocles' remark to the Andrians in *Plutarch's lives; translated from the original Greek . . . by John Langhorne and William Langhorne,* ed. Francis Wrangham (New York, 1822), 2:30.

2. Robert Burns, "Tam O'Shanter," line 60, first published in *Edinburgh Magazine* (March 1791), and later the same year in Francis Grose's *Antiquities of Scotland* (Edinburgh, 1791).

3. Joanna and Effingham's physical and character traits seem to be caricatures of the author and James Chesnut Jr., her husband, although none of the events of the Effinghams' married life parallel those in the Chesnuts'.

praise; oftenest when she had been doing something which jarred his nerves to the uttermost.

He was a charming person. She was pleasant too, nay brilliant, when her temper was not crossed; but sneering and snarling, when resisted or contradicted in the slightest degree. Their hospitality was enjoyed by all who could attain unto it.

Cavillers said: (there are such in every community), "That Mrs. Effingham, violent, high-handed, imperious always; nay sometimes almost vulgar in her outbursts; had a human heart in her bosom; but the quiescent, self sufficing, dignified, and polished gentleman—where was his?"

This was after the family catastrophe.

Regina Hartkopf, as Mr. Effingham now called his wife, had forced their daughter Annita into an excellent marriage which the girl from her soul abhorred. The father sided with his child, but the effort he made to save her, was thought by the lookers on to be faint and futile. They said Regina unclasped Annita's arms from around his neck, using her full strength to do it, and marched them off, father and daughter, to dress and be ready in time for the wedding ceremony.

As the story ran, Regina had in hand the best match in the country, and she would listen to nothing the poor girl could say against it.

She thought well of the French system,[4] she said, and from the first she had announced her plan of action. "Any one with common sense must acknowledge that parents know best what is for their children's true interest." "She had never yielded to a child of hers, and she never would." "I will conquer her yet." Discipline was the word ever on her tongue.

One motherly old soul had her feelings "awfully harrowed" as she expressed it, by Regina, when Margaret, the eldest girl, was not quite a month old. The young Mother asked, "At what age do you begin to discipline a child?"

Annita was the Godchild of her beautiful Aunt; she resembled that altogether lovely person in appearance; but unfortunately, she was of an acute sensibility and the cleverest member of the family. She was her father's pride, his joy, his life, his partner in all literary delights—a facsimile of him in mind as she was of her Aunt in person.

For many months father and daughter combined to wage a fruitless war with Regina's Iron Will. And then they succumbed.

Annita's married life hardly endured a year.

Frank Effingham never again alluded to this painful episode in his life.

4. I.e., marriage arranged by the parents.

From the time Regina placed Annita's hand upon his arm, and drove them before her, so to speak, up the aisle and to the altar, where he gave away his daughter, with his finest manner, cool, smiling, imperturbable, he was dumb—so to speak—and opened not his mouth on that subject.

One day he startled Joanna by a candid statement of his views when he said quietly: "Margaret—dear wife—is your own child. But the little ones—Susan and Emily—may be they have hearts to be broken."

"Now for it Frank. For many a long day I knew it had to come—we will have it out. I know you hold me responsible for Annita's death!"

"No—the Doctor said she died of typhoid fever—slow fever—no low fever—that was what he called it—low fever was the Doctor's way of putting it."

"Tut—tut—I am amazed you should talk such nonsense. I am a woman of my century—I do not believe in broken hearts."

"Neither do I. She lived longer than I expected. Three months of that dismal swamp—with that awful bore would have killed me. She stood it three times as long as that."

"Oh Frank! What a good man he is! How can you!"

"Surely—he is good—or coward as you must think me I would have slain him. There is not the smallest speck of evil to be perceived about this immaculate person. So he had to be endured."

"The man is no fool—you will confess that, now that it can do no good."

"Yes, and the most sensible thing I know of him is that he owns the most beautiful place on the river. He is a member of the Legislature, and a Colonel of Militia! But for all that he could not see when a woman loathed him, even though she told him so. Nor could he feel it, which is denser stupidity. He thought her shy, modest, timid."

"He was devoted to her to the very last—they say he rarely left her side, night or day."

"Yes—thanks—he put the poor child out of her misery sooner by that. He was compounding a tomato salad when she died. I sought him to say— she was dying."

"He is faultlessly handsome."

"Dear wife—have we not had an enough of him? Yes—and so had Annita; I never could like him, and she died—trying to do it."

"Oh Frank—how wrong headed you are! Our son in law is an honorable man, so he must be honored. He is respectable, and commands respect."

"Now you have mounted your high horse. Loveable and must be loved? Devil take him!" cried the hard driven Frank. "That is, with your leave," he added blandly smiling. "But I will have rest now—I have sacrificed enough—for a quiet home. I mean to die in peace. My life has been all a mistake; I let things drift, I did not assert my true and lawful power. A bolder stand on my side would have ensured a more solid tranquillity. But dear wife—how we have wandered from the point—I came to tell you that the Doctors are consulting in the Library. I want you to find out from them what they think of my condition—*my case.*"

"Are you ill? You have sent for a Physician! Doctors in this house!"

"I left them, two of them, together, when I came to you. Two heads better than one."

"What is the matter? Are you ill?"

"I fancy it is the same incurable disease, that killed Annita. They will give it some fine name. A disinclination to live. Want of vital power? My blood has not enough Iron in it—like my will."

Joanna was stricken down. Surely her shackles were shaken off; he dared to show her plainly wherein she had been wrong.

He was ill, he said. She would not believe it. Without a word of consultation with her—he had called in outside aid. She felt bewildered. He smiled significantly.

"Frank you are laughing! and at me!"

"No, I am escaping you. Did I laugh? I thought I had lost the trick of it. It was at your expression of face—you look baffled at last. I was thinking how differently the Amazon Queen looked that day, when she stood like a warrior pointing her sword, I mean—beggin your pardon—her parasol, at our pile of luggage on the Wharf. Annita and I hoped to put the Atlantic between us and her unlucky suitor. She wanted to slip away from you and spend some years abroad. The whole escapade was of Annita's planning. I knew you better; as well try and evade one of the forces of nature. You caught us of course—resistance was vain. I see you now—your triumphant air, as you marched away with your captives! Your runaways."

"Do you not feel, dear Frank—" cried the thoroughly frightened Joanna. "This is a very disagreeable surprise to me."

"No, dear. I have not felt since that morning you dragged my child's arms from around my neck—Yes. I do feel! her arms are clinging, her soft cheek is pressed to mine—now."

His wife arose [and] left the room hastily.

She soon returned with a paler face—but she had regained her composure.

"Frank—my dear boy—you have called me your helpmate—I will still be so, in this dark hour."

"No. You can not help me now. I will have to make my way alone—No need to worry. Fancy me on a battlefield. You could trust me alone there— Eh?—I would not disgrace my blood. You have found me a failure—in life.

I am going to do better about dying. I have looked death in the face—already. With the firmness of a Christian—and the coolness of a gentleman—I may reproach him that he has kept me waiting so long. That is all."

Mrs. Effingham sat down. She was at her wits' end—conquered at last. Could this be Frank? her husband! In the article of death,[5] so the Doctors seemed to fear—and no one had warned her! He least of all—and absolutely he seemed to enjoy her discomfiture! That faint smile which had been the trial of her life playing fitfully around his lips, as he calmly confronted her.

"Look at those pictures, Regina. Your poor fool of a son in law! the man who took Annita's shuddering aversion for maiden modesty; in here the other day, while he was posing for a grief stricken man of the world, and at a loss for something to say, asked, 'Which of those ladies up there was Eugénie?[6] I mean the Empress Eugénie you know,' he said striking an attitude. 'Neither.' My God—Annie and Annita—and he prates of his Empress. She has small eyes they say. Look there—large—soft—wide open—glorious southern eyes—Have you forgotten? Babbling! A sick man and his dreams! No—no—it is not of the eyes that are closed forever, that we need take heed now. It is of—Emily, dear, I meant to warn you—she has a will of her own too. When Greek meets Greek, you know.[7] The tug of war I shall not see—but it will come. Harshness will not frighten her. Tired now—I have told you what I think. Have I not? No, then some other time—"

But no other time was vouchsafed him.

Next day they thought him better. He was seated in an invalid's chair near the fire, his wife beside him. She looked up. Something in his face startled her. She sprang towards him. He waved her back, with an effort. A pale smile hovered over his lips, the smile which had baffled her so often.

"Regina! For one thing, I know you give me credit. I take no stock in Mahomet's Paradise—Houris and all that sort of thing—never did—Eh? What a failure I have been. I deserted Annita in her bitter hour of need. She forgives me now. She and I will meet in the Christian's Heaven. Maybe,—where there will be 'neither marrying nor giving in marriage.'"[8]

5. I.e., the crucial moment of death.

6. Eugénie (1826–1920), the wife of Napoleon III, daughter of a Spanish grandee and an American mother, married Napoleon in 1853. She was considered an intelligent woman and a great beauty.

7. Allusion to a quotation in common parlance, "When Greeks joined Greeks, then was the tug of war," meaning that the contest will be fierce when great warriors are evenly matched (Nathaniel Lee, *The Rival Queens; or, The Death of Alexander the Great* [1677].) Frank predicts that Emily will prove a match for Joanna.

8. See Mark 12:25 and Luke 20:35.

They saw that his strength was rapidly failing. He was sinking.

The Doctor softly touched his hand. His wife was inarticulate with grief.

Then for a moment he opened his eyes, and with the faintest touch of that inscrutable smile, he said, "To the Christian's Heaven, you know."

3

Yea, ere the night, greater the joyance grew:
For to the throng of heroes came there two!
In no wise worse than any of the best![1]

At her husband's death, Mrs. Effingham was left with three daughters. *She thought* Margaret—the counterpart of herself; she was her equal perhaps in intelligence; but alas weak and wavering in will, with a touch of sentimentality foreign to both parents (and this last trait had already led her astray more than once). She had neither her Mother's strength to battle with trouble, nor her father's fashion of standing aside to let it go by. When she was in a scrape, she would only plunge deeper, at every struggle to be free. After all her most dangerous characteristic was a tendency to fix her mind on one thing, to the exclusion of all else—until this thing assumed unnatural proportions, indeed until she became on the absorbing subject scarcely sane.

Emily the youngest was as beautiful as her father foretold she would be—happily she had the courage of her opinions as the French say; and so was in no danger of being "coerced, compelled" after the fashion of her unhappy sister. Emily's face was cast in the same mould as Annita's, even to the long tangled lashes veiling those great grey eyes. Emily's, though soft, were wide open—fair and fearless—glorious southern eyes, [with] lashes which have been pronounced "'trop de déluge'[2] for the breakfast table, they should be kept for full dress." The sisters had been trained in all modern accomplishments. In addition, Emily had inherited an indescribable beauty, which consists in a subtle grace and charm; a gift to woman which since the days of Helen [has been] all powerful to ensnare helpless men.

Perfectly good natured and always laughing, Susan (she was Emily's senior by two years) spoke ever, in gold. "She had been taught all that a poor child was ever forced to learn," she would say. She played upon the Piano—and sang when she was asked: and her friends wondered how Mrs. Effing-

1. William Morris (1834–96), *The Life and Death of Jason* (London, 1867), book 3, lines 327–29.

2. Fr., too abundant.

ham could allow her "to make so painful an exhibition of herself." She
painted in the same style, principally for fancy fairs. The amount of perfectly useless needlework that she did was immense; as her Mother remarked when paying bills for her "materials." She was without malice, or
thought of her own; but she conscientiously made herself the constant
chronicler of the wit and wisdom of others. She had no tact, and trampled
with hobnail shoes in the most sacred corners. Her father quoted—"fools
rush in, where angels fear to tread"[3]—but she was no fool; far from it.
Every body loved her. She beamed alike on the just and the unjust—one
person was the same to her as another, *if* they admired her amiability. A
good word from their cowboy delighted her as much as a compliment from
the "President of these United States." Her father said of her, "When she
meets Judas Iscariot, she comes home, and plumes herself; 'He behaved
to me with so much more consideration, than he did my beautiful sisters,
and my brilliant Mother. The attention of such a man is a compliment. He
does not like every body. Why—he even treated our Savior—shabbily.'"
When the neighbourhood rose in its wrath and was pouring out hot vials,
upon some malefactor's head, Susan would say, "Don't expect a word from
me against him—he was always a friend of mine."

Mrs. Effingham had enlarged and improved the drawing room of that old
house, whose woodwork and carving had all been brought from England in
the Colonial days, by throwing out a bay window on the South side. The
library opened into this room. While Mr. Effingham lived he kept the door
of the communication between the two rooms locked; and further more
barricaded himself by placing his writing table against it.

After his death this door was opened, and the table, turned against the
side of the huge old chimney, which being all built into the smaller room,
projecting itself so far into the middle, seemed to threaten to cut [it] in two.
Otherwise it was a snug, cosy little retreat from the drawing room. The
table with its writing materials, in that sheltered corner, not one step from
the drawing room door, proved itself a great convenience, among a people
who never risked a message; but wrote notes upon the most trivial occasions, thanks to the "peculiar institution's" aptitude in making mistakes.[4]

The house was roomy, quaint, and comfortable. The live oaks, the shrub-
bery of camellias and cape Jasmines; the orange grove, and the long cedar
avenue leading to it was trimmed up into the likeness of the transept of a
cathedral—under whose shade you could walk with head uncovered at

3. Alexander Pope, *An Essay on Criticism* (Dublin, 1711), line 625.
4. The "peculiar institution" is, of course, slavery. Chesnut's statement here may inadvertently offer evidence of covert slave resistance.

noonday. These gave the local coloring; within doors there was of course little difference between ladies' surroundings there, and those of ladies every where else over the world.

As Mrs. Effingham sat at her husband's table in the Library one day with a huge pile of plantation account books before her, diligently writing, Susan flew in, followed slowly by Emily, who in an absent minded way was arranging the drapery of her riding skirt.

"Oh, Mamma!" cried Susan. "The very nicest man Johnny[5] has ever had with him yet! He is simply the handsomest creature I ever saw, though his face is half covered with brown beard; he is ever so tall and strong but he is as fresh and rosy as a girl. Margaret had him all to herself—I rode with Johnny. Ah, Mamma! Don't turn away from me—I can tell you more than Margaret can. He could not talk to her all the time himself, and dear old Johnny did to me—he told me every word there is to know about him— he said so."

"Margaret," said Mrs. Effingham, as usual calmly looking over Susan's head, "What does it all mean?"

"Susan as usual appears to rave, Mamma, but she has not exaggerated in this case I assure you. She has been talking like mad ever since we left them at the gate. For once, she has some reason."

"About this new man?"

"Indeed, he is all Susan says, in appearance; his manners are very different from Dr. Johannis' style—but as good; he is very clever. He arrived to day. I asked them here tomorrow."

But Susan had regained her breath and interrupted.

"Johnny says, he is jolly—he is a horse—you know when a Kentuckian wants to say all for you that is good in one word he says 'old horse.'[6] He explained it by a story of Macready, who was playing in Louisville. The pit was frantic with delight and called Macready before the curtain and he brought his friend with him."

Susan was standing just within the drawing room; Mrs. Effingham rose majestically and closed the Library door in her daughter's face. Emily was caught by that strategic movement *in* the Library. Without a pause Susan continued her story turning to Margaret, who found it hard not to laugh.

"The people cheered like mad, for that 'Horse.' Macready acknowledged

5. Johnny or Dr. Johannis is based closely on MBC's husband's nephew, John Chesnut. See *MBC,* 142–46.

6. In James Kirke Paulding's 1830 play *The Lion of the West,* Kentucky backwoodsman Nimrod Wildfire declares, "I'm a horse" (ed. James N. Tidwell [Stanford, Calif.: Stanford University Press, 1954], 27).

the compliment gracefully, and said, 'here was his Ryder.'[7] Was not that good? the other actor's name was spelt with Y—but the crowd forgot that. As if I care for Macready?—Was not Mamma rude? Only in my own family am I so treated! Every body likes me best. Binky Anne says behind backs Mamma calls me 'the fool of the family.'"

"How can you let her tell you such things? She ought to be ashamed of herself." Susan's tears were flowing now freely but [she] wiped them soon.

"Come with me now darling," said Margaret, soothing her as best she might. "Let us talk of that nice new acquaintance of ours—Cheval de race[8] —our Kentuckians, Eh? You can tell me all of Johnny's stories. You will tell the whole truth always and people hardly ever want it all."

"Ah!" said Susan. "You know they were ever so long in Paris together. And in New Orleans last winter. Johnny calls him a guitaring fellow, because he sings divinely. But he does a quantity of other things. I know this— he did something or other while they were abroad. But Johnny is so ridiculously discreet—I could not make head nor tail of it. This I remember—it was very amusing. There was the duel with the little creole who led the German[9]—No—Mr. Collingwood led, and a fractious little New Orleans Frenchman quarrelled with him. That was the laughable story. Ask Johnny to tell you. He swims beautifully and saved somebody—up some where. That's the wager. Oh on Red River—such frightful names—Nachitoches[10]— it sounded like that. That was South. But the boat race—and he was stroke whatever that is. He seems to be always some where. Like Johnny after being abroad he takes his time about going home. I have made it all as short as I could to leave any sense in it. Johnny wound up with this: 'He is such a pleasant tempered fellow—that is the best of him.'"

To return to Emily and her Mother.

"You do not seem to have been with the others—you know my rule. You must keep together."

"Young Blockington and a city lad he has with him joined me. We were never far away: not fifty yards; at least not out of sight."

<hr/>

7. William Charles Macready (1793–1873), famous British actor, made an American tour in 1843 and again in 1848–49. On both tours, he appeared in Louisville, and on both tours he was accompanied by fellow actor John Ryder. The incident Susan describes does not appear in *The Diaries of William Charles Macready,* ed. William Toynbee, 2 vols. (New York, 1912).

8. Fr., literally, horse of pure blood lines.

9. The German is an elaborate social dance similar to a cotillion.

10. The Red River, the southernmost main tributary of the Mississippi River, flows from Texas through Louisiana. Natchitoches is the name of both a city and a parish in northwest Louisiana.

"I know—you never disobey me."

"Let me tell you how young Blockington talks of his home life. He calls Blockhouse 'a high pressure Mississippi steam boat; jarring, creaking, puffing, snorting, every thing straining and quivering, steam whistle blowing. Steam letting off. With an explosion imminent at any moment.' The boiler burst this morning, he says. He asked his friend, 'Did you think the house was on fire? Well my father who was kneeling at prayers, facing a window, saw a negro boy ride his horse to water—you know he ought to have led him. He shouted out of the window in the most excited manner, "Ah! you little rascal—I see you." Cuffer got down in an instant and was out of sight as soon. And my father resumed family prayers. Never seeming to give the strange interlude another thought.

"'With all this noise, this sound and fury, nobody is afraid of him but my mother and sisters; they have not found him out. He is kind hearted—absolutely soft hearted. As for Cuffer, whose moral sense is none of the clearest at best, he is bewildered when he finds mislaying a spur raises the house—and stealing a horse can do no more, you know.

"'My sister says just now—the rice needs rain. And he can't get at the weather conveniently, so he takes it out in railing at those of us who are handy.'"

"Did the Charleston man have a father to uncover?"

"Yes, Mamma. He said his father, he knows, is famous, for he is always reading what he does and says in the papers; that he is awfully proud of him—but then he rarely ever sees him. A lawyer is so busy."

"And you—what did you complain of?" said Mrs. Effingham dryly. "Did you describe your home?"

"Why not? I told them we lived under the sway of a benevolent and beneficent tyrant—who had few laws, and enforced them rigidly. There was no uncertainty, no meddling in trifles. And no unnecessary fault finding—that I did not know so happy a household."

"Then young Blockington said, 'Peace reigns in Warsaw.'"[11]

"He did—or something very like it—but who told you? Susie was barely in sight."

"I know the sneers of all sophomores. You did not meet this admirable Crichton?"[12]

---

11. From Alexandre Dumas père (1802–70), *Mémoires d'un médecin,* second series (Paris, 1846–48), 4:3.

12. James Crichton (1560–82) was given the name "Admirable" by Sir Thomas Urquhart (1611–60) in *Discovery of a Most Excellent Jewel* (1652).

"Oh yes! only for a moment—at the gate. But Margaret in her high and mighty way is worse than Susan—she liked his manner. She said he had a natural ease and grace—(not like our formal home bred youths) which she had heard, never failed to accompany perfect physical beauty."

"Tut—Tut. Their heads are turned," said Mrs. Effingham. "Every one of them."

4

Yet be merry. Strive not with the end.
Thou canst not change it.
For the rest, a friend
This year has won thee, who shall never fail.[1]

As they rode away from the gate at Effhall, Dr. Johannis spoke sharply. "You were indiscreet Collingwood. You must not tell tales out of school. I propose to forget the nonsense we talked in Paris. I never dreamed of your repeating what I said then."

"Are those girls ordinary samples of humanity, as it manifests itself along this coast?" said Collingwood, ignoring the rebuke.

"I have never heard them called ordinary before."

"As mere samples—they are astounding—my eyes are dazzled."

"'Revenons à nos moutons.'[2] I could have added a supplement to your story of the bachelor dinners. Do you remember your terms? They were short—sharp, and decisive. 'An heiress. An orphan. And a woman who would be satisfied with one husband!'"

"What an awful fool I was! Terms indeed. I surrender at discretion; I lay down my arms. I know my wife will be good and beautiful. The rest is 'as God wills.' Benedick says something like that in the play.[3] Eh?" He was blinded still by that radiant vision—those glorious grey eyes, through which he fancied he caught sight of a soul.[4]

---

1. William Morris, "The Love of Alcestis," from *The Earthly Paradise* (London, 1868–70); in *The Collected Works* (London, 1910–15), 4:113.

2. Fr., literally "Let's return to our sheep," here means "Let's return to the point." The saying comes from an anonymous French farce, *La Farce de maistre Pathelin* (1470), in which a judge, confronted by a complainant who seeks reparation for some lost sheep, but who has become confused in court by a devious lawyer, directs the plaintiff to get back to the main business at hand.

3. Allusion to Shakespeare, *Much Ado About Nothing*, 2.3.30–38.

4. Chesnut here adds "&c &c" in pencil, apparently a note to herself to expand the section.

When Margaret came down to the drawing room next day, somewhat earlier than the others, for she had her own especial duties—the wine, and the arrangement of the cards on the table; she looked brighter and happier than she had done for many a day. Certainly, she was far more elaborately and becomingly dressed. At all times however she wore the self satisfied air of a beauty, and that goes far to delude a world little given to think for itself.

Her hair rippled away from a fine forehead, well formed and white. Those who did not like her said—she had a cruel mouth. Be that as it may, the teeth within that red line of their lips, were beautiful. Her face grew colder when she smiled. She had the Murdstone eye.[5]

People did say—when, patience exhausted, she swooped down on Susan when the latter was too exasperating, to put an end to her intolerable gabble, that Margaret had the fierce expression of a bird of prey. The younger girls were "Em" and "Sue." Not one letter of Margaret's name was ever bated.

"We are a handsome family," Susan was wont to say.[6] "Every variety of style. And Mamma has had us stuffed with all available knowledge. We were carted off to Europe with Mrs. Blythe, who was to ensure our seeing— well—everything. I was a fearful failure; but the others can tell you of the Pictures—the Galleries—the Alps, and the Churches. Margaret can tell you."

But we will leave the girls for awhile and say something of "that dear Johnny," and his friend who, according to Susan, had only to come, to see, and to conquer.[7]

Charles Johannis inherited a fine Estate, and with it an establishment so perfect in all its appointments, so picturesque in all its surroundings—as to be the show place on the river and the desire of all mothers' hearts. It was so near Effhall, that, but for the live oaks, it might have been seen from the drawing room windows.

Johannisberg was not even a hill. And it could not boast a grape vine. Why should it? The family were driven away by Malaria by the fifteenth of April—every year, and never returned before November. But the cellar

5. Allusion to Charles Dickens, *David Copperfield* (London, 1850). Edward Murdstone, David's stepfather, is described as having "that kind of shallow black eye—I want a better word to express an eye that has no depth in it to be looked into."

6. A penciled marginal note that occurs about here in the text indicates that MBC apparently intended to move portions of this material and include them in chapter 3. Since it is not clear exactly what she intended to move, or where she intended to place it, these marginal notes have been ignored.

7. Julius Caesar's observation on his conquest of Gaul, "*veni, vidi, vici*" (I came, I saw, I conquered). Suetonius, *Divus Julius,* 37.2.

justified its borrowed name—there "green seal" and the "yellow seal" were sufficiently abounding.[8]

When these young people were babies still, Mr. Effingham said, "Wife, if either of these children takes a fancy to Charles Johannis give her the land; and divide the money between the other three." From a man whose face was so rigidly set against match making, this hint spoke volumes for Johnny. At that time he was spare and slightly made,[9] with fair hair and a pale face. Without the appearance of health or strength, yet he was a consummate horseman; there could be no finer rider in the world. The pride of his life was centered in his stable. Even the owner of that princely estate was thought to exceed the limits of prudence, when he touched horseflesh; but then he had no other weakness. He was too inert to hunt, too lazy to row upon the river. His boat however was well manned by a crew of trained black oarsmen.

He had a magnificently shaped head—for all that, he was neither clever nor cultured. With a beak à la Wellington[10] and a most winning smile, this courteous, loyal, well bred gentleman won his way. He would have died a thousand deaths on a point of honor, or right. If he considered his personal honor implicated, words were vain. He was devoted to the society of women and ever devising some new pleasure for them. The Effinghams were all the world to him.

He was apt to make love to young women, when they were pretty or agreeable, but he had never been known to propose to any of them. In spite of his real humility and unexaggerated self estimate, he could take care of himself. Once, when she was about eight years old, for her health, Mrs. Effingham sent Emily with her Maumer,[11] under his care to an aunt in town. With this beautiful child upon his knee, as he drove along in the balmy spring morning air—even then he had resolved to make her his wife, at some future day. Of course this wise resolution he kept to himself.

8. Johannisberg is located in the hilly Rheingau district between Bingen and Wiesbaden in Germany. The noted vineyards of nearby Johannisberg Castle, situated on a hill, yield one of the finest German wines, Rheingau. The vineyards still produce various qualities of wine, which are labeled with seals of different colors.

9. This description of Johannis corresponds closely to MBC's descriptions of John Chesnut in her revised Civil War journal. See, for example, *MCCW,* 485, 511, 523–24, 558. It should be noted that the revised Civil War journal was written after *The Captain and the Colonel,* long after John Chesnut's death in 1868. Therefore, MBC's portrait of John Chesnut in the revised Civil War journal may well have been influenced by the character Charles Johannis in the novel.

10. Arthur Wesley (later Wellesley), first Duke of Wellington (1769–1852), Anglo-Irish soldier and statesman, defeated Napoleon at Waterloo in 1815. His prominent nose is evident in a number of portraits, including that by Goya in 1812.

11. A "maumer" is a slave nursemaid.

Emily alone had some inkling of the high honor in reserve for her; but she did not impart her knowledge to a human being. She was too much afraid her Mother would favor the idea; and she said to herself, "I could not—you see—I could not."—

"Mamma," cried the amiable Susan, already oblivious of that rude door shut in her face. "What do you think Mr. Collingwood told us!—there, out at the gate while we were waiting for Emily. He said, 'In Paris, Johnny informed them, that he was waiting for his little wife to grow up; that he had always intended to marry at home, because there, every body knew every body else's circumstances.'"

"Very impertinent of Dr. Johannis upon my word! his 'circumstances' in this connection means money."

"Oh yes!" said Susan. "Mr. Collingwood comprehended 'the circumstances' as soon as he saw us, that drew Johnny home. And, he said—he did not blame him." Ruefully regarding her Mother's unsympathetic face—Susan hastened to add, "If you find any thing wrong in this, set it down to my blundering. I am the family repeater, you know. Margaret said it was a beautiful compliment to us all."

Here the gentlemen were announced.

As Margaret led Mr. Collingwood away to inspect some new music, Mrs. Effingham remarked to Emily with a smile, "The stranger does not fall below public expectation, although Susan has tried to raise it as high as the skies."

Emily did not respond. She was thinking "how old, and ugly, and faded, Johnny looked aside the newcomer; this specimen of youth, health and manly beauty."

"I saw you but for a moment yesterday," said a voice at her ear. "You joined us at the gate only; to atone for that cruelty, on your part, let me take you down to dinner."

"I would like it. But that is, as Margaret pleases. She arranges the cards. It would never do to leave our guests to accident, you know."

"And Emily arranges the flowers," interposed Susan. "That is her household duty; I help her. Mamma objects to a pyramid of flowers cutting the table into four parts; but we pile them high some times. It is such a convenient hedge to hide behind. We are never doing any thing wrong; but then when Mamma looks round severely; and her grim face is depressing; though half the time, she is not angry at our small flirtations, but patriotically defending her adopted country. So we raise a rampart to be out of view of the enemy."

Leaving Susan in the midst of her uncalled for revelations Emily went into the dining room and made a quick investigation of Margaret's plan of battle. She saw that Collingwood and Margaret were on one side of the huge mound of flowers and Johnny and herself on the other. She quietly substituted a couple of elderly neighbours—and placed Johnny and herself in full view of his friend. After accomplishing this strategic movement she returned to the drawing room, hoping her brief flitting had passed unobserved.

At dinner, Mr. Blockington and his contented lady friend never knew they had sustained any injury. The view of Collingwood's handsome face was nothing to them. They ate in solid peace and comfort, from Gumbo Soup, to Pineapple ice—through oysters, terrapin stew, shrimp pie, ham and turkey, wild ducks and partridges; with Scipio[12] at their elbow to replenish their glasses, with silent celerity. He knew Mr. Blockington's cellar and appreciated its excellence, hence he gave him the oldest Madeira. I think the old wine was one of Johannis' "circumstances."

Margaret was surprised, but supposed she had inadvertently made a blunder. She said to herself "that Emily would make eyes at strangers," and yet when she put her behind the pyramid of flowers—she knew in her heart that it was not true.

So Collingwood listened devoutly to Margaret, and occasionally caught Emily's eye and smiled. Across the table he heard something spoken of, for the next day. To ride some where?—he scarcely heard what, or cared indeed. He meant to ride one of those fine horses of Johannis, and with that girl, over there; he settled that positively in his own mind.

They were all gone—and the girls were lighting their bedroom candles.

"I say Mamma! You know Emily ran down to the dining room just before dinner." Margaret turned and looked steadily at Emily, who flushed scarlet.

"When she came back, there was the whole length of the room between us, and she had to walk across to join Mr. Collingwood and me—he was talking to Johnny, he did not know I heard. He was watching Emily and he said, 'She is a high stepper.' Johnny scowled—but nothing daunted the Kentuckian added, 'She picks up her feet so daintily.'"

Susan having made every body thoroughly uncomfortable, in sweet un-

12. One of James Chesnut Sr.'s most trusted servants was named Scipio (a common name for slaves). MBC mentions him in her revised Civil War journal. This is apparently the same Scipio who revealed a plot designed to instigate a slave rebellion in Camden in 1816, and who was secretly granted his freedom for his action (L. Glen Inabinet, "'The July Fourth Incident' of 1816: An Insurrection Plotted by Slaves in Camden, South Carolina," unpublished paper delivered at a Conference on South Carolina Legal History, University of South Carolina, December, 1977.) Scipio, as a very old man, delivered the last prayer at the death of James Chesnut Jr. (Isabella Martin, introduction to first edition of *A Diary from Dixie* [New York, 1905], xix).

consciousness kissed them all "good night." As Emily went up the stairs she called. "Stop Em! I have more to tell that you did not hear. Did you ever read Pelham?[13] As you rode up to the gate, he asked if we remembered what Pelham said to himself when the people stared at him. Johnny said it was a young man's book! And Margaret knew nothing about it."

"Is that all?"

"No indeed! Pelham told them to look as long as they liked, and if they could find any fault with man or horse they were cleverer fellows than Pelham. It was his nice way of saying you and the Arabian were faultless."

"I see," said Emily in a rage.

"Kiss and make friends—I have offended you—and I did not mean it."

Here Susan caught her Mother's eye, and fled from the wrath to come.

The next day Emily rode with Johnny, in spite of Collingwood's fixed determination otherwise. Johnny nodded—and called "little Hartkopf" and she smilingly responded. Susan's disagreeable suggestions of the night before were still in her ears. And Margaret's eye, when her small manoeuvre with the cards on the dinner table the day before was laid bare.

At the place of local celebrity, which was the object of their expedition, Collingwood adroitly managed to gain a few words with the lady of his love. For to that it had come already. "Love flows like the Solway but ebbs like the tide."[14] This thing had seized Collingwood by the throat at a bound; with the grip of a blood hound. No cruel crawling tide, no ebb and flow. There had been one quick spring and all was over. This was Collingwood's fine way of putting it—to himself.

He saw chance was forever throwing him with Margaret and he hoped to improve the time, by making her his friend. If she was not the rose—he told himself—she lived with her.

The game of cross purposes was so innocently played. Margaret exulted in her appropriation of the handsome stranger, and sounded his praises. Mrs. Effingham saw that Emily was sure of Johannisberg whenever she chose to take it. She preferred of the two, to send Susan away to Kentucky—but one can't have every thing exactly as one desires, and Margaret should not be crossed. Joanna Hardhead would be amiable, and carry out dear Frank's wishes. What a delicate sense of propriety he had! And how hard driven he was sometimes; but anger him as she would, never once had an allusion been made to that letter of hers to which he had so promptly responded. And yet in the hands of a vulgar soul how she might have been

13. *Pelham; or, The Adventures of a Gentleman* (London, 1828), by Edward Lytton Bulwer, later Edward George Earle Lytton Bulwer-Lytton (1803–73).

14. Sir Walter Scott, *Marmion* (Edinburgh, 1808), canto 5, stanza 12, line 20.

harried. A few months after her marriage she came across this letter in his Portfolio. She hastily consigned it to the flames. She blushed now a hot brick dust red as she remembered that act—And yet it had all ended so well.

This was the one unsatisfactory retrospect of her life.

Annita?—No—there she did her duty.

5

The real woman whose first touch
Aroused to highest life
My real manhood. Crown it then,
Good angel—friend—lover wife!

And so weeks passed away: still no word of love had been spoken by the stranger to Emily. Perhaps his love scrape lost nothing by the constant excitement of outside arrangements to evade.

They felt the disturbing influence; and—it may be—their planetary course swerved slightly from its prescribed course. Only instinct at last. No thinking was done—none whatever.

Collingwood meek as a lamb let Margaret lead him to pasture, with a blue ribbon round his neck, as it were. But he kept a quiet look out: in the melee, there was always a sweet word to be snatched from his own fair one.

Dr. Johannis owned a beautiful Arabian. One day, he brought this horse to the house as a present to Emily.[1] Her Mother promptly forbade her accepting so costly a gift. So—it was taken back—but kept in Johannis' stable for Emily's sole use. At the same time it was an understood thing—when that horse came to the door for Emily she was expected to ride with its Master.

Collingwood averred, since the world began, he had never witnessed any thing like Johnny's devotion to his horses. "I have read L'Hermite de la Chaussée d'Antin[2]—while for hours he sits on a fence—and watches his stable boys."

"Why does he not take a chair?"

"That would be a preferable 'coign of vantage'[3]—but—the top rail of a fence—he says is not so uncomfortable as I think."

So the Arabian came up. And Emily fed it with apples and lumps of sugar.

1. John Chesnut presented MBC's niece Mary Williams with a horse in the summer of 1865 (transcription of a memoir by Mary Williams Harrison Ames in the possession of Martha Williams Daniels).

2. Etienne Jouy (1764–1846), L'Hermite de la Chaussée-d'Antin, ou, Observations sur les moeurs et les usages parisiens au commencement du XIXe siècle (Paris, 1813–18).

3. A position well suited to observation or action; cf. Shakespeare's Macbeth, 1.6.7.

It knew her, certainly. And the greeting between the two was remarkable. "The Arabian gives a horse laugh when he sees Emily coming down the steps," said Susan.

"He imitates the sound as nearly as he can," answered Collingwood.

All this was very pleasant. Not so the inevitable consequence. She must ride with Johnny. In his company alone, "she swayed the Arabian's rein with dainty finger tips."[4]

Never was a Kentuckian so tired of horses—as Collingwood soon came to be.

This day however—the ride was postponed. Margaret had to be waited for.

Mrs. Effingham had borne Margaret away with her to pay visits with a full understanding that the riding party was not to come off until she returned.

Johnny and his Cupidon déchaîné[5] came hours too soon. What else had they to do?

"My boat is at the landing. Let us spend a delightful morning on the water—and so get rid of all the bore of waiting for Margaret," suggested Johnny.

"Do. It is such a pity to waste a moment of this perfect day," pleaded Collingwood. In a thrice the girls were ready. "We can't say—as Louis XIV did—'almost we have been kept waiting.' You are models—for all women," said the grateful Kentuckian.

And the group sauntered down the cedar walk.

Johnny risked this sage observation: "The Garden of Eden—now I wonder if it was very different from this?"

"I dare say they did have live oaks—and cape Jasmines—and red bud—and white fringe trees—and Carolina Jasmine—and crab apple blossoms—and opopanax[6]—and roses and violets—and bay blossoms—and Camellias—and sweet olives—"

"Take breath, Susan."

"A breath of the Sweet South."

"Do not forget that wisteria—in your enumeration of the beauties of Johannisberg. See it hangs like huge purple bunches of grapes. Can any thing be sweeter than that Paulownia? The leaves are so much larger than fig leaves. If Eve had any Paulownias—I know she would have made her clothes of them!"

"At any rate now as then—whenever Adam wakes—there is his Eve—still."

"He always finds his Eve. Yes—and he finds the devil too—with her—sometimes."

4. Allusion to Tennyson's description of Guinevere in "Sir Launcelot and Queen Guinevere," *Poems* (London, 1842), 40–41.

5. Fr., unleashed lover.

6. An "opopanax" is a popinac tree or fragrant mimosa (*Acacia farnesiana*).

"Oh the devil! He taught Eve to distill apple brandy, from her apples of evil. Alcohol you know. The Devil made his first appearance on Earth with Apple Jack. Shabby Adams survive the fall—they accuse poor Eves still of all they do wrong."[7]

"Colley, you are not getting along as nicely as I could wish with your Eden—try something else! Leave Milton; try Tennyson."

"Why not?

> In curves the yellowing river ran
> In crystal vapour every where:
> Blue Isles of heaven laughed between,
> And far in forest depths unseen,
> The topmost Elm tree gathered green
> From draughts of balmy air.[8]

Inhale it! And with it a thousand sweet odours, and glimpses of a sky and a sunshine Launcelot and Guinever never conceived of in their wildest dreams. They only knew English skies, you know."

"That was a bold leap from Eve to Guinever. How this poetical fever grows on you."

"Why do you let him call you Colley?"

"Because a colly is the most faithful thing known among men or beasts. A colly knows but one master, and is true unto death. I like the name, but Johannis gave it to me, and I allow no one else to use it."

"What do they call you at home?"

"Bertie—and it might have been worse—Rob, Bob, Bobbie, Robby, Wobberty were all there to choose from."

"What is your M or N. name as the catechism has it? I alluded to that."

"Robert St Alwyn. My parents are Virginians—and they say, you know, they give us fine names. It is their all; they have nothing else to give."

"Why Emily says you have horses—and blue glass!"

"Yes—I live in a glass house and I never throw stones."

"Susie! he is always laughing at you. I said 'blue grass.'"

"I see—but it amounts to the same thing. Who cares whether it is grass or glass; so far away as Kentucky."

"Susie lend me that superfluous glove I see dangling from your pocket? I want it. Emily is wrong! you are so kind, nobody ever laughs at you."

"You let your conceit be seen pretty plainly—my glove fit you!—oh modest youth! Why you are as vain as a peacock."

7. Allusion to John Milton, *Paradise Lost* (London, 1667), book 10.
8. Tennyson, "Sir Launcelot and Queen Guinevere," line 15.

"What has he to be vain of?" said Collingwood.

"His small hands—to begin with—and his large house."[9]

"You forget his horses—he risked his life for four mules today."

"How?"

"Oh! We have had adventures to day early as it is. In the first place, we have had a ducking. We wanted to cross the neck, and met one of the Johannisberg wagons. The driver, Philip, said we ought not to venture—the water was too high. His master replied, 'I know all the high water marks,' and we got in the wagon. Johnny then asked Philip if he could swim. 'Like a fish.' And so we drove in. We were soon out of our depth. Johnny ordered Philip into the wagon and he took the saddle. He managed those mules splendidly—but it was a risky thing to do. He accused Philip of being scared. Philip looked indignant—oh you are a queer people down here."

"Were you in any danger?" inquired Emily.

"No. Not at all. We could all swim. Yet Johnny and the mules were in great danger—I thought."

"Not a bit of it—the mules swam like good fellows. I could not leave those valuable animals in Philip's hands. I saw he was frightened."

"Nor risk Philip's life in driving them? I did not expect to see such skilful driving—or as fearless, out of Kentucky."

"Oh—please don't brag, Mr. Collingwood. Emily detests people who brag."

"Then I will not. I never mean to do any thing Miss Emily Eff dislikes."

As they reached the landing the boat came slowly down the river. The crew wore red shirts, and their black, brawny arms moved in concert with the wild weird music of their song.

"From whom do they learn those tunes?"

"Brought them from Africa—maybe. At least no one ever hears an 'Ethiopian Melody' so called—on the plantation. Nor do you ever hear music like this from the Negro Minstrels."

"This I call Bonny doon weather[10]—with any grief, or any thing on one's conscience—on such a day, and in a scene like this—with that wild music."

9. John Chesnut prided himself on his small hands; cf. *MCCW,* 511.

10. Allusion to Robert Burns, "The Banks o' Doon," in *Johnson's Musical Museum* (Edinburgh, 1787–96), which begins:

> Ye banks and braes o' bonie Doon,
> How can ye bloom sae fresh and fair?
> How can ye chant, ye little birds,
> And I sae weary fu' o' care!

Burns's songs were sung frequently by Chesnut and her contemporaries in South Carolina. When she quotes Burns, she does so from lyrics learned by ear, rather than from any particular edition of Burns.

"Never mind doing poetry for me Johnny," said Susan. "Look behind you. Those two are out of hearing and I am glad of it. What did he mean when he talked to you of Houyhnhnms?[11] While Emily was giving the Arabian that sugar. I did not know."

"And you need never know," said Johnny shortly. To be left alone with Susan was more than he had bargained for.

"These two moved off without tap of drum!"

Suddenly Johannis remembered he had never mentioned Emily's name to his friend. How should Collingwood know, that for her was the great honor reserved—that she was intended for the future Mistress of Johannisberg!

Again Susan applied the lighted match. She seemed to wish to fire the train.

"Margaret calls these her halcyon days. She says that man hangs over her chair, his soul attuned to harmony. She will not be delighted with this day's work. With her Mozart and her Beethoven—sometimes I wish the clever Margaret could see with the back of her head—how her fine faith in Mr. R. St A. C. would vanish! He is always watching Emily—so are you. What did you say? It sounded like swearing. Don't now—I am not at all sure of him. He will give you a hard fall yet. He is in love with Emily."

"Stop, Susan. Do not insinuate doubts of Collingwood's loyalty."

"He looks like an Englishman, he is strong, healthy, rosy, trim, and he has an honest face. He goes in for fair play. Eh—Johnny? That's the way you talked."

"No—no. There is no harm in Colley—he is a mere boy—rather too frank and headlong. He never takes an unfair advantage. He could not do a shabby thing if he tried."

"He has temper of his own—though you say he is so good natured. Did you ever notice his discontented expression when Margaret hangs on too long?"

"Heavens what a kettle of fish! Who is to hint this to the absolute Regina. I would not like to be there when she hears it," said Johnny who had to say something. Then, "By Jove! he is taking her hand."

"It was only for a second. But we have no right to play spy."

"Hello there! Come back! the boat is here waiting—I say—you philanderers come on. We are ready to go on the water," shouted Dr. Johannis.

"Listen to me Johnny. When Mamma harangues, they slip out on the pi-

11. Horses with superior ability to reason, inhabitants of the last country Lemuel Gulliver visits in Jonathan Swift's *Gulliver's Travels* (London, 1726).

azza and I go too as quietly as a cat; but he sees me fast enough. She sees nothing; her eyes are glued to the ground. He shows his annoyance at my approach pretty plainly."

Johannis was hearing more than he could bear. But after all; how could Collingwood be a traitor. Johnny had never [mis]trusted him in the slightest; or any one else indeed.

In society where the laughing is forced, and most people sit with a fatuous smile, Dr. Johannis' grave face was always a rest to the weary eye. Now the smile which had fixed itself upon his face was of the kind called sardonic. Susan had never seen it there before.——

But we must go back and take heed of those radiant ones under the trees.

"Why did not Johannis tell me of this Earthly paradise of his? He only said, 'Come to my old bachelor barrack.'"

"And yet he is proud enough of it! He never could bear to talk of himself. He can be silent—with out murmuring—as the Frenchman said. His forefathers were the original sinners—settlers I mean—they were exiles; may be they ran away. At any rate they were the right thing—but in the wrong time or in the wrong place. Republicans when the world was mad for a King, or Royalists—when loyalty did not pay. Do you want to hear all about it?"

"Not the least bit in the world. We see each other every day—but so many people are always in my way."

"Let us go back. See they are waiting for us."

"Watching us—you mean. I wish the Earth would open and swallow them."

"That sounds friendly."

"No matter now. I have no time to waste. I must speak to you to day. Do you like me as well as any?"

"Yes. But what an odd question."

"Do you like me better than any?" Here she drew her parasol nearer her face, and turned away.

"May I try to make you love me?"

"That is just as you please," she answered lightly. He took her hand, and then came that seemingly uncalled for shaking of hands which caused the staidest gentleman south of the Potomac to whoop, suddenly like a wild Indian, for their return.

"If we must go—take my arm. Give me your parasol; you have been using it for some time as a fire screen. Susan? Oh no. She is a hundred yards off still. It is hard, we may not walk unmolested under this shady avenue. May I speak to your Mother?"

"What about? Why do that? What have I done?—I have said nothing."

"You have not said—No—and every thing else means—Yes.[12] Do not say another word please."

This was love making under difficulties—but the game was won. The mischief done.[13]

6

The universal topic—in 1861.
The gates ajar.[1]

Late that night as the dusky damsels brushed out their young Mistresses' long hair, Susan began. "While you and young Collingwood strayed to day—Johnny and I had such a talk! I like people that I have known all my life. I have faith in Johnny. We have always lived so near. We know every body on his place."

"No doubt. And if there was any harm to be said of him you would know it. His people like him, but they watch him and tattle about him as only the negroes can. I wonder if there was ever a secret in a Planter's home. Negroes are all spies. Not single ones—but they come in battalions. They have their own underground telegraph.[2] Now these girls can tell us every thing that has happened in the last twenty four hours for twenty miles around."

"Let the 'Irrepressible conflicts'[3] slide—I have something else in my head to night."

12. In an autobiographical memoir written for her nieces and nephews following the death of her sister Catherine in 1876, entitled by Chesnut "We Called Her Kitty," MBC ascribes this remark to James Chesnut Jr., prior to their marriage. (Williams-Chesnut-Manning Collection Collection; transcribed in Muhlenfeld "MBC: The Writer and her Work" [Ph.D. diss., University of South Carolina, 1978], appendix C.)

13. Possibly an echo of line 195 in Samuel Taylor Coleridge, "The Rime of the Ancient Mariner" in *Lyrical Ballads* (London, 1798), "'The game is done! I've won! I've won!'"

1. Title of a best-selling novel (Boston, 1868) by American writer Elizabeth Stuart Phelps (1844–1911).

2. Chesnut refers throughout *MCCW* to the information-gathering abilities of the slaves. In March 1861, for example, she and William Henry Trescott speak French, and describe what they are doing as "using French against Africa. We know the black waiters are all ears now, and we want to keep what we have to say dark. We can't afford to take them in our confidence, you know" (*MCCW*, 36). It is worth noting that throughout this teasing conversation, the girls speculate and comment on the shortcomings and sins of the slaves while slave women are brushing their hair!

3. The phrase "irrepressible conflicts," alluding here to the slave women in attendance on the sisters, derives from a speech delivered in Rochester, New York, in October 1858 by

"Oh Johnny—well he belongs to the best abused race that ever existed. It pays politically as well as otherwise to abuse slave owners—as Mamma says."

"Ah Mamma! Methinks I see her now. That is always your way—your refuge in time of trouble giving us Mamma second hand—we want neither her wit nor her wisdom here to night—I am going for you!"

"Uncle Von Enden said slavery hung over me like a pall—and it embittered Margaret—to hear her home life abused. I was beaten back from siding with him—because it made me so angry—that he did not believe a word of Mamma's facts. Theories are free to all—and he did not believe what he saw—because he chose to think these exceptional plantations. The winters are so comfortable here. And our easy going life seems to fascinate northerners. And the climate and all that—but *we,* the home folks, are rather over done with climate. We want to go away—and we do go—unless we have a houseful. We are in town in winter—and off to the ends of the Earth in summer," said Emily talking against time.

"But my lady—hold on awhile. It is blue grass and horses—toward which you now tend? Any slaves in Kentucky?"

"To think these smiling creatures behind us are supposed to tremble and obey. They do not resist—of that they are incapable—but their docility misleads and betrays."

"I hate deceitful people," said Susan—who did not take the trouble to hate any body or any thing, except perhaps to hold her tongue.

"Oh—Papa said that was a part of their peculiar position. Cunning was self defense. He was amused at one fact. The forlornest african on the place by sheer force of cunning could circumvent him."

"I like Daddy Paul's way of putting it. He says, 'Any body who is obliged to dodge will lie—dat buckra tell trut cause dey aint afeard er God—Man—er debil.'"

"I like Mrs. Blythe's comfortable theory. You know she has been as Governess or as Housekeeper—with all kinds and conditions of southern people. She says—be they hard, or soft, rigid and exacting as Mamma, or careless and extravagant as Johnny, in either case their people get their fair share of all that is going. She has never seen it fail. Delightful—Eh? poor things. When it is not given to them they take it."

"I call that pleasant tidings."

"Susie. We are not in the least high-toned. By this wild talk we may encourage evil deeds—you forget our *entourage.*" The girls were laughing.

William Henry Seward (1801–72), later to become Lincoln's secretary of state, that characterized the political division between slave and free states as an "irrepressible conflict."

Binky Anne came forward with a log of wood to replenish the fire. She looked up—as she put "light wood" in to hurry up the blaze—and said, "If black people tek from dey own owners—it is different—it is pulloining—not stealing."

"Binky Anne—take all your cases of conscience to your Methodist 'circus rider'—as you call him—he is the best man in the world. I do not feel equal to putting you straight on the relative merits of pulloining or worse—to night."

"I dare say not," said Susan. "Generally you jump at a chance to preach. While you and your new friend were taking forever and a day to walk up from the landing, Mrs. Blythe was trying in vain to interest Johnny in old Johannisberg stories. He did not seem to take much pleasure in hearing anecdotes of his grandmother's cook."

"Oh! I can tell you plenty," said Binky Anne who continued to kneel before the fire—that she might see their faces, as well as hear all they said.

"Binky Anne will put in her mouth," said Molly[4] disdainfully.

Then Binky Anne volubly narrated the history of the "Jansbug" black people, how they were stuck up. They were descended from servants the first Mrs. Johannis brought from New York. They were proud that their forefathers were from the "big norrard," long before "the resolution war." Ole Miss Johan's maid was her own "frum de fust"—but on her first visit home she induced her husband to invest in a splendid cook and butler in Philadelphia. "That's the reason they can teach any body. Now these here learned fum the Philadelphia negroes."

"Mrs. Blythe's story illustrated that fact," said Susan in a glee. "You know Mamma came down here like a wolf in the fold. She swept like a new broom—Mrs. Blythe says anger and consternation was depicted on every dark countenance. One day she was seated on the stile between this house and Johannisberg—like the Irish Emigrant's lament[5]—and our cook's son came running from 'Jansbug' as hard as he could stave. She halted him and inquired—the reason of his hot haste? His Mother had sent him to ask Jansbug Philis for some butter for her breakfast hominy. And Philis sent it to

---

4. Chesnut's own slave maid, also named Molly, was with her throughout the war and remained afterwards as a house servant until Chesnut's death.

5. Helen Selina Blackwood, Countess of Dufferin (1807–67), "The Lament of the Irish Emigrant" (*The Irish Emigrant* [London, 1840]), begins with this stanza:

> I'm sittin' on the stile, Mary,
> Where we sat side by side
> On a bright May mornin' long ago,
> When first you were my bride.

her—with the taunt—'that she must be a poor cook indeed, who could not save enough of the Buckra butter—for her own hominy.'

"Mamma laughed. The dear old B was shocked. And she ventured to remonstrate with her ci devant[6] pupil—and urge her not to take in sail too rapidly.

"Johnny's perfectly appointed Establishment[7] is an inscrutable fact to our dear Mother. According to all rule of right reasoning it ought to be otherwise."

"Oh bother!" said Susan.

"She can not forgive him. With all her genius for organization—her law and order mania; he does quite as well without any. Nobody takes care of his little negroes—and they grin and grow like young monkeys, and increase and multiply beyond ours. Ours who are cared for like young princes. He has no army of sempstresses and yet his people look as tidy and comfortable as ours. And then their own pigs, and gardens, and balls and prayer meetings, are not regulated—and no harm comes of it. It is Mamma's despair."

"Stop Emily. Johnny has his Mother's cook and her housekeeper and the old grey headed butler. But you know it requires four people over there to do what Mamma requires of one. I own that she finds it hard to forgive him his dinners, which are so much better than ours. His roses too—they are all thorns to her."

"One little item we must set to Mamma's credit. Johnny swears that his negroes are indebted to him for the sum of fifty thousand dollars. He sells his forefathers' accumulation of stocks and all that, every year. Now Mamma makes investments—north, constantly, she calls that her common sense, her superior method, her thrift and her economy."[8]

"You are trying to hold me off? Johnny?—I love him as a brother. You are drifting away from him."

"Marry him yourself."

"He would as soon espouse Mrs. Sebbes' green parrot. What made him study medicine—it seems so senseless to speak of him as a Doctor."

"Only to keep away the longer from this dismal swamp and dull plantation life. They were awfully jolly in Paris—and even in Philadelphia I dare

6. Fr., former.

7. See *MCCW,* 32, where John Chesnut, on whom Charles Johannis is based, is described as a lax, softhearted slave owner.

8. In the preceding comparison of the Johannis plantation to the Effingham plantation, MBC contrasts what she sees as Yankee management techniques aimed at efficiency, order, and profits with more easygoing patterns comfortable to southern gentleman planters.

say. I wonder if he ever sowed any wild oats any where—he is preux cheva-
lier here—sans peur et sans reproche.[9] You remember Mrs. Blythe called
him 'guindé'—which you translated into good American—as 'stuck up.'"

"Heavens Emily—you said that yourself. You are talking against him.
Give the devil his due, the slave owner and all his works—you'll have none
of him. You tend now to horses and blue grass; toward people who die and
conquer agony—oh no—I mean to say—come, see and conquer."[10]

"Now—speaking of this interesting race—"

"Good Lord deliver us," cried Susan—holding up both hands devoutly.

"Binky Anne," said Emily—nearly at her wits' end, "what book was that
you had under your apron today?"

"Lord Miss Emily. Nobody thought you'd care. It is old an wore out. Heap
of the leaves is gone. It is Santa Sebastiano or the N'Young Protector."[11]

"Would you like something new?"

"No Ma'am. We like de ole ones bes. Scottish chief—and Magdalena the
ward er Delamere.[12] Some likes stories like Tar gal and Ber Fox—and Ber
wolf, sitch as begin:

> Once upon a time
> When Pigs was Swine
> And Turkey buzzards chawed terbacker."[13]

"I have heard them myself—down there—so often, when I was a child."

"Molly reads for herself. She teaches me. I can read some, but my young
lady—wont—'she hates learning and she hates teaching'—thems her own
words. Aunt Leah sings.[14] We like that as well as being read to."

"What does she sing that you like best."

9. Fr., valiant knight, without fear and without stain, a phrase usually applied to Seigneur
Pierre Terrail de Bayard, an early sixteenth-century French military hero.

10. See chap. 4, n. 6.

11. Catherine Cuthbertson (fl. 1803–30), *Santo Sebastiano; or, The Young Protector* (London, 1806). The capital *N* preceding "Young" indicates pronunciation, and is representative
of low country Gullah speech.

12. Jane Porter (1776–1850), *The Scottish Chiefs* (London, 1810); Elizabeth Sibthorpe Pin-
chard, *The Ward of Delamere: A Tale* (London, 1815).

13. See Guy B. Johnson, *Folk Culture on St. Helena Island, South Carolina* (Chapel Hill, 1930),
134. Blacks found on St. Helena often began stories with "'Once upon a time, a very good
time, / Monkey chaw tobacco an' spit white lime.'" Johnson records a couplet "Once upon
a time de goose run blin', / Monkey chaw tobacco an' de cat drink wine" that begins a story
about Buh Rabbit (137). Elsie Clews Parsons, *Folk-lore of the Sea Islands, South Carolina* (New
York, 1923), cites and records several versions of the Tar Baby story, including one in which
the tar baby is a tar girl with whom Buh Rabbit falls in love.

14. Leah was MBC's grandmother Mary Whitaker Boykin's seamstress. In "We Called Her
Kitty" she writes:

"Oh! 'Lord Lovel'—and 'Cruel Barbry Ellen'—and the 'Nice brown maid'[15]—a heap of tunes like that."

"Negroes never affect Ethiopian Melodies—I wonder why?"

"Time is up—girls—you may go. Em I will not be staved off any longer. The grand smash has come. The Lord help us!"

"What do you mean?" said Emily at the highest pitch of her voice. But even as she said so—her face grew red as a rose, and a radiant smile illumined it. In spite of her knowledge of the trouble to come there was light within from some untold source.

"I am not clever—we give that up. I hear it often enough! But I am up to your high jinks. Nobody can hear when Margaret is thundering her mighty music; but I can see that creature drag himself to the Piano when she demands his presence there, to turn over leaves. And indeed she does it as if she owned him body and bones. His eyes are free. Heavens! How they looked in the boat to day. He fairly devoured you. He came down the Cedar walk treading on air. What a winning good humor he was in; he was gay and frank enough to win all hearts. To tell the truth he always is. Our dear Johnny's manner was awfully repellent. When Johnny called to you to

---

the head sempstress used to sing—& talk—& sometimes crack any sleepy headed youngster with her thimble—the wool seemed so thick we used to hope it did not hurt—very much—She rode to Camden on horseback & make all the purchases & get new fashions—& tell her young ladies to hold up their heads with the best—& did her best to see they were sufficiently fine—boxes came from Charleston from a colured lady Mrs. Hannah McKenzie who was then to us what Worth is now to American & Paris—& our Leah tried to imitate I know now that Leah was a slave—but I could not have found it out then for myself—her eldest son—bought himself—they made him a tailer—& he soon paid some nominal price for himself—he came back to see us—he was a baptist clergymen—talked dreadfuly through his nose—but that seemed to have been no hindrince to his rise in the Western religious world.

15. "Lord Lovel" and "Barbara Allen," both traditional ballads, were extremely popular in the South. Both were published in the *American Songster,* John Kennedy, comp. (Baltimore, 1836). Both ballads are recorded with variant wordings in Reed Smith, ed., *South Carolina Ballads* (Cambridge, 1928; reprint, Spartanburg, S.C., 1972). Reed does not record any South Carolina versions of "Barbara Allen" that include the name "Barbry Ellen," but such a version has been recorded in Kentucky (see John Harrington Cox, *Folk-songs of the South* [Cambridge, 1925], 101). The "Nice brown maid" may possibly be "Lord Thomas and Fair Annet" or "Lord Thomas and Fair Elinor," a traditional ballad of Scottish and English origin recorded in Percy's *Reliques,* which was, along with "Lord Lovel" and "Barbara Allen," one of the most widely distributed ballads in the United States, and which occurs in South Carolina in many variations. It tells the story of Lord Thomas and his fiancée, a "brown" girl who kills her rival and is herself murdered by Lord Thomas. MBC may also be referring to the anonymous English poem "The Nutbrowne Maide" (or in Percy's *Reliques* 2:26, "The Not Browne Mayd") which dates from about 1500, and which may have been set to music. See Smith, *South Carolina Ballads,* 109–20.

look out for your head, he said to me in a low tone, 'A queenly head it is'—
you were Regina's own daughter. It was high falutin—but Mamma likes
that. He can not begin in that quarter too soon."

"Stop Mrs. Nickleby!"[16]

"To think you are my own sister and the one I love best—and that till to
day I did not know what a beauty you are. When you and that Kentucky
chap came back to the boat—I wish you could have been painted. It was
worth it—I would call the picture—'Soul made manifest in the flesh'—
for you were just too splendidly lovely to be human—Johnny looked blue
black!"

"Who, and what are you alluding to?"

"Mr. St Alwyn C. Has he become *Bertie* to you—since the walk up the
river—under the Cedars! now!"

"Johnny is in love with us all. He is an old bachelor—he is thirty years
old!"

"How you forget—I am older than you."

"No—dear Susie—you never let us forget any thing. Your memory is
implacable—I will change your name—Miss Cellaneous Reminder!"

"That guitar ribbon—the coolness of the creature! As he removed it
from your neck; he cut a little scrap of it and tied it in his button hole. He
informed me again. 'Those were his colors'—and to me!—'Give me what
this ribbon bound—take all the rest the world goes round.'[17] I have spoiled
it? I dare say. What does it matter? I always do—quotations. He made himself very plainly understood when he sung 'Napolitaine I am dreaming of
thee.'[18] But his dreams were with his eyes wide open."

All the blood in Emily's body seemed to have rushed to her face. She
clapped her hands to her ears.

"Margaret is awfully interfering. She tells Mamma so much we do not
want her to know. Johnny and his boat were too much for her to day. And
he was a little too clever for his own good; he gave some people a chance
they have hankered for many a day."

Emily sprang to her feet. "I will go into another room. This is simply in-

---

16. Mrs. Nicholas Nickleby, widow of Nicholas, Sr., in Charles Dickens's *Nicholas Nickleby* (London, 1839), interprets actions and remarks of other characters as romantically mo-
tivated.

17. MBC's niece Serena Williams had a suitor in Columbia in early 1865 who wore a red
scrap of ribbon she had given him in his buttonhole, "his 'colors nailed to the mast'" (see
MCCW, 703). Edmund Waller (1605–87), "On a Girdle," in *Poems,* 2nd ed. (London, 1664),
3:11–12.

18. "I am dreaming of thee" by A. Lee, included in the eight-volume Franklin Square song
collection published by Harpers, 1881–91.

tolerable—insufferable,"—but she failed to find peace. Susan left her and her own maid Molly reentered.

"Miss Susan talks a heap but she dont know every thing. Peyton tole me Miss Margaret was down on the strange gentleman to ole Missis in the carriage this morning. Clarissa is going to be married to Yaller Sam—his true true name is Sambo for his father who is name Guinea Sambo—but he calls himself Yaller Sam because his father is that black. Mr. Collingwood did say—'glossy black.' And his mother is another sorter brighter than me. Our people do say he stole ole Missis' cochum[19] Chaney here—but mum's the word. For Old Carrabo—his Mother is Mars Charles' Nuss—and we dont want her down on us—no how."

Emily groaned.

Molly then with a thousand amplifications and variations told of Margaret's having heard through Clarissa, who had it from Sam—of the gay bachelor life at Johannisberg. Even the number of bottles emptied each day at the dinner table. Mr. Collingwood drank Rhine wine, which he said was of the most innocent description. The vin du pays[20] of his country was corn whiskey. Sambo declared his preference for that "fan, and give it to him reverent too," having no weakness for "rind wine—which was pore vinergry stuff after all."

When Margaret began to describe the unusual dissipation which Johnny now permitted himself, Mrs. Effingham stopped her instantly—saying it would never do to condemn a friend and neighbour on "negro news." According to Clarissa, "Ole Missis snapped her up short."

Margaret hastened to the river bank but soon returned. Mrs. Effingham was at this time seated at her desk in the library—and Margaret standing before the fire began her second story—an account of what she saw and heard from the river bank: Collingwood's songs—and Emily's guitar accompaniment. Such conduct was a double insult. They had no father nor brother.[21] This came from Big Judy the cook who going in for orders, discovered her Mistress and Miss Margaret in earnest conversation. Judy wishing to hear stood back, screened by the chimney but near enough to step into the drawing room and say, "she this, this, minute come in, she heard Miss Margaret tellin I cant tell you what all. He was a butterfly—but the hysterics come on an Ole Missis got up, and shet the door—Slam—big Judy had dodged long befo dat—but she heard Miss Margaret a screamin."

"I do not want you any more to night—never mind my slippers. I do not

19. Coachman.
20. Fr., literally "wine of the countryside," popular wine.
21. I.e., no chaperone, no paternal or fraternal protector.

mean to hurt your feelings when I stop you. I know you felt it right to warn me. If I ever go away from here—would you like to go with me?"

"Miss Emily—do you think I would lef you?"

"Well—on one condition I will take you—promise never to tell me any more tales."

7

> Un lion de haut parentage
> En passant par un certain pré,
> Rencontra bergère à son gré:
> Il la demande en marriage.[1]

When Mr. Collingwood called next day, he asked for Mrs. Effingham.

Never again did he experience such trepidation—such sinking of heart. And in his after life he stormed some bristling batteries as we shall come to see.

He tried to state his case clearly; but then he was not altogether as cool as the judge before whom he pleaded. In demanding the hand of her daughter in marriage, he named the amount of his income; and made known his power to support his future wife in the comfort and affluence to which she was accustomed. He referred to his friend Dr. Johannis, who had known him for years, and not long ago made him a visit of several weeks. She showed no inclination to interrupt him.

She was truly formidable that day.

At last she spoke.

"I have been a witness to your devotion to my daughter. She is old enough to be trusted in this matter. So if my daughter Margaret has given you her consent, I will not with hold mine."

She smiled grimly at his unspeakable dismay. Collingwood saw he was in for it now! How was he to remedy his blunder?

"Since the day I met her first—I have openly sought Miss Emily Effingham's hand. There has not been a shadow of concealment on my part.

"Yesterday she gave me permission to ask your consent," said the poor fellow, who felt he had made an awful bungle of it—after all.

"Yesterday! And not one word of this has my undutiful child spoken to me. No—I will not consent. No. You are a stranger to me. My daughter

---

1. Jean de La Fontaine (1621–95), "Le Lion Amoureux," *Fables* (Paris, 1668): "A well-born lion / On his way through a particular meadow / Met a shepherdess to his liking / And asked her to marry him."

is only seventeen. I know you only as an intruder who has caused our hitherto discreet neighbour to be harshly criticized, in consequence of your
bachelor revelries. And then your extraordinary behavior in this house! I
see you forever dangling after one of my daughters, and you are here to ask
permission to marry another! It is an insult to my understanding—to my
penetration, and my prudence—indeed to my watchful over sight as a
Mother. This equivocal position of yours justifies my distinct refusal—without further reason. The account of your riotous life at Johannisberg no
doubt displeased Margaret; and then you turn and beguile my simple
hearted Emily. Should one of these children disobey me, and marry without my consent, she can be cut off from her inheritance. You do not know,
probably, that I have absolute control of my husband's property."

"No—Madam—I did not know it, but I am very glad to hear it. It clears
my way amazingly. Miss Emily Effingham does not think of me as you do."

"My children think as I choose them to think. Scipio you were slow in answering the bell. Show the gentleman the door."

The girls were to dine next day with a friend of theirs; Margaret and the
ever faithful Johannis were always accounted capable of taking care of the party.
Soon after breakfast Susan hurried off, for a long day, with her youthful crony.
She said "she knew Emily's trial was coming on that day and she wanted to
be out of it." She bestowed parting advice, in her own peculiar fashion.

"Stand up for yourself! Remember that queer smile of Papa's—you have
it to day. No one could ever tell when he was in earnest—that day he was
defending the poor old opium eating Fronin. Mamma lost her temper. She
cried, 'You do well. Your everlasting classics. Your poems and your novels—your self indulgence, and your ease at others' cost. Your life is as sinful a deadening of the soul, as old Fronin's opium is of his body.' We hung
our heads—but he smiled. 'Go away you babies.—Stop—I will do one
duty. When I am gone—stand up for your rights—do not let her crush
you.' He was so kind. *I* mean to take his advice. I will give you a capital
hint—give her back one of her own lectures—as you did—last night. You
remember them so well. Keep her off as you kept me at bay last night. She
is always preaching sermons on Matrimony. I am not afraid of her. Great
Heavens! She is coming up the back stairs. I will escape by this door. I will
pray for you while the battle rages. Remember—Don't be crushed."

The day however passed without disturbance, and unmarked by any unusual event. There was a heavy feeling prevalent in the house—it was as if
a death, or some calamity hung over them, until Margaret opened the
Piano—She had received some new music. She found it difficult, apparently, for she persisted in mastering it, the live-long day. And her noise was
a relief to all parties.

Mrs. Effingham ruled, with a strong hand. Peace, plenty, and happiness to the greatest number was the result of this strictly personal government. She was order and punctuality incarnate. Every wrong was righted by whomsoever committed, black or white; and as far as her laws extended every crooked thing was made straight. There was no appeal from her despotic decisions however.

Emily found the atmosphere of the house oppressive; but she dared not leave it. Johannisberg was so near; she felt that Collingwood was hovering in the air ready to pounce upon her if she emerged, and her Mother was equally ready in such a contingency, to have her ignominiously dragged back.

After all, this day spent in Solitude was a respite. She could take counsel with her own heart and settle her plan of action. That she meant to stand to her guns, was certain.

She was sure she would meet her accepted lover at dinner, and they would consult as to the future.

8

> But it is all in vain—The battle is done.
> The day is lost!—the day is won!

"Emily are you ready? Margaret is waiting," cried Johnny from the foot of the stairs. As soon as she appeared he ran half way up to meet her, he took her hand, and they walked at once to the carriage; he whispered, "You remember the old song—

> She never blamed him never,
> But received him when he came,
> With a smile as sweet as ever,
> And *he* tried to look the same."[1]

When they arrived at Mrs. Sebbes' door, without giving a glance behind him, he walked off with Margaret. As they drove up, he saw Collingwood waiting for them in the piazza, and he magnanimously cleared the way and left the field open to his successful rival. Johnny moved quickly—as Collingwood sprang down the steps; but Margaret looked back at the exact moment, when Collingwood bent his head over Emily's hand and pressed it to his lips. She started as if stung—in the drawing room, after speaking to the lady of the house, she turned and fixed them with a stony stare. For

1. Nathaniel Thomas Haynes Bayly (1797–1839), "She Never Blamed Him Never," in *Songs, Ballads, and Other Poems, by the Late Thomas Haynes Bayly, Edited by His Widow* (London, 1844).

her pains she saw two gloriously beautiful human faces, radiant in their new found happiness.

Susan had been as mysterious all day; but the strong necessity of speaking overcame her good resolutions.

"May—dear—do ask your Mother to send Mr. Collingwood down to dinner with Emily. As for me, I would not object to him as a brother, I like him so well."

"Oh! Oh! Is that so. Are they really engaged?" May was wild with excitement, and wanted to know all about it at once.

"Not positively, I am sure—Mamma may give them some trouble—you know—but never mind."

At dinner fate threw them again along side of Mr. Blockington, who, when he laughed shook himself all over, he shook his chair, he shook the table, I am not certain that he did not shake the house. And then he whispered audibly his joke. "Love and a cough can't be hid. Look at Miss Emily —she was never before, half so handsome."

There is no redress for the injured under these aggravated circumstances.

"Brief time had Conrad now to greet Gulnare."[2] And yet he was inclined to waste the precious moments as they flew, in vain repetitions. He was so contentedly happy, she could not make him properly apprehend the rocks ahead. She knew better—she knew they would not be allowed to see one another—or even to write—that is, if her Mother proved obdurate. Though Emily herself had alway a happy knack of hoping.[3]

Mr. Blockington—in a low tone suggestive of distant rumbling thunder—remarked to Susan, "It is easy to see what is going on there. I suppose they have settled it. He looks so—they always do—so foolish and so happy. He has what you young ones call 'the love light in his eye.'[4] From what I hear, your dread Mother will quench that soon enough."

"Yes—he does not know yet, what Mamma amounts to, in our house."

All this was rather hard upon the "newly engaged couple." Fortunately they had no time to hear or to resent liberties taken with their affairs or their appearance. Emily promised to do all in her power to rectify her Mother's misapprehensions. If he failed to hear from her, all was lost for the present, and it would be wisest for him to go quietly home for awhile and let the storm blow over. They could wait. She would not give him up. He had already asked her that. At the worst—when she was twenty one she could act for herself. She asked why he did not confide in Johnny?

2. George Gordon, Lord Byron, *The Corsair* (London, 1814), canto 2, stanza 6, line 1.

3. "Alway" here may be an intentional archaism or allusion, and has therefore not been changed by the editor to "always."

4. Helen Selina Blackwood, "Lament of the Irish Emigrant," line 8.

"I have tried. He is very considerate. You saw him arrange it so I could take you out of the carriage? But if I approach the subject he freezes the very marrow in my bones."

"I see—never mind. I will put him straight going home. I am to drive with him."

"No. Let him alone. You are not to have any other friend than me."

"Proprietorship already?"

"Yes—that hand you let me take, yesterday, has turned my head."

Then came what she called "Nonsense—Nonsense."

"I have one fear!"

"You need not. I am sure of myself!"

(Seventeen!)[5]

To Margaret there was not the faintest allusion—for very sisterly shame. Johannis likewise treated that part of the late drama as if it had never been. The elder sister's mistake had been so humiliating. He would not so much as think of it.

As they drove off—Emily said to Johnny, "I know you are going to be my friend?"

"Yes—and all that I settled with my self last night. Every thing has been fair and above board. I had to acknowledge that—to myself. For the last month we have lived in a fool's paradise. Some of us—those who were not wanted—got in—and we have been kicked out. Treachery was on the end of my tongue all day yesterday. Thank God! I did not utter it—for it is false. My pillow was a raging billow of bad words last night; the tide ebbed before day. Did you ever hear me make so long a speech? I, who never walk when I can ride, or talk when I may hold my tongue. You have the floor now."

"And you have really forgiven your little 'Hartkopf Emily'?"

He put his arm around her and calmly kissed her. She bore it as coolly, as she would Molly dusting her mantle. Between Johnny's fraternal embrace, and some of her late experiences there was so little in common that one did not even recall the other.

When she grew too old for Johnny to take her on his knee, he knew, he ought also to put an end to the petting and kissing; especially when he began to entertain other hopes. He could see that it left him in the same boat with the dear old parson and the good old Doctor, the two most intimate and trusted friends of the family, and to whom parental privileges were accorded. But he had never been able to sacrifice the present for the future.

"Now listen—to me. Mamma has the experience of three successful

5. MBC had herself been seventeen for only three weeks when she married James Chesnut Jr. in 1840.

campaigns. She spoke peremptorily to Aunt Annie—who believed her every word. Pappa called it 'damned iteration.' She had a brilliant success there. Uncle Von Enden says—she came up with Papa—touched him on the shoulder as a corporal does a deserter—and marched him into camp. These are family 'twice told tales.' How strong she is—and how good. I am not wanting in filial piety. Annita?—How can you? That is too pitiful. Still it is a warning. Johnny, let her marry you to somebody. She will I know. She always succeeds."

"Hold on—there is no question of me. You are number four."

"No—no—no. She is invincible when match making. Mine is a case of match breaking—in that she is a raw hand; and she will fail. I dread the trial of strength between us; for I do not mean to disobey her—for awhile. She will be routed in the end. I am made of different materials from Annita— I will not die—I mean to live, and be happy ever after."

"Last night," said her friend, "I planned for myself a foreign tour. I wanted to be out of the row I foresee. Did you hear that old dunderhead to day? He recalled the outside world to my wandering senses. A fellow cannot leave home now. They all said war was inevitable. Did you hear the ghastly picture drawn by our parson. The horrors of war! 'Ah! I don't mind all that,' said old Mr. Blockington cheerfully. 'I am afraid of those damned heroes who are going to infest the country for forty years after the war.'"

"I cannot believe there will be a war."

"You might as well accustom your self to the idea—it is at hand. I am a quiet citizen—not given to shouting—or singing—*Enfants de la patrie.*[6] That is not my style; but I must abide the brunt. I do hope they will let me do my fighting on horseback."

The carriage wheels were grating on the gravel, at her own door.

She stammered, "Johnny befriend me? You are the only one I can rely upon. Eh?"

"You may." He put her hand on his heart; it was beating like a sledge-hammer. She was dumbfounded—and fled in silent consternation.

Before breakfast next day, for the first time in her life—we had almost said—Mrs. Effingham voluntarily sought an interview with her daughter Susan. Margaret's narrative had been so highly colored, and of such condensed bitterness it defeated its own purpose. She told of the man's rudeness; he only acknowledged her presence by a distant bow. "Their brazen effrontery." (In her heart Mrs. Effingham believed nothing of the kind about Emily.) And the nods and becks and smiles of the lookers on.

6. From the first line of Claude-Joseph Rouget de Lisle's "La Marseillaise" (1792), which became the national anthem of the French Revolution.

Susan knew no good would come of her revelations. She tried the "Know nothing" method—but she failed. Her mother soon entangled her in a hopeless muddle of "Dawson told Philip to stand where Doctor Johannis put him; that is behind our carriage. Somebody else made Philip drive round the circle. So in reality he was in front of us. Emily went in the wrong direction."

"By herself?"

"It was Philip's fault—he moved. Every body was hunting—every body. At last Johnny found them waiting not very far from our carriage. He drove Emily home." The story was preposterously confused; for the want of a missing name.

> And the omission like that of the bust
> Of Brutus, at the Pageant of Tiberias
> Made Joan wonder—as no doubt she must.[7]

"Go—and send Emily to me."

"My dear Emily—I am afraid Mr. Collingwood has not dealt candidly with you. I positively refused—to give my consent, to this engagement."

Emily trembling from head to foot and by no means the cool and self possessed young warrior she so calmly outlined to Johnny the night before, [spoke]. "He told me. Ah Mamma, how could you be so rude. He said it ended by your showing him the door, or something very near it."

"And yet—last night—before the assembled world—you behaved as—affianced lovers."

"Oh no. We did not. That is we are—The truth is I do not know how affianced lovers do behave. I behaved as I always do. I was troubled in mind. Mrs. Sebbes sent us down together—at dinner I mean. It was Johnny who told him to put me in his Phaeton. He drove me home. Dr. Johannis of course."

"Never let me hear another word of this nonsense. You understand me?"

"Until I am twenty one I will not marry without your consent."

"You astonish me! I was totally unprepared for such impertinence! Without my consent, you will never receive a cent of your father's money. Did you know that?"

"Not until he told me—and we are so glad of it. Now—he has no scruples. He will persevere. The world will know he cares only for me."

"And I am to be defied in this way, for a stranger, a mere bird of passage, a man who began by misleading, and then trifling with your sister's affections."

---

7. Byron, *Don Juan* (London, 1824), canto 15, stanza 49, lines 1–3. MBC has substituted "Joan," short for "Joanna," for "Juan," and changed "he" to "she."

"I did not expect that from you, Mamma, you who are usually so clear sighted. Even Susan saw from the first that he was only trying to make friends with my elder sister. She is three years older than he is. You have often told me, that I am as old for a woman, as Johnny is for a man. Oh how could she humble herself as to complain of him?"

"This is idle raving—and it must cease. We will speak of this thing seriously. Perhaps, we are not as far apart in our views as you suppose. I look upon marriage as more than a copartnership; although I cannot understand a love sick fool. You remember when young Mrs. Marron, who married one of the finest young fellows I ever knew, pitied herself as the wife of a pauper. You know—I was the one to take it up. 'Yes,' I said to her, 'he is poor indeed, his wife did not bring him so much as the dowry of her heart.'"

"*He* will be satisfied with that dowry—which I can ensure him. You may keep the Estate."

"Fiddle sticks!" said Mrs. Effingham angrily.

"No—dear Mother—but may be I am a chip off the old block."

"Emily you amaze me. Do you aim at being a woman of the period— pert, flippant, a garçon manqué,[8] not half a woman—scorning true wifehood and maternity. Irreverent to parents? My child—take heed of my words. I forbid this engagement absolutely—solemnly—This man at best is but a dissipated idler."

"Dr. Johannis knows that is a false charge. Why not ask him?"

Emily paused suddenly. It flashed across her that in their touching reconciliation, and eternal swearing of friendship last night Collingwood had not been named. And the latter only spoke of Johnny to shiver at his coldness.

In a moment she regained her unshaken faith.

"Send for Johnny."

"My daughter I loved you more than all. And now you turn upon me in this flippant fashion, with out shame or sense of propriety. You may go— Surely this must be Susan—not my obedient sensible Emily?"

"Why not? For two days, my own Mother has not deigned to see me. And my heart has been sorely tried."

Here breaking down utterly, Emily turned and fled.

During the childhood of her brood, Mrs. Effingham had found blindness to their presence a punishment which terrified them into submission sooner than any other; now it seemed to have lost its power, and efficacy, in a most unexpected manner.

8. Fr., a tomboy.

9

Sweet is childhood. Childhood is over.
    Kiss and part.
Sweet is youth—but youth's a rover
    So is my heart.
Sweet is rest: but by all showing—
    Toil is nigh.
We must go—alas the going—
    Say good b'ye.[1]

When the smoke of the battle field had blown away, Mrs. Effingham felt she had used her great guns in vain. Victory had not perched upon her banners. The foe was in motion all along the line. To herself—she was constantly saying, "To think a child of mine could be so insolent—so insubordinate. But I will conquer her yet."

When sent for Dr. Johannis came—a little absent minded and quiet—but "with a kindness true as ever." To her close questioning he answered, "I can only repeat, my dear friend, I have never heard any thing, known any thing, or seen anything which would prevent my giving Collingwood a sister or daughter of mine—without scruple or misgiving." No more than this could be wrung from him.

But he was evidently not at his ease: he had taken a letter which he saw Collingwood give Philip—and to save Emily—in Philip's eyes—he had handed it himself to Emily. Consequently he felt guilty in Mrs. Effingham's presence. She trusted him and he had gone over to the enemy. Mrs. Effingham had sent for her counsellor in all plantation matters. Mr. Tame[2] the overseer was a rare character; he began life with Frank Effingham's father; bluntly honest and straight forward, fils de ses oeuvres,[3] he had risen to a most respectable position. In his youth he had been counted the strongest man on the coast; his shoulders now were somewhat bent by age, but he was a dangerous man to meddle with, still. His hair was white, and his dark eyes bright and piercing. Some one said, "That dreadful big black eye of Jim Tame's looks through you."

1. Jean Ingelow (1820–97), "Sweet is Childhood—Childhood's Over," in *Mopsa the Fairy* (London, 1869), chap. 11, 148.

2. Mr. Tame is based on the Chesnuts' overseer, Adam Team. Apart from what MBC says of him in her revised Civil War journal, little is known about Team. Apparently the son or grandson of Adam Team (?-1844) who served in the Revolution in the first Battle of Camden, Team had at least three sons who fought in the Civil War.

3. Fr., a self-made man.

Whenever Dr. Johannis left home he placed his affairs in Tame's hands. And they were said to thrive, consequently—when Johannis travelled.

Mr. Tame had an immense respect for Joanna Regina—whom he always addressed as "My lady." Her administrative ability, and her common sense in the conduct of affairs won his admiration.

He advanced swinging his huge straw hat. And he announced in stentorian tones a startling fact. "You can hear the cannons firing—my lady!"[4]

There was a dead silence. Then Mrs. Effingham said solemnly, "God help us! 'As our days so shall our strength be'—This is the death knell of slavery."[5]

"Yes—my lady—and which ever side has the sense to put these people right in the field[6]—make soldiers of 'em—will win."

"What do you mean?"

"Old Mr. Blockington says—we are five to seventeen—and Napoleon said, 'Numbers will tell in the end.'[7] Tell every man on the plantation, if he will go into the Army, you will free him and his family. See what a number you get right off."

"The field they had better go in—will be the rice field," said Johnny. "If white men can't do our fighting—we had better look out."

"Why Johnny. I expected you would agree with me. They say this is a rich man's war."

"And I will go in the ranks, to set an example to those who say so."[8]

"Well I have always heard you call Negroes a nuisance—you said they spoiled the landscape," said Susan. "In Paris—he told us—he wished somebody would send them all to Heaven in a hand basket. That was his way out of the difficulty; he wanted to get rid of them before his money was all gone—he said he was a practical man and the thing did not pay. Took his bonds to pay for his plantation."

4. Mr. Tame's remark suggests that the Effingham plantation, Effhall, is situated somewhere near Charleston, as he must be referring to the firing on Fort Sumter, which began in the predawn hours of 12 April 1861, and continued throughout the day. MBC gives few clues to the location of Effhall in *The Captain and the Colonel*.

5. Deut. 33:25. MBC writes in an entry dated 7 December 1861 in the original Civil War journal, "Teams thinks the war may leave us a great & independent nation but *slavery* is over. I have thought so six months (& *hoped* it)." *TPMC*, 214.

6. See *MCCW,* 255–56, for a good description of Adam Team and his opinions concerning slavery. In the original Civil War journal, in an entry dated 6 December 1861, MBC records that Mr. Team "is for arming & freeing the Negroes to meet the Yankees" *TPMC,* 213.

7. At the beginning of the war, the South had a white population of approximately 5.5 million, the North of approximately 18.9 million. The proverb "Providence is always on the side of the last reserve" is attributed to Napoleon. See also *MCCW,* 297, where Adam Team mentions the adage and attributes it to Napoleon.

8. John Chesnut went into the ranks as a gentleman private with Maxcy Gregg's 1st Regiment of South Carolina Volunteers (see *MCCW,* 64–65).

"Johannisberg supported itself and sent money to Europe while Johnny stayed there," said Mr. Tame significantly. "Now my way out of the scrape you have heard. Steam boats will run up these rivers and carry them all off—as the British did—and the road is now open from the Potomac to the Rocky Mountains.[9] If you don't utilize them you will lose them. Lord what tall swearing old de Bosquet is doing on the road out there. I propounded this theory to him. He don't care for any thing on this Earth but sacred property. He will let his son go—I believe he has gone—but don't you touch a hair of Cuffer's wool or his patriotism goes with it. 'Where a man's treasure is there his heart will be.'"[10]

"Oh I am so glad," said Susan. "They need not jump on blocks of ice now.[11] All the Uncle Tom's Cabin people *now* have only to pick up their hats and go out of such a Hell upon earth as she describes—I am so glad the road is open."

"Hold on Susie—you are going ahead too fast—But Mrs. Effingham we must attend to our business or I will lose the train," said Johnny.

The booming of the guns had affected Joanna Regina most painfully. She understood better than they did what a declaration of war meant—and showed it by her demeanour. The others took it lightly. They were preoccupied. Dr. Johannis turned to Mrs. Effingham. "We have pulled the house down on our own heads," she said.

"I am no politician—but that does not matter now. We must stand up to it—as one man," he replied. Dr. Johannis was on his way to town, but had some business matters to arrange with his neighbour Mrs. Effingham; they had bought some plantation supplies in partnership. The papers necessary for a settlement he brought in a small black leather travelling bag. As she opened it, Mrs. Effingham spied a rent in the lining, and at once offered to mend it. They then walked from the hall where they were standing into the drawing room—to look for her work basket; which was found on its accustomed table in the bay window.

9. During the Revolution it was British policy to consider slaves belonging to the revolutionaries or Whig sympathizers as public property. When Charleston was occupied by the British, from 1780 to 1781, such slaves were assigned to work on public projects or on sequestered estates. Promised their freedom at the end of the war, most either died of smallpox, yellow fever, and other diseases, or were sent as slaves to the West Indies. When the British evacuated Charleston, they reportedly took with them more than 5300 slaves. (See George Livermore, *An Historical Research Respecting the Opinions of the Founders of the Republic on Negroes as Slaves, As Citizens, and as Soldiers* [1863, reprint, New York, 1969] and D. D. Wallace, *South Carolina: A Short History* [Chapel Hill, 1951], 330.)

10. Matt. 6:21.

11. Reference to an escape across a river in Harriet Elizabeth Beecher Stowe (1811–96), *Uncle Tom's Cabin,* serialized in *National Era* (1851–52), published in book form, Boston, 1852.

Margaret emerged from the library at that instant, almost immediately followed by Emily. Johannis stared, he had not expected to see those two together; he smiled inwardly, and hoped the sisterly misunderstanding was amicably adjusted.

Margaret as she passed it, nervously caught up the bag; her Mother armed with needle, thread, and thimble asked for it. Margaret clutched it convulsively as her Mother attempted to take it. She cried, "Mamma don't do that! give it to me."

"Give you Dr. Johannis' hand bag. Surely I live among lunatics! Take these keys. Go bring me my porte monnaie.[12] I will busy myself mending this, while you go for the money to pay my debts."

Margaret returned out of breath, with haste, but their restless visitor had departed unpaid.

Scipio, the butler, came in with a tray of burnished silver, and a chamois leather thrown across his arm.

Margaret, after her fruitless errand, had fallen in a chair, in a sunken attitude. She revived.

"Please daddy Scipio, have Susan's horse and mine brought to the door, at once."

Emily was still in the porch where she had gone to give Johnny her letter; he had held out his hand, and put the letter in his pocket—continuing to say nothing. Internally he was swearing; this should be his first and last appearance in the part of go between, promoter of clandestine correspondence. This behind backs game was repugnant to him, and he was ill at ease. He had a sulky hang dog look unbecoming to his open honest face. And all this to please Emily! In his heart he knew that he would prefer to break every bone in Collingwood's body rather than help him.

The letter received by Emily—ran thus:

Dearest. You say there are lions in our path, and I ought to cower in fright before them! But joy bells are ringing in my heart instead. If you love me what does it matter? And you do—don't you? I beg pardon. I am never to ask 'silly questions' nor to sing silly songs. So says my wise Emily—'Thine to the core of my heart my beauty—Thine—all thine—for love not duty.'[13] I will see you in town, come what may. Do you think it better for me to go home now for awhile, and wait until the storm blows over? If you are prevented from writing, one word to Johnny will do. He is an old, cold, polar

12. Fr., pocketbook.

13. Mrs. Dinah Maria Mulock Craik (1826–87), "Plighted," lines 1–2, in *Poems* (London, 1859).

bear; and it is your fault that he is not the least fond of me now; but he can be trusted. We defy time and tide. Nothing can harm us now. That touch of your hand, under the old oak, has made a man of me. No more boyish folly henceforth.

God bless my darling.

Au revoir. Yours, yours only and forever.

R. St A. C.

10

Deux coqs vivaient en paix; une poule suit,
Et voilà la guerre allumée.
Amour! tu perdis Troie; c'est de toi que vint,
Cette querelle envenimée
Où du sang des dieux même on vit le Xanthe teint.
[. . . . .]
Tout vainqueur insolent à sa perte travaille,
Défions nous du sort, et prenons garde à nous.
Après le gain d'une bataille.[1]

Emily's letter written in haste at her father's table in the library:

It is all over. She will not consent. I will see you in town day after to-morrow and explain it all. I was firm—so be of good cheer. Keep my precious *first love letter.* I dare not—and I had not the heart to burn it. Take care of it for me.

Au revoir—faithfully.

Your Emily *Hartkopf*

Johannis found his friend Collingwood at the gate; they were on their way to the station, and he promptly delivered the note entrusted to his care.

1. Jean de la Fontaine, "Les Deux Coqs," *Fables,* 2d collection (1678–79), book 7, fable 13:
Two cocks got on until joined by a hen:
And then ill will flared into hate.
Love, your power burned down Troy; so these cocks in a pen
Made war which none could abate;
Xanthus flowed red with blood of gods the gods had slain!
. . . .
And vaingloriousness may work one woe.
Hold your fire; beware; you'd better be demure
When you have struck a decisive blow.
(Tr. Marianne Moore, *The Fables of La Fontaine* [New York, 1952], 160.)

To his amazement, when this triumphant lover turned his face toward him, it was as dark as a thunder cloud.

Strange to say, these two men had long ceased to mention the name of Effingham. Long ago Collingwood had told Emily of this peculiarity of her friend, openly pronouncing it a preposterous absurdity. After his first visit, he had ventured the original remark, "Those are beautiful girls Johnny." The latter stared at him in silence—and seemed deeply pondering the subject. After a long interval and an evident internal struggle he replied, "Those are beautiful girls. So we discuss French women—and all sorts of women—but those girls—never." "If you could have seen his high mightiness, when I dared to call you the 'Divine Ineffable.'"

Now they drove in a constrained and sulky silence. "Confound this fellow!" thought Johnny. "He ought to be the happiest rascal alive. When I think of the face I left on the Porch—all tears and smiles. What a lovely look she had in her eyes. If she had but let *me* love her—little would I reck of Joanna's wrath. Did this boy expect the Queen Mother to hand over her beautiful daughter at his first word?"

Collingwood looked him straight in the eye.

"What message did you bring me."

"None whatever. She might be dumb, for aught I have heard her say to day. But Man! What the Devil do you want with a message? Have you not your letter?"

Again a dead silence. Then, "The happiest days of my life have been spent under your roof. Thanks—my friend for that. Shall I go back to Kentucky for awhile? I will write to you. For my life I cannot comprehend it!"

"You are the best judge of your own affairs."

This was awkward—to say the least of it. Collingwood recovered from his surprise.

"I am your debtor all the same for the happy month—passed at your house. Good b'ye." They shook hands cordially, as the whistle blew.

When the family arrived in town this scene was fairly wrested from Johnny. They had hard work with him—he did not wish to tell—and they were all determined to hear—from different motives indeed. Collingwood had gone home!

The enemy triumphed all along the line. Mrs. Effingham expected nothing better from this adventurer, this butterfly—this trifler.

"Ah Emily—how you wasted heroics on this fine lover of yours who laughs and rides away." The good lady was absolutely hilarious. The logic of events had proved her sagacity and foresight.

Susan was ready to cry.

Emily took a very cheerful view of things, which was exactly the most provoking thing she could do. Nor did she conceal her view of the situation: when they met, all would be explained. That would soon happen. The clever ones had outwitted her cruelly. There was a conspiracy, evidently. Johnny was not in it—he was loyal and true. "Oh Johnny is your 'tame snake,'[2] as the girl in [the] play called her love. No she did not—she called the other girl's lover so," said Emily gayly.

And she made not the slightest change in her outward behavior. Besides—the rubadub—and the row had begun. The very air was aflame. Who had time to think of a trumpery love affair now.

Johnny failed to secure a place among the horsemen. But he volunteered among the first, in Gregg's regiment—a private, and on foot. He wrote home in excellent spirits—he was glad to find how well he bore the hardships and privations of camp life; his health was never better; his hands were blistered, with ditching near Manassah. When Gregg's regiment disbanded, which very soon happened, he had the luck to be made a Captain of Dragoons.[3] And he was satisfied.

As we have said before Mrs. Effingham was Joanna Hardhead of New York. Naturally she had hated and opposed the dominant party in the South[4] with her whole heart and soul. Now it was all different. The reaction was a silent one. She wished to send her daughters abroad, but they refused to leave her. She chose for her self a position she was eminently fitted to fill with credit and usefulness, namely the head of one of our largest Hospitals.[5] Happy were those who fell into her kind and capable hands. Her gift of organizing and governing so profitably displayed on the plantation, had now an ample field. Her head was clear, her will indomitable, her indus-

2. Allusion to Shakespeare, *As You Like It*, 4.3.71.

3. Maxcy Gregg (1814–62) was a Columbia, South Carolina, lawyer who helped to draft the Ordinance of Secession. Promoted to brigadier general in December 1861, he was killed at Fredericksburg in December 1862 (Jon L. Wakelyn, *Biographical Dictionary of the Confederacy* [Westport, Conn., 1977]). After Gregg's regiment was disbanded in June 1861, John Chesnut joined a cavalry unit organized by MBC's uncle, Alexander Hamilton Boykin, with the rank of captain. Boykin resigned his commission in 1862, and Chesnut assumed command.

4. The original passage read "in South Carolina"; this revision is indicative of MBC's intention that her novel be representative of the South as a whole.

5. Joanna Effingham's position as head of a Confederate hospital resembles that of two women MBC knew well: writer Louisa Cheves McCord (1810–79), who ran a large hospital at the South Carolina College in Columbia, and Phoebe Yates Pember (1823–1913), matron of the Chimborazo Hospital in Richmond, the largest Confederate Hospital. Mrs. Pember was a friend of Mrs. George W. Randolph, wife of the Confederate Secretary of War and a friend of MBC's. Mrs. Pember's memoir, *A Southern Woman's Story*, was first published in New York in 1879, and MBC could have read it only after the writing of *The Captain and the Colonel*. MBC served with Louisa McCord at the Columbia hospital in 1864 and early 1865.

try a proverb. Nor was the element of tenderness lacking; so much pain and suffering evolved it, at last, from even her stern nature.

Margaret was her Mother's right hand. She proved herself an efficient and faithful second in command. She needed no rest. Of diversion, she never seemed to dream. They called her "our Confed Nightingale."

Susan brought them by snatches Emily's unguarded speeches. She professed unshaken faith in her false lover and declared herself engaged to him still. She had a calm way of looking for him to turn up at every minute, and then there would be an explanation of his abrupt departure.

"But Margaret, Mamma. What a persistent creature she is. You remember that black bag you mended for Johnny—you know she fell in love with it, and at the depot that day she absolutely asked him to give it to her. Of course he did so, and sent Sambo for it. Heavens! What a row and a rummage we had but it was lost. She held me; she would not let me go near Mr. Collingwood; he looked stupid, unlike himself; he kept away from us. How she does hang on to a fad, when it once gets in her head. She is a monomaniac."

Captain Johannis lying on the snow with a saddle for his pillow and a saddle blanket for his covering, forgot both cold and hardship. "His heart was sore within him. The world was full of care; and the burden laid upon him was more than he could bear." He arraigned himself for two high crimes and misdemeanours. First—he introduced that fellow at Effhall. Secondly—he volunteered to be the letter carrier in Philip's place, and thereby thrust himself in what was not his affair. He had played an underhand game for the first time in his life—He had lowered his Flag—And for what? To see Emily at last left in the lurch.

> Der Captain he ortered no hymn nor no Psalm—
> But his lips he opened and priefly say—"damn."[6]

The perverse délaissée[7] was apparently contented. She could give no enemy of hers the satisfaction of seeing her unhappy.

Joanna Regina remonstrated. "It is hard lines! I have always gone forth to meet my foes with flags flying, and drums beating, and waged an honorable and open war. My own daughter suspects me. I am a plotter, a conspirator—a poor creature who intercepts letters and undermines by strategy—eventually I may turn out a bush whacker."

6. Unidentified. A slightly different version, without attribution, appears in a daybook MBC kept in the late 1870s and 1880s, which begins, "Der Shinral he ortered." In this version, the last word of the couplet appears as "d——-m."

7. Fr., jilted girl.

With scorn and derision she laughed aloud.

"Mamma!" cried Susan, "how can you! Emily does not talk that way about you. Indeed she does not. She tells how careful you were of us when we were young; that you made the nurses keep us clean and quiet. And how proud you were when we were handsome and healthy, and a credit to you. And afterwards you overlooked the Governess in the same spirit. But you never cared what we thought, or felt, or wished."

"Leave the room. That false Kentuckian has done incalculable mischief. Emily is losing her senses."

Giggling outside as she walked away—Susan said, "For the first time in her life she has heard our side."

11

The Confederate Drawing Room.

The mind has a thousand eyes
The heart has one.
And yet the light of a whole life dies
When day is done.[1]

The hour was an early one—and the crowd was just beginning to come; Emily found her self standing at the lower end of the Grand Piano—in front of whose Ivory keys Mrs. Davis was receiving her friends.[2]

A military magpie, with two stars on his collar chattered at Emily's side. He knew every body—and he knew every thing. She was watching the faces of those who spoke to Mrs. Davis, and not listening very attentively to the flood of gossip he poured in her ears: but of this fact he was unaware.

"That group in the centre of the room—they have chosen a conspicuous place truly. Let me point them out to you. They are the four magnificent Kentucky generals.[3] Look at Breckinridge—and Gnl. Preston! And yet they say we have degenerated on this side of the water—bodily, and mentally.

1. Francis William Bourdillon (1852–1921), "Light" (place or date of first publication unknown), lines 5–8.

2. Varina Howell Davis (1826–1906) was one of MBC's closest friends until the end of her life. The two women had come to know one another in Washington in the late 1850s, when their husbands served in the Senate. During those periods of the war when MBC was in Richmond, she lived near the White House of the Confederacy, at one point directly across the street; the Chesnuts and the Davises frequently entertained one another. Throughout the war, Mrs. Davis held regular receptions in the Confederate White House.

3. William Preston (1816–87), John Cabell Breckinridge (1821–75), Simon Bolivar Buckner (1823–1914), and John Hunt Morgan (1825–64). MBC describes the impact that the

If that kind of thing goes on—after a while the average will be seven feet out there. Here comes another. Did you ever see him before? He is splendid—Eh? He is young Collingwood—Colonel I see by his stars. They say Albert Sydney Johnston gave him a letter asking for his promotion—gallantry in action—you saw an account of it in the Examiner. The President never fails to honor drafts from that quarter.[4]

"There are no end of romantic tales about him. No wonder—with that face, and that figure! There is a young lady in the case—she jilted him. She must be hard to please. He has been in prison and he escaped—with wonderful adventures.[5] He has been desperately wounded; I see he has saved his legs and his arms. A letter from Sydney Johnston. A fellow might keep that as a patent of nobility—to show his children. Laudari a viro laudato."[6]

Emily was as pale as death, and nearly as cold. Every thing around her seemed to rock and roll; she steadied herself by the Piano. The stream of this man's talk sounded afar off; her senses were deadened. They did not leave her however, and with a deep drawn breath she strove to regain her presence of mind.

"Hood[7] has taken his arm. See—he is presenting him to Mrs. Davis. How those western chaps hang together. By Jove! he is bowing to you. He bows low—but it was gracefully done. We will give him that credit."

Kentucky generals had on social life in December 1863 and January 1864 in *MCCW.* She and the Preston daughters, who were staying with her at that time were frequently in the company of one or more of the generals.

4. Albert Sydney Johnston (1803–62), killed on the battlefield at Shiloh, had been at West Point with Jefferson Davis, and had served with Davis in the Black Hawk War of 1832. Davis regarded Johnston as the South's finest general, and felt that his death at Shiloh was a national calamity. Johnston's son, William Preston Johnston, served as one of Davis's aides-de-camp. The *Richmond Examiner,* under the editorship of John Moncure Daniel (1825–65), was extremely critical of the Davis administration.

5. Collingwood is later said to have served with John Hunt Morgan, who led a raid into Ohio in July 1863, was captured, and imprisoned in the Ohio State Penitentiary in Columbus. Morgan escaped by tunneling on 26 November 1863, and returned to a hero's welcome in Richmond in January 1864. This chapter of *The Captain and the Colonel,* then, probably takes place in January 1864.

6. Properly, *laudari a laudato viro,* to be praised by a praiseworthy man, Cicero, *Epistulae ad Familiares,* 5.12.7.

7. John Bell Hood (1831–79) was promoted to brigadier general in March 1862, and to major general in October of the same year. He was severely wounded in the arm at Gettysburg in July 1863, and lost a leg as a result of wounds sustained at Chickamauga two months later. In Richmond to recuperate, he fell in love with Sally Buchanan Preston, a beautiful young Columbia woman who, with her sister Mary, was staying with Mrs. Chesnut in Richmond. The romance of Hood and "Buck" Preston plays a major role in MBC's revised Civil War journal.

"I see you know our reigning beauty," said Hood.[8] "Help me to that sofa. There sits a kindly old soul who sends me rice pudding, and I must not lose this opportunity, to thank her. Now off with you. Hand me my crutches."— And he has gone—as straight as an arrow from a bow—as it were.

"I am blazing out a road for you to the beautiful Miss Effingham. I am one of her devoted Admirers," said another of the handsome Kentuckians. "You know her already? Ah! I see—lucky dog," and he received a friendly poke in the side—to speed him on his way.

The Military News Monger rapidly effaced himself as he saw Collingwood approaching.

"I wonder if she can be the girl—then I have been bringing coals to Newcastle—with my information."

"I came to night hoping to meet you," said Collingwood holding her hand somewhat longer than was necessary. He saw his ring[9] was still upon it, and at the same instant her eye, that she was not able to raise to his face, took in the scrap of pale blue ribbon in his button hole—a memento of her guitar, and the walk under the oaks.

"I saw you when you spoke to Mrs. Davis," she managed to say—vainly trying to subdue the tremulous motion of her lips.

"They say she is awfully clever.[10] I found her very kind," he replied.

"Yes. We are devoted to her at our house. Mamma you know is an infallible judge of character." Up to this time she had been cold, and white as her handkerchief, shivering as with a nervous chill, and supporting her trembling frame against the Piano.

---

8. It is not clear who is speaking here. This appears to be a direct conversation in which Hood speaks to Collingwood, but it may be intended as a continuation of the "military magpie's" monologue to Emily, in which he reports the conversations he overhears or imagines.

9. Although no ring has been mentioned before in the novel, the reader is now made aware that Emily has been wearing Collingwood's seal ring. MBC probably inserted this detail because such a ring was worn during the war by Mary Preston while she was engaged to Dr. John Darby. A letter copied in MBC's hand from Mary Preston dated 18 September 1863 tells of her engagement and continues, "Now I wear a seal ring which is not too small for me. And which I am told will be becoming enough to my hand [until] the solitaire comes to replace it. This a secret, dear Mrs Chesnut—so please don't tell any one—that I am engaged." (Letter book in the possession of Katherine Glover Herbert.)

10. Varina Howell Davis was often criticized during the war as "common" or "rude" by those antagonistic to the Davis administration, and in 1861, MBC was critical of her for a time. By late 1861, however, MBC once again regarded her very highly. In the revised Civil War journal, she writes: "Mrs. Davis has been so kind to me—I can never be grateful enough. Without that I should like her. She is so clever, so brilliant indeed, so warmhearted, and considerate toward all who are around her. After becoming accustomed to the spice and spirit of her conversation, away from her things seem flat and tame for awhile" (*MCCW*, 429).

Citing her mother's insight into character to Collingwood was so absurd a malapropos, all things considered, she looked up in despair. As their eyes met—suddenly both laughed outright. The hot blood surged over her face. How she longed to cover it with her hands.

"My colors you see are nailed to the mast," he said—putting his hand upon the ribbon.

"Why did you not stay in town to meet us? as you said you would."

"My letter was returned to me—without one kind word to break my fall—and I fled in dismay."

"But I asked you to take care of it for me; there was no harm in that?"

"I do not understand you. My note was sent back to me in a blank envelope—directed in your own hand writing."

"I answered your note—and enclosed my note with yours. I put those two notes in the envelope my self—and sealed it." She recalled the whole scene vividly in her mind's eye. She spoke slowly—and with deliberation.

"It is very extraordinary—I can not comprehend it. When Johannis gave me that envelope it contained nothing but my own letter of the morning. I asked him for a word, explaining the trouble; he did not waste many upon me. He said he had no message for me—that he was told to give me that letter and he had complied with the request. He seemed to be eyeing me with some curiosity. And I thought at the time, with considerable disgust, and so we parted. As soon as I had time to think, I wrote to Johannis. Afterwards, I heard of him at Manassah—but I received no answer. Then I was taken prisoner, and escaped only to be painfully wounded in the next battle. I had an unsatisfactory letter from him. I wrote again and enclosed one to you. To these I had no answer. So I came to see."

"He told me that he had written to you soon after we came here."

"Did he say why?"

"He was wearied probably—I was—with the eternal changes rung upon your—name."

"What did they think of me?"

"I do not know. I know what they say. They called you false—fickle—mercenary—a butterfly—and a designing villain."

"What did you say?"

"Nothing. I thought in some way you had fallen in a trap—laid for you. I knew whenever it pleased God, that we should meet. You would explain it."

There was a momentary silence—but she did not go unthanked if eyes can speak.

Again her pale face was crimson—the blood came rushing back from her heart. After all these long years! this anguish of patience! He had made it plain—why he appeared to desert her when she bade him stay.

"Why did you return me my letter without an answer?" He took her hand again for a second.

"Did I not tell you? I wrote to you—as kindly as you had any right to expect! and I enclosed the two letters—begging you to keep yours for me. *I could not*—and I saw you take the envelope from Johnny's hand at the side gate. There!"

"It is very odd—only my own—was in that envelope; insultingly returned; and by her, who had a few hours before promised to be my wife. I rushed off like a fool, in a rage. I was a madman. But my punishment has not been of the lightest. Do you forgive me?"

"What have I to forgive? I distinctly refused to be miserable. And I did not doubt you! It is such a comfort no one could pity me. If there was any misery, you had it all to yourself." She was proudly herself once more—and she coolly added, "'Sans la foi—l'espérence, et la charité point de salut *dans ce monde* ni dans l'autre.'[11] This I said to myself night and day for two years."

"Youth, love, hope," he answered laughing lightly. "That's a free translation. We have all that. But Emily! Are we never to meet, but in a crowd—and the eyes of the ten tribes of Israel[12] upon us."

"Oh I don't mind that—I am glad to see you. What does it matter? They can not hear what we say."

"Will Mrs. Effingham continue forever to condemn me unheard?"

"I think not. Why should she? She has been cruelly unreasonable in this; but she is rarely unjust. Sans la foi! remember. Have faith—and all will come right. Do go now and speak to Susie, I know she has been dying to join us."

"Emily, are you sure you had no conjurors at Effhall. This mysterious disappearance of a letter while it is in a gentleman's hand is necromantic."

"If it had been any body but Johnny! I would as soon doubt King Arthur. We have enemies—but we may trust Johnny—he is the soul of honor. And this feat—was too shabby for the lowest."

"If I leave you for a moment to speak to Miss Susan Effingham, will you wait for me here. I do not intend to lose a moment of your sweet company, that I can help. May I walk home with you?"

"Mamma, does not allow Susie and me to separate, the carriage is here—but I will declare my American independence and take you with us."

---

11. Fr. Without faith, hope, and charity, there is salvation neither *in this world,* nor in the other. (Unidentified.)

12. Ten tribes are promised Jeroboam in 1 Kings 11:31, but there were, of course, twelve tribes of Israel. Possibly Collingwood alludes to Bathsheba's exhortation to David, 1 Kings 1:20, "And thou, my lord, O king, the eyes of all Israel *are* upon thee."

From Susan he received a cordial welcome; to lose no time he went at once to Capt. Johannis who stood—with his hands behind him—in somewhat of a Napoleonic attitude. He had never moved or taken his eyes from that pair since their first greeting.

Collingwood held out his hand with a smile. Johannis bowed politely.

"You do not mean to speak to me?"

"I have spoken—but the hand of Douglas is his own."[13]

"Oh I know," said Susie at his elbow, "'Douglas Douglas tender and true!'[14] As Em says the best thing in Miss Mulock."

"Leave us—for a while—please Susan."

"Did you ever? After this no one can say that I do not know how to take a hint." And she stalked away with Captain Cropper—as nearly offended as she had ever been in her life.

"You know my hands are tied," Collingwood began as soon as she moved off. "I cannot afford a row with you. My affairs are sufficiently complicated already. If you choose to play dog in the manger it is your own affair. But I suppose I may ask a civil question. Why did you not answer my last letter?"

"Because you said in it what I know to be untrue. I put that letter which you deny having received into your hand myself. I regret from the bottom of my heart that I ever took you to Effhall—and as fervently I deplore that I was ever fool enough to be your go between and carry your letters. Is my answer civil and satisfactory?"

They looked each other straight in the eye. The devil that dwells in most men had come to the surface. In a moment more they were calm and smilingly polite.

"Your regrets are natural! But I did not receive that letter from you."

"I believe the evidence of my own senses."

"Come down from your high horse. If you have my letter handy, give it to me," said Collingwood in a low tone and with a smile more insulting than a blow.

"Quarrelling is stupid—Col. Collingwood—at any time. Here it is absolutely vulgar. My friend Capt. Wilson[15] will see you tonight."

"A vos ordres."[16]

---

13. Scott, *Marmion,* canto 6, stanza 13, line 27.

14. Dinah Maria Mulock Craik (1826–87), "Too Late," line 4, in *Poems* (London, 1859).

15. MBC has probably deliberately chosen the name "Wilson" as surname of the man who will serve as Johannis's second. John Lyde Wilson (1784–1849), governor of South Carolina from 1822 to 1824, published *The Code of Honor; or, Rules for the Government of Principals and Seconds in Duelling* (Charleston, 1838).

16. Fr., at your disposal.

12

Ten Paces.

Is death more cruel from a private dagger,
Than in the field? From murdering swords of thousands?
Or does the number slain make slaughter glorious?[1]

Early the next morning before any one else was stirring Susan flew into her Mother's room.

"Oh Mamma! Something dreadful is going on! Yellow Sam is down stairs; he tells Binky Anne that his Master, and Dr. Guilliard, and John Wilson went off in a carriage at sunrise; they had a small mahogany box—he knows it is a pistol case. He heard them tell the driver to take the road towards Mr. Lyons' farm."[2]

"Let Dawson bring my carriage to the door at once. How dare they make my child's name a bye word! Am I never to be rid of this man? First a guest—then a burden—then a pest![3] Did you hear anything of this last night?"

"No. They seemed all right. Johnny insulted me. When I left them they were quoting poetry, 'Douglas, tender and true—drop down from Heaven like dew.'[4] Surely when people are going to take each other's lives they do not talk nonsense such as that."

"You are absurd to the sublime point to day. Have beds ready. I may bring wounded men here. Did you see Col. Collingwood? After he spoke to Johnny I mean?"

"Oh yes—he wanted Emily to walk home with him; she would not; but he came home in the carriage with us. Johnny sat by me—of course I did not speak to him. Those men were telling army stories, comparing the Western Army with Gnl. Lee's.[5] Collingwood repeated what the soldier

1. Colley Cibber (1671–1757), *Papal Tyranny in the Reign of King John* (London, 1745), 3.1.331–33.

2. Probably "Laburnum," the country home west of Richmond of James Lyons (1801–82), a member of the Confederate House of Representatives. MBC records in her revised Civil War journal Sally Buchanan "Buck" Preston's distress over a duel fought in 1862 outside Charleston between Major Alfred Moore Rhett and his former superior, Col. William Ransom Calhoun (*MCCW,* 431).

3. Attributed to Édouard de Laboulaye (1811–83), *Abdullah* (Paris, 1859).

4. See chap. 11, n. 14.

5. Robert Edward Lee commanded the Army of Northern Virginia from May 1862 until the surrender in 1865.

out west said to Gnl. Morgan. 'That the cavalry raced around and brought the news. The artillery made the noise—and the Infantry did the fighting. And they gave all the glory to a General.'[6] I thought them in splendid spirits. I noticed one thing—they did not behave as engaged people do in novels. He had his hands on his knees—and she had hers clasped against her breast as if she were praying. She did not open her lips.

"Johnny and I came in the house, but those two stayed out in the cold.[7] I looked out from the window, he was standing on the pavement, but leaning in the open carriage door. I lost my patience and called out what a shame it was to keep Emily there—snow on the ground. When I turned round Johnny was gone."

"Send to hurry Dawson."

Mrs. Effingham, as she came down stairs, met Sambo—hat in hand. He was very glad that she was going and begged to go with her. He had heard of the quarrel through Ben who lived now at the President's[8]—and listened on the other side of the door against which Captain Johannis was leaning. They talked very low; but Ben was on the alert to hear every whisper in that house. Sam insisted that they had words about a dog—even the word mange—had been called.

"Get on the box with Dawson. We have had enough of such stuff."

Mrs. Effingham was at home again in a surprisingly short time. She met a furniture cart, escorted by John Wilson and Dr. Gailliard. The wounded man was therein. She captured the whole party.

Her first idea was to suppress all rumour of the duel. And there she had no difficulty; but few persons knew of it. And upon them secrecy had been enjoined. Collingwood they said had gone back to the West. And a wounded man was an every day matter in Mrs. Effingham's house. The Doctor pronounced the wound painful, but not at all dangerous.

When things had subsided the irrepressible Susan broke into Emily's room.

"My darling child! I do not blame that dear fellow at all. Who can stand

6. See Muhlenfeld, *MBC,* 157, for a full discussion of this sentence. Chesnut played with it on several occasions, recording it in a daybook of the 1870s, and eventually using it in a slightly different version in her revised Civil War journal: "Cavalry are the eyes of an army. They bring the news. The artillery are the boys to make a noise. But the infantry do the fighting. And a general or so gets all the glory" (24 February 1864, *MCCW,* 573).

7. A similar tableau involving General Hood and Buck Preston is recorded in the revised Civil War journal, *MCCW,* 562.

8. As many of these notes indicate, MBC is here drawing heavily upon the material in her Civil War journals for January and February 1864. There, the President's servant is named "Jim," and is mentioned only when he runs away to the Yankees (see *MCCW,* 535).

the supercilious Johannis! What could Capt. Cropper have thought of me last night! His impertinent 'excuse me.' He put me in so false a position."

Emily mutely looked at a chair. Susie seized it by the back.

"I saw him—he wanted to know what you said. 'Oh nothing at all,' I told him, 'but she sobbed so I thought the house would come down—it was a bitter cry'—and I told him so. And I said you were not a weeper—not the least bit in the world given to shed tears.

"He looked pretty foolish. I was really sorry for him; he says he was awfully wrong and would like to beg your pardon on his knees. He thinks Johnny has the best of it—lying here, with a trumpery shot in his leg, for us to coddle and nurse. What would he give to change places with him. He is off, but he will not be gone long. He wants you to understand once for all. Johnny's life was safe in his hands; he seems to think he can hit people where he pleases. He did not mean to fire at all; but Johnny was just too provoking. He hates duels—but there are limits beyond which! As he walked up to Johnny he saw him turn white with rage. He says—the very sight of him now upsets Johnny. When I spoke of that awful fit of crying, you fell into—when you heard of the duel—I came near offering him my handkerchief, he needed it—but a Colonel of cavalry promoted for gallantry in action—to wipe away a tear—Ah never! Though he acknowledges that Johnny is at times too much for human patience—still he was not harsh—he spoke of him in the highest terms. He admitted that he was dogged and narrow minded—but he was considerate in all his remarks—evidently shooting him had satisfied him. He says, 'Johnny seems to feel that—his'—Collingwood's—'abrupt departure was a slight put upon you. He had the impudence to go away when he was given permission to stay. That was a great liberty for any man to take with the Effinghams.'

"You see he justifies Johnny in fighting him because he says—from his point of view—that you had been insulted—Johnny was right to resent it.

"I said, 'Did you not explain?' He laughed. 'The difficulty is when an idea fastens itself in that roomy loft where Johnny keeps his brains—it is nailed there to the wall—and clings outside—only an Earthquake can dislodge it.' I called you our heroine.

"'No. Nothing has preyed on her damask cheek.[9] Her beauty last night was absolutely dazzling. Heaven be praised! Then she is so healthy and hearty, and not the least helpless or mysterious. She is cruelly direct and straightforward. She sternly refused to be crossed in love. She would not wail for me—in prose or verse—she does not write poetry or quote it,

---

9. Allusion to Shakespeare, *Twelfth Night*, 2.4.111–12, "let concealment, like a worm i' the bud, / Feed on her damask cheek."

or extract it, in a blank book. And all these things heroines do.' I had to put my hands to my ears. This man wants to talk of nothing but you. He is awfully glad he did not hurt Johnny seriously—and I think he is not sorry that Johnny did not kill him. He did say, 'after all his airs it would do Johnny good to limp awhile—and—that fellow is not half as much in love with Emily as he thinks he is, but it is not in his nature to give up.'

"Our young friend is delightfully high falutin—but I put it plainly. 'Emily—is truth—and—faith and love—certainly—take away those elements of her being—and her old Confed hoops would stand as empty as a bird cage. There would be no Emily there.' He seemed staggered at that view of the subject, but he laughed. All at once he cried, 'You are a dear little thing,' and he put his arm around me and—would you believe it—my rash young hero—kisses me then and there—at the corner of Clay Street[10]—in broad day light—I looked to see—who saw—but there was nobody in sight. And I forgive him. He did it only because I showed him I appreciated you."

Emily had been listening without sound or motion—stretched on a sofa with her handkerchief thrown over her face. Susie gently removed it—and passed on so to speak that fraternal embrace. This affectionate demonstration not being resented she drew a chair and felt emboldened to speak freely.

"Emily that letter is mixed up in somebody's papers. It fell out some where. It is all a stupid blunder."

"I never want to hear of it again. It is not of the slightest consequence—since I know that he did not receive it."

"Consequence indeed. Can you be willing it should lie about nobody knows where. However, you barely knew Col. Collingwood then—so it could not have been too affectionate. Heavens! if it had been? and now nobody knows who has it." Emily sighed.

"How I felt for you last night, while Capt. Cropper was showing round that love letter picked up in the deserted enemy's camp.[11] The girl's name in full—awfully love sick. 'I would not *thus*.' I had never seen 'thus' except in print before—'but I know full well no eye save thine will ever rest upon this page.' And there it was kicking about among the horse boys.

"He asked if Mamma had relented at all since she was forced to see—that he was neither false nor fickle—nor a fortune hunter. I replied—that she still shook her head—and said—'sly and slippery.' How his face blazed."

10. The White House of the Confederacy was located on the southeast corner of 12th and Clay, a principal east-west street in Richmond.

11. Cf. *MCCW* 108, where MBC describes letters brought from the battlefield at Manassas.

"May God forgive you Susan—for you are an intolerable mischief maker. How he will hate Mamma now. You know she was speaking last night of that odious surgeon[12]—that horrid man who quarrels with her at the Hospital—not of Collingwood. Pray go—and look after Johnny."

As the door closed upon the discomfited Susan—Emily cried aloud, "Could I have lived under it many minutes longer?"

She did not go near Johannis—but one day he sent for her.

"Come little Hartkopf—smile once more on your old friend! You are disobeying Collingwood. Susie says he sent you word to take good care of me for his sake. You see before you a repentant sinner. Collingwood has taken good care I shall not go on my knees. I am to blame, Em!—for it all. That night—and the next day. He came up to me light as air—smiling—in his Colonel's stars—and I had seen it all before. His bit of blue ribbon flaunting—hanging his banners on the outer wall. I behaved like an ill conditioned brute; he tried awfully hard to keep his temper. Even while I was telling him I did not believe him—another self sat in judgment within me—and cried, '*You do*! and will be ashamed of this.' I sent the challenge—and I fired the first shot. On the ground he came up and began, 'We were both in a passion last night and said what neither of us really thought.' I turned my back on him. Cropper says he laughed 'at my airs.' He deliberately aimed, and shot me below the knee. He had no idea of risking the life of *your* friend. So I must thank you at last. Hereafter I will have faith in Colley—even if a miracle is performed by him—such as that flighty letter of yours slipping out of a sealed envelope. You wrote doubtless in 'moving tropes.'"[13]

"It was a slim sheet of this note paper," said Emily.

"Whatever writing material you used, it certainly was not stationary."

"I could almost wish I had never been taught to write—I am so wearied of this thing."

"We are all in a muddle—but I began to see daylight. There may be a way to make it all right—and not a disagreeable way either. Am I forgiven? It was rank treason to attempt the life of that splendid soldier of the Confederacy. There now the color has come back to your cheek! and your smile is as sweet as a May morning. When you write to him—will you write?"

"Most assuredly."

12. Phoebe Pember in her memoir about her service in the Chimborazo Hospital frequently mentions unscrupulous or incompetent surgeons who challenge her authority and interfere with her duties. MBC may well have heard such complaints from Mrs. Pember herself in Richmond, during the war.

13. Byron, *Childe Harold's Pilgrimage*, (London, 1812), canto 2, stanza 34, line 303.

"And mail it yourself—use sealing wax of the toughest—but not your sky lark signet ring. Those 'winged words' of yours need no outside aid from the sky lark's 'flying power.'"

When Emily came into the room, before going up to shake hands with the wounded man—she stopped before the fire to warm her hands. And then she stood still; all of his eloquence and all of his penitence had failed to draw her an inch nearer to his couch.

"Come here Emily. I think you might pass round that fraternal kiss Colley gave Susan—It is all in the family you know. No?—Implacable little Hartkopf. Well I am tired of firing at long range. Send me my flower of womankind. Send me Florence Nightingale—the best nurse in the Confederacy. One good thing in all this wrong doing. Margaret's health seems breaking down under this terrible hospital work—she can rest now and take care of me."

Emily turned to obey his mandate.

"The miracle I am willing to concede since I am tied here by the leg is this—I saw Collingwood take a letter out of that envelope—but if he says he did not—perhaps I was laboring under mental hallucination. He took that letter from the envelope; he glanced at it—he crumpled it up; and stuffed it in his pocket, with a smothered curse. Now he says—I gave him no letter from you."

"Poor fellow," said the lady in clear soft tones. "No doubt it was a dismal disappointment."

The captain continued.

"Then he sulked awhile. I asked him to light a match for me. I was driving—and my cigar had gone out. He drew that letter from his pocket and burned it to cinders. Throwing away the remains with any thing but a blessing—but if you require me—"

"What nonsense! Did any body ever doubt your word? I believe you as thoroughly as I do Col. Collingwood."

"Thanks," murmured the exasperated Captain.

"I always believe what a gentleman says."

"When two gentlemen give contradictory evidence?"

"I believe both. I know there is a mistake some where."

"Little Hartkopf, your pink of perfection[14] is handsomer than most men, otherwise he is not different—My dear girl, you have lavishly endowed him with every heroic virtue. If he could see the picture you have made of him for yourself—he would be amazed and exalted—or he might go hang himself in despair at its want of verisimilitude—at his own short comings, I

14. Oliver Goldsmith, *She Stoops to Conquer* (London, 1773), 1.1.

mean. A man's a man for a' that.[15] And he is nothing more. Susie![16]—a regular primrose by the river's brim—Eh? Now Em—you really believe you know this gallant Colonel after a few days' acquaintance as well as you do me?"

"Better."

"He is a fine fellow—after all said and done; but how did you—I mean how do you explain that?"

"By this token: He understands me, you never could. Not a word was needed when we met—at a glance—"

"Oh! Oh! A deaf and dumb couple would not have lacked words then, to come at a complete understanding. Neither animal magnetism, nor occult science was needed. Those that ran could read. It was visible to the naked eye—to the dullest intellect. You were ticketted. He with his bit of dirty blue ribbon—and you with your hand half covered with a seal ring, bearing his initials only marked thereon."

She interrupted him abruptly. "Now I will enlighten you. In that envelope was the letter you brought me from him an hour before. I thought one from me accompanied it. That was intercepted—when or by whom I know not. I had but a few moments to think. I had a horror of Susan's lynx eyes. Neither she nor I ever owned a lock up place in our lives—not to speak of the researches of Binky Anne and Molly. The fire was at hand. I ought to have burned it—but in a fit of sentimental stupidity I could not. Hence all of these hateful complications. What annoyance to every body would have been saved had I thrown it in—I had no common sense then—I know better now."

"Oh! Fool that I was—I see—But how the devil was I to know? Hereafter—"

But she was gone.

Outside she was saying to herself, "He thought I would take his hand—the one he so insolently refused Robert—and with that silly stagy speech! He did not try to hide that he intended to kill—the one I like better than myself—and he wanted me to kiss him! I could as easily have touched a rattlesnake." And she walked away shivering. "How I wish that wretched letter was at the bottom of the Red Sea!"

"The Christian religion ought to eliminate duelling," said Mrs. Effingham.

"And War," answered Emily.

15. Robert Burns, "For a' that and a' that," line 12, in George Thomson, ed., *Scottish Airs* (London, 1795).

16. It is not clear why Dr. Johannis says "Susie" here; there is no other evidence that she is in the room or enters the room. He may be characterizing his own quoting of poetry as being like Susan's conversation.

"I see—you are preparing for an attack upon your admirable Crichton."

"No my dear Mother—but in a state of civil war one's ideas grow confused. Right and wrong seem to change places according to circumstances—even in keeping the ten commandments."

"Honor thy father and thy Mother?"

"No Mamma. I was thinking of—Thou shalt not kill."

"Duelling to me means—murder and suicide—compounded. These men had none of the excuse given by hot blood—or rash action, they were as cool and smiling as in a ball room."

"Or on the battlefield."

"Surely you do not defend them?"

"Ah No! My dear Mother. It was a bitter disappointment to me. In my heart I called them—fools and madmen. The foolishness of their conduct I see—fortunately for Col. Collingwood it was a *duel*. That is Johnny's way to right a wrong. Col. Collingwood's Western civilization leads to shooting a man on sight in the streets. In this silly adventure—however—*one* cannot be a monster—a murderer or a suicide—and the *other* a martyr and a victim—so I do not defend my friend. I know you will not be harsh to Johnny's evil deeds."

"Revenge an insult when 'tis given, Aye even in the courts of Heaven," declaimed Susan.

"I do not know what would be done in such a case in the courts of Heaven but it would have been a dangerous experiment in Mrs. Davis' drawing room. From the appearance of my friend—his broad shoulders, and powerful frame—I fancy knocking people down would be an easy matter. But Johnny is not a man to stay knocked down—Susie, darling, leave Mamma, and me—Do you not think dear Mother that you have made a mistake in Col. Collingwood's case. The army, and the generals, and the President think so differently of him. And you ought—I mean—will you not, consider me a little in all this? How I do wish you could see him again. He had changed—and for the better in every way. You spoke of his fine frank face, and his manly appearance the first night you saw him. He wears now a heavy military moustache, showing his well formed, clean cut chin. It is a vast improvement."

"She has lost her senses. Clearly she is daft—She thinks my judgment of this man can be influenced by the cut of his beard! And he red handed from an attempt to murder my best friend."

Emily fled.

13

La faim épouse la soif[1]

Marry not
In haste; for she that takes the best of husbands,
Puts on a golden fetter.

The next day before Susan and Emily were out of bed, Binky Anne rushed in out of breath.

"News! News! A Wedding!"

"What is it?"

"As I was standing at the foot of the back stairs—"

"What is it?"

"Oh let her tell it, her own way or we will never hear."

"Big Judy call down over the banister, 'The Captain's got religion.'"

"Why did she think so," asked Susan.

Binky Anne replied by describing the sounds which were heard coming from his room, "like preachin and prayin for dear life." She said Philip told he had carried Mr. Minnegerode[2] a note yesterday evening—and he had let him in a short time before. Binky then determined to see for herself. So she armed herself with a dozen towels and entered the room. Nobody noticed her—so she stood stock still at the door. Miss Margaret was kneeling by the bed—where the Captain was lying flat of his back. And Mrs. Effingham, "like a Judge or a Queen—or something grand—sat stately in a chair." But she was fearfully dishevelled, as Binky Anne worded it, "Everything crooked." It was too soon for her maid to be there to see she was all right. As soon as the thing was over, she, Binky Anne, flew, to be the first to bring the news.

"A runaway match!"

"No," said Emily—lost in amazement. "Not *that*—one is stretched at full length—the other kneeling. And Mamma presiding in a cap all awry. Why did they do it? Why did they not tell us? What can they mean?" Binky Anne was not able to answer; but she averred that her "ole Missis—did not like it." She knew her face like a book. Still unless "she pleased" no wedding could take place in that house. "Look how she is holding Miss Emily back."

1. Fr., hunger marries thirst. Proverbial, said of a poor couple.

2. Reverend Doctor Charles Frederick Ernest Minnegerode, rector of St. Paul's Episcopal Church in Richmond, the church in which President and Mrs. Davis worshipped, as well as MBC and many of her other friends.

She was positive that her ole Missis was scared. This Wedding scared her; though she permitted it to take place. "Old Missis held up her finger and shake it at Miss Margaret and she give her the scripture (red hot) as says, 'go down on your knees—and thank Heaven fasting—for a good man's love.' You see it was before breakfast."

"Come we must dress and go. The bridal party are to be congratulated. Every body—even this flighty Abigail[3] thinks me fair game. It is hard to bear."

"Miss Em," said Molly as she began to brush out her young Missis' hair, "Dont you mind Binky Anne. She is so mouthy—sitch a news toter. Lord how you did hit it. She is esackly that kind of a gal."

"What kind?"

"Oh—you know. What you jis now call her. Abigal! She is all gab."

"Emily," said Johnny—with a hectic spot on each cheek. "The coast is clear. We married to get out of every body's way."

"I see. I see—my dear brother," said Emily with that face he knew so well—all tears and smiles. "'Example is better than pretext,' Mr. Minnegerode says. I may follow yours. I will ask him, to go with me, if I hear my fiancé is wounded. And with Maum Aneke we will take care of him— but I will have to be married before I can play nurse."

"Maum Aneke is a splendid nurse—but she called me a tartar to day. At least she said—Johnny had caught a tartar."

"Called the bride a tartar!" cried Johnny laughing out in the fullness of his heart. "What a shame."

"I hope you will never call me a Crim tartar,"[4] said the bride with an odd expression.

"Emily knows—my name for you. The noblest woman in the Confederacy."

"Let us go," said Emily. "Susie we must remember—the honeymoon is on the horizon's edge! See."

"Stop. Let me explain Maum Aneke's wrath. I would not let her have a game pie Mrs. Allan sent the invalid—at least what was left of it. He will want it again—his appetite is prodigious. She says, 'If people would only give you what they can't eat theyselves—but no. They'll let it spile fust.'"

Johnny was still hilarious. "That's her way of accounting for the obliquity of the ecliptic, Mrs. Effingham says. 'If you could hold your own.' She was fresh from one of her daily battles with the Hospital surgeons—her

3. A lady's maid in *The Scornful Lady* (London, 1616) by Francis Beaumont and John Fletcher.

4. Margaret here refers to a Tartar of the Crimean region, and is punning on the word "crime."

mortal foes. Emily—who does not come near me! says, 'Beware of meddling with Cavalry officers—pleasant tempered fellows—who never quarrel—but shoot a friend occasionally.'"

Captain Johannis soon recovered and joined his company. A braver man or a better soldier never sat in saddle—but he was Captain, still.

One day while Emily and Susan were walking up Franklin St. the latter began.

"Why did those two people marry? They are not wildly in love certainly. He is so kind—so considerate—he will be a good husband. He must be proud of her—I should hate to live with Johnny if he did not respect me. The day of the wedding—I saw Yellow Sam louting low to his new Missis— she took his blarney coolly, but gave him a hand full of money. Now what do you think the bride said—of all things in the world! 'Have you found that bag for me as you promised?' She is constant to a fancy. How utterly insignificant we are—by Mamma—and Mrs. Johannis. For all that I think the hospital is Margaret's hair shirt. She is en pénitence[5] for something. What is it? Mercy—or Charity that is not strained.[6] Is it in the Bible or Shakespeare? Any how it is twice blessed. It blesses him who gives—and him who takes."

"You mean Clarissa—who still thinks herself engaged to Yellow Sam."

"Yes—as she saw him walking off with that money she curtsied down to the ground—and he bowed as low. They seemed dancing a black minuet, they flitted before each other so rapidly and so grandly. She said with a profound *reverence,* 'How does your corporosity seem to sagaciate, my Lord.'

"'Quite abflout,' he answered.[7]

"'What do they mean?' I asked. Binky Anne treated the whole thing with great scorn. She said they were 'playing ladies and gentlemen and talking dictionary.' She mysteriously hinted that Sambo was fooling Margaret. She said—he liked a cool climate and he did not care for home. 'He found Richmond temptiture very embracing.' She ended by saying, 'Sambo's got no sediment—that's the matter with him.'

"Now when you interrupted me—I had got as far as my grand question to Collingwood. 'If he had been—What they called him you know. Did he not wonder what you would have done?'

"That staggered him. After a while he laughed heartily and said he was

5. Fr., penitent.

6. Shakespeare, *Merchant of Venice,* 4.1.181. Susan may also be referring to 1 Cor. 13:4.

7. MBC here incorporates a popular form of dialect humor aimed at skewering "edjumkated" blacks "spouting tongue-twisting, mind-scrambling language." See, for example, Robert C. Toll, *Blacking Up: The Minstrel Show in Nineteenth-Century America* (New York, 1974), 70.

not a Judge nor a Maud Muller[8] and he would let 'the might have been' alone. Do you know—when he went to Jansbug—(he calls it that now) he liked Johnny better than any man in the world—I preached against duelling. And he agreed to every word I said. He acknowledged it was an evil.

"He said he had not been at a girls' school for the last two years—but out west with Morgan's Cavalry. Nothing prevented him taking Johnny by the throat the other night—but you. After all he thought we might as well make up our minds that man was a brute, and a fighting animal—like bears and tigers you know. He said he was the happiest man alive the night before, when Johnny came and poked his long nose in, and spoiled all.

"I do not the least wonder at your infatuation—now that I know him; he is charming."

"Particularly with his arm around your waist at the corner of Clay St.," murmured Emily in a tone that was almost spiteful.

"Now Em—*I* have never called your obstinacy unmaidenly, as the others do—I am sure if Mamma would give this creature a chance, he would talk her over, with his 'bonny blue e'en.'[9] He has winning ways—at least— I will say that for him. He is crushed by this unexpected and fatal termination of his visit. Without exception he is the handsomest man I know. And people are stupid enough to say *that* does not count.

"Some of these days—Mamma will like him best of her three son-in-laws—he will be the favorite."

"Three?" echoed Emily taken aback. "You have stolen a march on us. Who is the third party?"

"I have not the remotest idea—I was that near being engaged once—I thought about it. You see—Mary Sebbes—told me her brother Tom begged I would think about it—and give him an answer when he came back—poor fellow—he never came back—'Hame came the good horse—but never came he'[10]—that was literal in his case. It strengthened the link between Mary and me.

8. John Greenleaf Whittier, "Maud Muller" in *Maud Muller* (Newburyport, 1854), in which a Judge encounters a peasant girl. Each envisions life with the other, but because their stations seem to prevent their marriage, they go their own ways, wishing they had yielded to their impulse.

9. Richard Ryan (1796–1849), "O, Saw Ye the Lass" in *Eight Ballads on the Fictions of the Ancient Irish and Other Poems* (London, 1822).

10. Traditional Scottish ballad, sometimes called "Bonnie George Campbell," sometimes "Bonnie James Campbell," sometimes "Hie upon Hielands." MBC copies one version of the poem out in full in her original Civil War journal (9 November 1861, in *TPMC*, 195–96), probably one she learned as a child. The first stanza reads:

Hie upon Hielands
And lay upon Lay,

"When you go too—Mamma will turn her attention to marrying me—if she does not do it for me—I will do it myself—for I can not live alone with my dear Mother. She has such a contempt for me—I have lots always of what these girls call beaux.

"Well—to go back to what we were talking of when you interrupted me—Mercy being strained. It takes those two to the Hospital. That is they give themselves to the Hospital, and take themselves away from domineering over us. Margaret don't? May be not. When did she stop seeing you? To me she grows dourer every day. Marrying for spite has not improved our sister's temper."

"Do not say such horrid things!"

"No—dear I will not. I wish I could not think them."

A few months later at early morning prayers during Lent Emily was leaning, with her prayer book open before her—but her thoughts far away, when a card was placed upon it. She closed the book instantly, and put it in her pocket. She rested her face on her hands—so shutting out the world from her vision; but all the same she knew. Collingwood was kneeling in front of her.

When they came home—they met Mrs. Effingham at the door.

"Where did you breakfast to day?"

"At Mrs. Davis'. She asked us yesterday."

"Who put a note in your prayer book—in the Sunday School room this morning?"

Emily turned and gave Susan an astonished look.

"Come now Em. That is nonsense—I do tell a great deal—but I have had no opportunity. You scarcely think I wrote a note and warned Mamma at the Hospital that Col. Collingwood had come—and gone—for he left by the twelve o'clock train.

"After breakfast we walked as far as the Executive office with the President—he was by *my* side, and carried *my* prayer book.[11] And I mean to put it away as something sacred," said Susan. "Oh! Oh! See! There is that old blunderbuss—Dr. S—. Emily he is the busy body who ran to Mamma with tales."

Bonnie George Campbell
Rade out on a day.
Saddled & bridled
And gallant rade he;
Hame cam his gude horse
But never cam he!

11. Cf. *MCCW,* 549 (25 January 1864), in which MBC remarks that the President accompanied her home from church.

Emily took her book from her pocket. She opened it—read the card and handed it to her mother.

> "Nymph in thy orisons
> Be all my sins remembered.[12]

I do not see any thing so dreadful in that! I know Margaret is demented and you cannot receive him. Still you might trust me. He wants me to marry him at once. He is so urgent it is hard to deny him. But he is cut off from his home—by the fortunes of war—and I would have none. I cannot go trotting round behind him on his horse like Mysie Happer and Sir Piercie Shafton.[13] No—No. I will wait until this cruel war is over. I was so glad to meet him to day; he breakfasted with us at Mrs. Davis'. It was because I was with him that I forgot utterly that unholy quotation from Hamlet, until now."

"Mamma—he is all right. Every body likes him. I overheard him to day—he knew she was near him as soon as she knelt there, and he was mortified that he had to do something challenging to make her aware of his presence. If that was not—"

"Stop Susie, for pity sake. We have had enough of your overhearing," said Emily not far from tears of rage.

"Not quite. For I do want to know. He seemed to think you knew all about the story. He is really the horseman Atra Cara[14] got up behind. He was riding with Morgan's men you know."

Mrs. Effingham looked at Emily and fairly laughed out. She said to her, "Answer not a fool according to her folly,"[15] and walked away.

Susie went directly to Margaret's room.

"What is Atra Cara?"

"Why?"

"Never mind. Mamma has insulted me as usual—even Em laughed at me."

"An obscene bird, black as death comes behind you. You feel the flapping of its foul wings—but you dare not look back. You feel its claws grip-

---

12. Shakespeare, *Hamlet,* 3.1.91–92.

13. Characters in Scott's *The Monastery* (Edinburgh, 1820).

14. Atra Cura, or Care, a shrouded, winged figure seated behind a rider, from "post equitem sedet atra Cura" (behind the rider sits dark Care), Horace (65–8 B.C.), *Odes* 3.1. William Makepeace Thackeray used the figure in a poem, "Atra Cura," included in *Rebecca and Rowena* (London, 1849), in *The Complete Works of William Makepeace Thackeray* (New York and London, 1904), 17:115. Thackeray's "Atra Cura" appears separately as a poem in vol. 24, p. 165. The entire following conversation is part of an elaborate revision that Chesnut has not punctuated carefully and which is therefore quite confusing.

15. Prov. 26:5.

ping your shoulders. And you know its sharp beak—and its cruel eye lie in wait for you—if you but turn your head."

"For pity sake! Margaret you do say horrid things. When you married Johnny the dearest fellow in the world—I hoped you were cured of all that."

"Johnny—the dear good fellow."

"You surprise me—I thought you had gone over to the enemy."

Poe's raven—that put it in her head.[16] How well I remember what I read—

> Take thy beak from out my heart
> Take thy form from off my door—[17]

Em thinks I am not fair to Margaret. She broods over something. If she did not care, she could be as light hearted as I am.

Now for it. I mean to make a clean breast to Emily. She deserves it at my hands so I go to her at once.

"My dear sister—I have come back to tell you the truth. Don't get up—lie there—I have something to say—I came near telling you that day when I told you how near I was to engaging myself to young Sebbes—chiefly because he was Mary's brother. Somehow I had not the face—so I stopped short.

"My Marriage was more romantic than Margaret's. Don't faint—Old Tame always said I would be married before either of you. I had so many more offers than you had. Are you struck dumb?—Do say something! You can't? Then listen—I saw you were jealous when Collingwood kissed me. Oh you deny it! You need not work yourself up into a fury about it. I have a husband of my own—And he may kiss you—then we will be even!

"I did not once see him after I was engaged to him. It was done by letter—though we were in the same house. And after we were married—I had not one glimpse of him—from the moment the parson said Amen.

"Mrs. Blythe's brother performed the ceremony. They rushed off to the overseer's house to get his will witnessed. The whistle blew—of all the days of the year—they changed the schedule that one—my wedding day. And the train was an hour sooner than they looked for it. More's the pity. He had to run for it. No chance to come back—or to kiss me good b'ye. He sent me the will to keep however."

"Who is it—who is it. For God sake—stop and tell me that?"

16. Susan serves briefly here as a first-person narrator. The same phenomenon occurs in the last chapter of *Two Years—or The Way We Lived Then*.

17. Edgar Allen Poe, "The Raven," line 101, in *The Raven and Other Poems* (New York, 1845).

"Oh you have found your tongue. You know I went home awhile to stay with Mrs. Blythe. *He* came back unexpectedly."

"Annita's husband?"

"Now Emily—that is spiteful. How can Annita have a husband. She is in Heaven. Her former husband—Yes. But my husband now. Even Papa—said, "In Heaven there is neither marrying nor giving in marriage.'[18]

"The night before he was to go away he wrote to me—I tell you for an hour or so, we kept notes flying. You know how easily I write, quite as much so as I talk. Well—he found it so nice to see me at the head of his table—so nice by the fire at night. *He* liked my singing. He is so handsome—and so kind."

"And so stupid—and so conceited—and so rich," added Emily mentally.

"He has invested no end of money in England. Says 'It is not such a dead sure thing as we think it—our success in this War.' So his treasure is laid up where moth and rust doth not corrupt[19] over the water.

"Made it running the blockade? Why not?—now you are unkind again. The crown and the poun' are both for me—Auld Robin Grey?[20] Eh?

"Now if he had married any one else—*she* might have turned dear Mrs. Blythe adrift—I will take care of her to the last. You see how many unselfish reasons I had for my romantic marriage.

"I am not to tell any one—Mamma above all—until I choose. I made that a condition before I consented. He wanted me to go with him—but he had blocked his own game. Before he made up his mind to marry me—he spent his time telling us tales of the dark dangers of blockade running. So I dared not run it with him.

"I like *our* place so much better than *Jansbug.* Johnny's grounds are better but our house is finer than his!

"I do not pretend to say I would not prefer that young Sebbes had lived: then I would have married him. There is a drop at the bottom of every woman's heart—softest for a soldier, a hero—a man who fights his country's battles. I am no stronger minded than my sisters after all. As soon as I knew you were engaged—I made up my mind to vacate too—Mamma and Margaret with out you—never! You have said yourself how placid and contented my face was since I came from Mrs. Blythe—Peace of mind—all my doubts and difficulties solved. Now Mum's the word—you will never betray me. It will all come out in good time.

18. Mark 12:25, Luke 20:35.

19. Matt. 6:19. In her revised Civil War journal, MBC frequently mentions people who regard the war as an opportunity to increase their fortunes (see, for example, *MCCW,* 207).

20. Lady Anne Barnard (1750–1825), "Auld Robin Gray," line 8, in *Auld Robin Gray* (Edinburgh, 1825).

"Did I not tell you how I tried to find out from Johnny what screw was loose at his domestic hearth? Now I said—'Johnny—Why is Margaret so discontented—so fretful—so unhappy? You are a pattern husband you know?' He answered with a shrug of his shoulders. He learned that in Paris. And he told me what Faust said to Mephistophiles; or may be it was the other way. 'There is something in the heart of man the devil himself can not satisfy.'[21] That's Goëthe you know. Johnny said—Shakespeare refers to 'the Devil as a perfect Gentleman.' I asked where I would find that profanity. He said in King Lear.[22] I cannot live with my own dear Mother—without you. I shudder when I think of the kind of man she would be sure to think good enough for me. She is a match maker. Always has been. So I took time by the fore lock[23]—I did well for my self. Johnny was praising you. She agreed—she has such a contempt for me. He said you had charm—the sub-tile grace—no one could describe—but they felt it. And now would you believe it. The Rigid Regina adds, of her own accord, with a gentle smile— she gave authority—chapter and verse—that I forget, 'Love makes people better always—Religion sometimes. Power never.'[24]

"The Pious Captain—just out of his duel—rolls his eyes and says, 'The Christian religion is Love incarnate.'

"Now for 'the fool of the family' that is pretty well repeated. You stand for Love. Margaret, Religion. Mamma, Power."

14

La défaite condamne.
La victoire absous.[1]

"My trusty Scots!" said the King as he looked upon this melancholy spectacle; "Had they brought only man to man, all Flanders, and Burgundy to boot had not furnished champions to mate you."

21. Johann Wolfgang von Goethe (1749–1832), *Faust* (1808, 1832). These words do not appear in any English translations I have examined. They may represent MBC's own transla-tion from the German, or from a French translation; they may represent Susan's interpreta-tion of the play.

22. Shakespeare, *King Lear,* 3.4.134.

23. Allusion to Edmund Spenser, *Amoretti and Epithalamion* (London, 1595), sonnet 70, lines 7–8: "tell her the ioyous time will not be staid / vnless she doe him by the forelock take."

24. This quotation also appears in MBC's daybook of the 1870s, where it is ascribed to Walter Savage Landor.

1. Fr., defeat condemns, victory absolves. Unidentified.

"Aye—an it please your Majesty," said Balafre, who attended close behind
the King, "Maistery mows the meadow—few men can fight more than
two at once—I myself never care to meet three, unless it be in the way
of special duty, when one must not stand to count heads."

Quentin Durward.[2]

One day Mrs. Effingham astonished her daughters by walking in at an unusual hour.

She was thoroughly worn out. Emily brought a bottle of Cologne, the gift
of a blockade runner; she arranged the pillows and made her mother lie
down on a comfortable sofa. She rang for Scipio, and ordered a cup of tea.

"Thanks—dear. I am not a tea drinking character—and I care even less
for Cologne; but I do care for dutiful demeanour on the part of my children."

In an instant Emily's arms were around her neck, and her face covered
with kisses. It is to be doubted if the stout hearted and strong minded
Joanna had ever been so smothered in an embrace before. She coyly wiped
her tear bedabbled cheeks, her tears and Emily's mingled. And she began
to talk with great rapidity—that her weakness might be the sooner forgotten.

"To day, at the Hospital, young Paul drew my attention to the howling
and complaining of a man, not far off.

"'It is our overseer's son; he is lying there in a whole skin; but somewhere hurts him,' Paul laughed heartily. That poor fellow's leg you know
is hoisted up—on some surgical apparatus. And he can't move. He has a
terrible time of it. But he never says one word about himself; he is the same
well bred, pleasant, quiet creature we knew at Effhall. Death is there at
his elbow—waiting. We can not save him. I asked, 'What can I do for you?
I will not waste time on the shrieker.'

"'Nothing more—you have done all that a mortal can. And there sits
Tony' (hereupon Tony showed all his eyeballs and white teeth) 'who would
not let even a fly light on me.' Tony brushed with renewed vigor. 'They say
Lennox is no better; his lines have fallen in pleasant places. I saw him last
just before he was shot. He nodded to me and laughed. We were in a place,
and at a time, that was supposed formerly to try men's souls.[3] We take it
easy now. We were dismounted cavalry—put there to be shot. We could
do nothing. There was the rub. Why we were ordered there God only
knows. I hear six of us are left. In comparison—Thermopylae was jolly—

2. Scott, *Quentin Durward* (Edinburgh, 1823), chap. 28.

3. Thomas Paine (1737–1809), *The American Crisis,* no. 1 (Philadelphia, 23 December
1776).

and Balaclava a fox hunt.[4] Somebody suggested we were thrown out *to feel the enemy*. "Not ours to question why."[5] Lying here one must think.'

"In order to gratify his wish, and to have the latest news of Lennox, I proposed to put on my bonnet and look him up. He seemed pleased.

"'What message?' I asked.

"'Three cheers for the Light Dragoons.'

"I was amazed at the strength of his lungs.

"I found Lennox, with every comfort about him in those magnificent drawings[6] of the Macalpines. His bed is in [the] door way—between the folding doors. The room was darkened—and cool and fresh. Mrs. Macalpine and her daughters are the loveliest and the best of women. They try to anticipate every want of that poor Lennox. And they did not know him until he was brought there wounded; one of them knew his sister however. I remember him on his Mother's knee. He is perfectly still—reticent as ever—and as considerately polite. He received me on that rack—that bed of pain—as coolly and as calmly, as though we had passed each other on the battery.[7] His leg has been taken off—too late. I dared not trust my voice with Paul's message. I saw it was all over. A man came with his letters. He presented him to me.

"'My dear friend. I have lacked nothing—these noble Macalpines! And then this faithful fellow Madison—they sent him to me from home as soon as they heard I was wounded.' I spoke to him of Paul—as hopefully as I dared—and then I knelt and kissed his forehead.

"Tomorrow when you ask me, how these men are; the answer will be—they are dead.

"I have dwelt upon these two because you know them. But I cannot count the number of similar cases packed like sardines—in that dreadful hospital—and yet we do our best.

"The strain on heart, mind, and body—is awful. As I turned towards the Hospital, I saw coming from that direction a military funeral. I tremble

4. At Thermopylae in 480 B.C., three hundred Spartans and seven hundred Thespians were annihilated by the armies of Xerxes. Balaclava was the site of the battle immortalized in "The Charge of the Light Brigade" by Tennyson. The battle was fought on 25 October 1854; allied forces from France, Britain, Turkey, and Austria defeated Russian troops. In the course of the battle, however, a brigade of British cavalry mistakenly charged Russian artillery batteries and lost nearly three-fourths of the brigade.

5. Paraphrase of Tennyson, "The Charge of the Light Brigade" in *The Examiner* (9 December 1854), reprinted in *Maud and Other Poems* (London, 1855), line 14, "Theirs not to reason why; theirs but to do and die."

6. Drawing rooms.

7. Promenade at the tip of the Charleston peninsula, overlooking the harbor in Charleston, South Carolina.

when I hear the dead march now. Your Mother is growing nervous—she shook like a leaf. It was Hamilton's servant leading his horse—with its empty saddle! I did not know he was killed. The hearse—and the music— and the empty saddle—I meet them every day, and supposed I was callous. I must be breaking down. I did not grow hysterical, nor scream, nor tear my hair," she said with a pale smile, "but I can understand now the women who do."

After Mrs. Effingham—recovered her firmness of mind and body, and returned to the Hospital, Susan spoke.

"She is a trump. She is a veritable Sister of Charity. Emily why do you not send for Collingwood—Mamma would do it—her heart is softened— but she does not know how to give up yet. Now is your opportunity.

"Where is he?"

"I do not know. In the Army of the Tennessee. If by any miracle he is yet alive."

15

After this cruel war is over

> The Army like a lion from his den,
> Marched forth with nerves and sinews bent to slay—
> A human Hydra issuing from its fen
> To breathe destruction on its winding way.[1]

Once more they were all gathered around the breakfast table at Effhall.

In that beautiful dining room, there was now but a pine table and a few oak bottomed chairs. A yellow painted side board stood afar off in the distance, on it was a lonely white pitcher which had evidently suffered a recent divorce from its companion basin. There was not an unbroken pane of glass; panels were smashed from the doors—gloom and desolation every where.

And yet these people were not in as evil case as their neighbours—all of whose eggs had been in one basket. Many were now without bread— and all in consternation as to how it was henceforth to be earned. Every implement of agriculture had been destroyed; every cotton gin—every rice mill burned. And not a penny in the country to replace them.

Mr. Effingham had funds invested in New York. Since her widowhood Joanna had largely increased the amount. In Mr. Von Enden's care this was

1. Byron, *Don Juan,* canto 8, stanza 2, line 3.

all safe. Certainly she had sustained immense losses from fire and pillage. Still, for her, personal privation and discomfort were only temporary. She had saved the old Madeira. In her wisdom she stored it in the garret and removed the stair case.[2] The success of the device justified her foresight.

This day they were in strangely excited spirits. For years after the war few family parties met together without wild tales of their experience during the raids; accompanied by hysterical laughter on the part of the women—and may be—curses not loud but deep on the part of the men.

"Mamma has only been thirty years a southerner—at first she says herself—she was fearfully Yankee—now she misses her black courtiers more than we do. She is lost without those stately Maumers with their white turbans and gold ear rings, who curtsied low at her every word and replied, 'Yes! my Missis! Yes Ma'am! Enty my missis know! She know ebbery ting!'"[3]

"For shame! Emily—I may miss the servants I have labored so to train—for thirty years. But for awhile they will pay dearly in creature comforts for the glorious privilege of being Independent. I can dispense with their services more readily than they can with my help. We were a mutual aid society."

"How came you by Tony?" said Capt. Johannis, "you seem in unlawful possession of a slave."

"No. Tony declares whenever he sees a way to 'better hisself' he will leave us. Paul, poor fellow, you know was a lawyer; he made a will of a few lines only—leaving—"

"Ah—I see—he bequeathed Mamma to Tony!"

"He left his faithful servant to my kindness and care. Unfortunately such devotion as Tony's for his Master is not transferable. There is nothing like the feeling Tony had for Paul unless it be the Colley for the Shepherd. I am sure I have seen nothing human of the same sort. In respect to us—Tony says[4] despondently we are not—'de family' even. I have tried to do what Paul trusted I would."

2. This device was suggested to Chesnut by Louisa McCord, who planned to send her daughters upstairs during Sherman's occupation of Columbia and remove the staircase (see *MCCW,* 715).

3. Chesnut is recording the creole language, here a mix of African languages and English, of the Gullah people, blacks established as slaves on the Sea Islands of South Carolina and Georgia. Compare her use of the Gullah word "buckra" (white man, owner), and, in *Two Years,* "pender" (peanut).

4. The editor has emended "say" to "says," although Mrs. Effingham may here be imitating the dialect of the servant she is discussing.

"A black present came to Mamma, that astounded us.[5] You remember our compulsory sewing society. We had to ply our needles two nights in the week, for the negro baby basket. I think Mamma kept bales of baby clothes. If one was ill, the mother brought it here, and there was a consultation—resulting in small vials and small spoons. If things became worse, Mamma kilted her petticoats and with a water proof over her head followed by Maum Aneke, she descended on them with baskets, bundles, blankets. She was misunderstood—duty was mistaken for affection.

"One day—when we had scarcely begun to breathe freely—the army had just gone. We had for our dinner boiled ground nuts—we were not starving, for one of the negroes had given us a few hand fulls of hominy which we reserved for our breakfast next day.

"Scipio came in with the air of a benefactor—he was prepared to make our fortunes.

"'Come out Missis an see! I got somethin for you. I bin out after my mules—dey bin hide in de woods all de time of de raid. I fine my mules slick as a ribbin—and as I come home perusin de road—I pick up dese here for you.'

"Before the door stood a wagon filled with negro babies. Picture to yourself the show! Their eye balls rolling; the screeching—squirming, squalling, laughing black mass—

"We stood spellbound. Mamma was the first to recover her senses—she sternly inquired, 'Where are their Mothers?'

"'Oh—dey run long after de Army—babies too heavy to tote—so dey drop em long de road; an I pick em up.'

"The comical side was too much for me. I leaned against the Banister and laughed hysterically."

"What did Joanna Regina do?"

5. MBC mentions this incident in her original Civil War journal (see *TPMC,* 241–42), and in the revised journal (see *MCCW,* 806, 809). Chesnut's first recording of this incident, told to her by an eyewitness in May 1865, mentions nine babies, and Chesnut comments, "Surely the poor black mothers were forced to leave them." By the 1880s, the anecdote becomes "Quantities of negro mothers running after the Yankee army left their babies by the wayside—left them—did not not [sic] spring from block of ice to block—as Mrs. Stowe fondly imagines they do. So Adam came in exultant: 'Oh, Missis, I have saved a wagon load of babies for you. Dem niggers run away an' lef' dem chilun all 'long de road.'" This is one of the extremely rare instances of a total change in account between the 1860s diary and the 1880s book, here reflecting how gossip has become "fact," and that Chesnut has, at the very least, over the years put aside her doubts about this story. Myrta Lockett Avary's *Dixie after the War* (New York, 1906), 190–91, relates as fact other stories of negro babies being deserted by their mothers in the weeks after the close of the war.

"She did not accept them as a gift but she saw the little blackamoor castaways taken care of. How crest fallen Scipio looked that his handsome present was not appreciated."

"The mills of the gods grind slowly.[6] This was curiously well timed. They did not know Missis was free also."

"Ah," said Mrs. Effingham. "Even I regain my freedom with a sigh[7]—as the Prisoner of Chillon did."

"And as I always say—'I told you so.' The queen resigns her kingdom and her subjects with regret. Fancy Regina Hartkopf—and only Susie to reign over," said Susan with her usual sang froid.

"Othello's occupations gone,"[8] said the captain with a smile.

"Oh such a comfort that it's gone," cried Susan. "I never thought one moment about the right or the wrong of it—and I never would."

"That reminds me—You know dear old Miss Emily Eyebright. The exquisite beauty of her dinners. I rode over to see her yesterday. She looked more quaintly neat and prim in those bare rooms, from which her luxurious surroundings had all been stript. She recounted her losses. Somehow I find it hard to listen now—so she buzzed and droned about my ears until it became time for me to leave.

"'Dear child—to think I dare not ask you to stay and dine with me. But here. This is all I have left—not a spoon or fork—not a knife. Not so much as a salt spoon. Look here. This is every thing I have to eat with,' and she brandished aloft a huge carving fork—made more formidable by a steel prong which seemed to cock up in its back. 'Only this.' She daintily held out the fork to me with her little finger stretched at right angles—and a face of such abject misery! I fled. When once more in the woods—I waked the echoes. I know I did. I laughed till I reeled in my saddle. There are troubles and—troubles."

"Why did you not suggest chop sticks," said the hard hearted Johnny.

"You people that know—if we were not saints—were we ever the devils they painted us?" eagerly asked Susan.

"Virtue is a matter of latitude and longitude. Look at England—how she concentrates hers on Jamaica,"[9] said Johnny.

6. Henry Wadsworth Longfellow, "Retribution. From the Sinngedichte of Friedrich von Logali," lines 1–2, in *Poets and Poetry of Europe* (Philadelphia, 1845).

7. Allusion to the last line of Byron's "The Prisoner of Chillon" in *The Prisoner of Chillon and Other Poems* (London, 1816).

8. Shakespeare, *Othello*, 3.3.362.

9. The British colony of Jamaica was a center of the English slave trade until 1807, when importation of slaves was abolished. England abolished slavery in Jamaica in 1833, compensating planters at the rate of nineteen pounds per slave. In spite of such compensation, many

"She waved us back—as slave owners—but the moral effect of that was lost for the other hand was holding up Turkey,"[10] said Emily.

"She kicks and cuffs Ireland and India pretty fiercely[11]—in spite of her pious love of freedom," added Johnny.

"Oh!" said Susan, "that great traveler Mamma is so fond of—has queer ideas—he hints—that a fellow—sharp set[12]—at a hospitable board in the Sandwich Islands—*will* take a slice of cold missionary[13] too—Now! Those negroes! They pity us so; they think we are lost without them. And we are jumping for joy that we are rid of them. They say, 'Don't fret little Missis—white people want a heap er waiten on. We wont lef you.'"

"I told Tame to let every thing stand until January. To work with them on shares. Rid of them! That was an odious word."

"You never do Susie justice. She meant she was free. She no longer dreaded to be called an oppressor of the weak. Poor Susie who never hurt a fly."

But Susan could not let "well enough," alone.

"You know Mamma how angry that old woman makes you—who will pray for you. I know it is rather hard to be prayed for in spite of yourself. But I do think you might thank her."

"Take her off my hands Emily," said Mrs. Effingham. "We are a case of incompatibility of temper."

"You remember in England once," said Susan coolly to Emily ignoring her Mother's outburst, "Mrs. Blythe dismissed an unsatisfactory servant. We were relieved from annoyance, and we began to deplore our fate, for

---

planters suffered financial ruin over the next twenty-five years as a result of increased taxes, scarcity of labor, and decreased tariff protection. By 1865, widespread dissatisfaction with the government led to rioting on the island, and the British responded to the uprising with ruthless martial law.

10. In 1854, Britain and France allied with Turkey against the Russians in the Crimean War.

11. Methods used by the British to quell revolutionary activity in Ireland included the suspension of habeas corpus in 1847 and virtual police rule. In 1858, Parliament transferred rule in India from the East India Company to the Crown. Taxes and tariffs were levied to recoup losses expended in suppressing rebellion in northern India and, in 1862, the last emperor of India was deposed and exiled.

12. Eager for food, very hungry.

13. Samuel Wilberforce, Bishop of Oxford, and later of Winchester (1805–73), is the reputed author of the following impromptu:

> If I were a cassowary
> On the plains of Timbuctoo
> I would eat a missionary
> Coat and bands and hymn-book, too.

our own sakes—that we were slave owners. You know so many of them are so disagreeable. And we could never get rid of them. Old Quashie our coachman for instance; he drove us wherever he pleased and brought us home always before we wanted to come. And whenever we asked him to go any where, or to do any thing—he would say snappishly, 'No. Yo Ma dont low dat.'"

"And," now said Johnny, "he is old and blind and deaf as a post—and you will have to support him till his dying day."

"But hear me out—Mrs. Blythe came down on us. 'Silence young ladies—do your duty in that station of life'—and all that. She cured me of having opinions. We have shaken off our old man of the sea.[14] If we could get rid of the odious subject! Let us talk of something else."

"No. My dear—do not hope it. The ghost will be worse than the living body—I see they are proud of Grant.[15] Let them laud and magnify him! They cannot make a Wellington unless a Napoleon had been conquered."

"By numbers—at last," said Emily.

"Oh Mamma—Emily says—you would have made a splendid Abolition lecturer—and might have been now a power in the land and we might have been rich. We continue to be on the wrong side of every thing. Mamma declaims to empty benches."

"An impertinent speech! I was a good man's wife. The highest position a woman can attain."

"You are not a woman's rights woman? Margaret was always keeping us away from people who abused the South. But no body kept away from us. And in the abstract we ought to have been horrid. Did you ever see your wife's book Johnny? Emily calls it 'You are another,' or Margaret's answer to Sumner.[16] Slavery is the sum of all evil. So she looked out for wrong among free people—you see—and those who scorned slaves and slave owners."

"I have only seen the outside," said Emily.

"I would not touch it with a ten foot pole," said the Captain meekly. "I would ride a mile to avoid any disagreeable sight—I never read a 'bad accident' even in my life."

14. Reference originally to Proteus in book 4 of *The Odyssey.*

15. Ulysses Simpson Grant (1822–85), commander in chief of the Union forces, later eighteenth president of the United States, 1869–77.

16. Charles Sumner (1811–74), senator from Massachusetts, delivered a vitriolic oration entitled "The Crime against Kansas" in May 1856, in which he described Senator Butler of South Carolina as a Don Quixote whose Dulcinea was "the harlot slavery." In retaliation, Preston Brooks of South Carolina beat him severely with a cane, disabling Sumner for several months. Sumner became a martyr in the north, and southerners regarded his vituperative speeches against slavery as representing public opinion in the north.

"I saw her often—making her book. She cut out and pasted in a scrap book any thing dreadful she saw in a Scotch, English, or Yankee newspaper. She scorned Irish or Russian barbarities—she went in for the unco righteous,[17] and their misdeeds. Let me read you the table of contents," said Susie.

> "All that the mind would shrink from of excesses;
> All that the body perpetrates of bad;
> All that we read, hear, dream of man's distresses;
> All that the devil would do if run stark mad;
> All that defies the worst which pen expresses;
> All by which Hell is peopled, or as sad
> As Hell—mere mortals who their power abuse
> Was here (as heretofore and since) let loose.[18]

"Why did she not come with you to day? Queer she did not tell you the piccaninny story—but it was a thing to see, not hear."

Here Mr. Tame came in swinging his hat, in his sweeping bows. His hair was now white as snow, and his stalwart frame visibly bowed and bent by age; but the brightness of those wonderful eyes remained untouched by time.

"A strange tale, my lady! While the storm detained us in the Church Porch yesterday—Mr. de Bosquet went for the Parson; because he preached that Sherman[19] was Attila—and the Scourge of God—for our sins. De Bosquet held that it was flat blasphemy—to bring God in, that kind of way. He was not particular in his language."

"What a shame! and he has had all the luck!"

"Yes. The Yankee gunboats took off every soul from his place—somebody went there—and heard a solitary guinea fowl cry—Now to have the power to help taken away from you; and to be beset morning, noon and night by the helpless; is not the least of our troubles—Seeing want that we cannot relieve!"

"That is not the form in which he thinks the gunboats aided him. They made a clean sweep of all who could have put the Yankees on the track of his summer place where his five years' cotton crop is hid," cried Johnny—one of whose stable boys had led the soldiers to the spot in the swamp where the Arabian was concealed.

17. Extremely righteous. The nineteenth-century Scots writers used the word "unco" frequently; here MBC may be alluding to Robert Burns's poem "Address to the Unco Guid or the Rigidly Righteous," in *Burns: Poems and Songs,* ed. James Kinsley (London, 1969), 37–38.

18. Byron, *Don Juan,* canto 8, stanza 123, lines 976–84.

19. William Tecumseh Sherman (1820–91), Union general whose "march to the sea" and campaign through the Carolinas in 1864 and 1865 left destruction in its wake.

"His only son—has come back—safe, and sound, in wind and limb, not a hair turned," said Tame who had two sons killed in the war.

"He takes that very coolly—he brags that he won't be put upon—by God, man or devil. He only cares for his money," said Mrs. Effingham, "but we forget, you have a strange tale to tell."

Old Tame's eye, dilated and darkened—emitting lurid flashes. And he began to speak so rapidly that it was almost impossible to keep pace with him.

"Yesterday, while old de Bosquet was growling at the Lord, and the Parson, and the thunder storm which kept him from home, his wife and son were seated at a window, in their Summer house—consulting. The young one went off with his company, when he was only seventeen; he wants to go to Charlottesville[20] and get a good education—but his father wants him to begin money making. He pointed to that great pile of cotton bales.

"'What is that worth?'

"His mother answered, 'Over a hundred thousand dollars—*he* says—and you know he never makes mistakes in money matters.'

"Young de Bosquet says—while his finger was still pointing—there came a crash of thunder that stunned them; his Mother threw her arms around him—but he saw the lightning as it struck the cotton. It spread like lightning—the blaze—was all over that cotton in a second."

"Could they not put out that fire?" asked Susan.

"For a hundred yards round, it was hot as hell!" cried old Tame in his wild excitement. "Not a lock of that cotton is left."

16

The universal topic of '65.

Eternal summer gilds them yet
But all except their sun has set.[1]

"Margaret will come tomorrow. I left her highly amused at a good scolding my father's head man gave me to day. He pities me as an amiable weakling. I have allowed several men who went off with the Yankees to go back into their houses. He drew a picture of my father's face as he saw them coming—his shout which could be heard for a mile—the scamper of the delin-

20. Charlottesville is the home of the University of Virginia.

1. Byron, *Don Juan,* canto 3, song following stanza 86, lines 693–94.

quents—and if my father continued to storm at them by this time they would be half way to the 'Yallerbam.'"

"How Johnny glories in being a degenerate son. And how he likes to hear what a terrible old fellow his father was. What did you give him?"

"Nothing—for an excellent reason. But he gave me something. It seems some of Guinea Sam's rogueries have been unearthed. Cudjo has some things Col. Blockington made Philip bring away from Block Island."

"How we will miss our friends from the north. They seemed to like our easy going ways. Some of them were charming people. So many parsons came. The balmy air down here was always so good for their throats."

"And they were so ready to marry their sweet voiced southern cousins," added Johnny.

"They quieted their consciences by calling it a patriarchal system," said Emily.

"And that made Regina furious," said the Captain with a grave face. "She was no wise inclined to model her establishment on Abraham's or Jacob's."

"No indeed," said Emily. "She was more self righteous than the Puritans who resolved to live by God's laws—until the Indians gave them time to do better."[2]

"Where we, poor mortal men are concerned—things will not work according to rule. It was a painful experience of Mrs. Effingham—that my uncared for monkeys throve while her pets grew sickly and delicate. Now I claim that by sheer neglect of my duty I have fairly educated my people for freedom. They are shifty—and thrifty. They can take care of themselves."

"Old Aneke says she has but one thing against Mars Frank—of blessed Memory—he would not let them pray hard. I suggested 'Loud' and she immediately accepted the amendment. She says he told them the Lord was not 'deef' and they need not roar like bulls of Bashan.[3] She thinks he was a very polite man," said Emily.

"By the way, why did that exquisite colored gentleman Sambo refuse to marry Clarissa—after all."

"He said—your marriage 'busted hisn.' It seems he had always expected his wife to be an excuse for being out every night. Now she was in the yard. He would have none of her."

"But," said Mrs. Effingham, "he is free now."

2. In *Two Years—or The Way We Lived Then,* Helen Newtown voices strong sentiments against the Puritans, whom she considered hypocritical, and in favor of the Indians, whom she regarded as having been ill-treated by those who called themselves Christian.

3. Allusion to Ps. 22:12–13.

"And he means to stay so," replied the Captain. "Who can blame him."

"Poor Clarissa," said Susan.

"Ah! they will take all the credit now."

"Let them have it. The thing goes out by the same hole it came in. Who brought Africans to America?"

"I try to forgive Genl. Lee—but I can't,"[4] said the sensible Susan. "Why did he do it."

"You will after a while. He had only a handfull. Grant was drawing soldiers when he wanted them as a juggler pulls ribbon from a bottle. The supply seemed illimitable. We were at the end of our row. It was of no use. Now Regina—answer me. I have all the faults of the typical slave owner— and more. We did not, after all, form the larger part of our Army. The flower of all the southern youth was there—in the ranks."

"Now Johnny! What did you fight for? Did you know?"

He bore this interruption of a not very complimentary nature with perfect equanimity.

"I thought this was *our* Country. And so I fought for the Confederacy. Nobody thinks much of the cause of a row after they are well in it. That I confess."

Again he turned to Mrs. Effingham.

"You saw those fellows in the Hospital. For five long years[5] I was with them; sleeping in the sleet and snow—barefooted, ragged, starving, wounded, dying—dead. Can you find no better motive for this, than a desire that other men should hold africans in bondage? Man is a queer creature; but that is unthinkable."

"No—not to people who are restless until some one comes to them with a tale of our depravity more horrible than the last. It is an agony to them to hear any good of us. If we do right it hurts them—and they receive the news with shouts of incredulity and derision. Like the rattlesnake in August they are blinded by their own venom. We shall be in the power of those who hate us."

"Don't you wish Uncle Von Enden was here? Mamma has her blood up. We would have a field day."

"Do not misunderstand me. It is better so. We must drie our weird.[6] We could never keep a standing army on that long line of Frontier. John Brown's

---

4. Lee surrendered at Appomattox on 9 April 1865.

5. Johnny of course errs in stating that he fought for five years; the war lasted almost four years exactly.

6. Scottish dialect, "We must endure our fate." Scott uses the phrase in *Guy Mannering* (Edinburgh, 1815).

ghost will never be laid.[7] It is better so. Time will—I mean we will learn of Adversity—Energy, Thrift."

"And getting along in the world virtues," hastily interposed Susie. "We need them certainly. But I want Johnny to tell us of his own Company because we knew nearly every one of them."

"At first they were like Philip of Orleans,[8] who feared the dust and the sun more than he did the musket balls. Then they laughed at their hard life, and took it as a matter of course. Addington would say in that hoarse voice of his, as our ranks thinned, 'Well! What did they expect? If they did not want to be killed why did they come here.' He soon joined the great majority—poor fellow."

The Captain's face blazed up—in spite of himself. That feeling was too strong. His pride in his "Company" could not be hidden; strive as he would. Susan even was forced to respect his love for his comrades in arms.

"Ah!" said Emily. "What a blessing to be sure of any thing in this world. Johnny believes in his company."

"Literally—we were company A. 1st. Cavalry. We went in to win. To have saved their flag, those fellows would have gladly freed the world, white and black—down to the Prince of Darkness himself—The Devil—and—"

"Come—now—no bad words," screamed the excited Susan.

"Rough times—rough words. Armies are always in Flanders. We have a bad name in the world. We behaved like gentlemen in Pennsylvania. You have just seen what an army of Philanthropists means."[9]

"Why were we defeated?"

---

7. On 16 October 1859, John Brown (1800–59) led a group of thirteen white men and five blacks to seize the federal arsenal at Harper's Ferry. An uncompromising abolitionist, he intended to arm the slaves and instigate a massive slave rebellion, though he seems to have had no specific plan in mind. He was tried and, in December 1859, executed. Years later, Mary Chesnut remembered learning of Brown's raid: "I remember then I saw the charleston papers, an account—of a speech from Senator Chesnut—& John Brown raid—I was so stupid—I did not read the raid at all—engrossed by my own small affair—& yet John's Raid—meant a huge War—revolution—*ruin* to us all & death to millions—& the speech—well it was a good speech—& there was the end of it—" ("We Called Her Kitty," MS p. 33).

8. Probably Phillippe de France, Duc d'Orléans (1640–1701), brother of Louis XIV, or Louis Phillippe Joseph, Duc d'Orléans (1747–93) called Phillippe Égalité, the two most famous of a line of Philips of Orleans (including Louis Phillippe Albert d'Orléans who came to the United States and fought in the Civil War under McClelland). MBC's source for this anecdote is unknown. Her reading in French history was wide.

9. Laurence Sterne, *The Life and Opinions of Tristram Shandy, Gentleman* (London, 1760–67). Uncle Toby repeatedly speaks of the armies in Flanders. John also refers to the campaign of 1863 which culminated in the Battle of Gettysburg, 1–3 July 1863, and to Sherman's campaign through the Carolinas, in which the Union forces plundered and burned southern property.

"Because they were too many for us. My pride increases every day."

"That's bad," persisted Susan.

"For I see how fullblown theirs has grown since we gave in."

"She dodges the word conquered; she uses paraphrases," again interrupted Susan.

"Grant is a Titan among them. He forced Lee's hand—and won. Let them blow their trumpets. Every blast is an indirect compliment to their dangerous, indomitable, and dauntless foe—or the trumpeting has no meaning at all."

"It is hard my dear Madam—hard on them; they have every thing else; but they may not have the comfort of despising their enemy, while they glorify their victory. They know it was hard won. The Death roll tells that."

"Tame says, 'We whipt our weight in Wild Cats,'"[10] said Susan complacently.

"Let us talk of something else—"

"Johnny," said Emily, "has Margaret told you—Guinea Sam chose to take his forty acres and his mule[11] on Mr. Blockington's Island place. When the old Colonel went over to see about it, there was not a white man on the plantation—and swarms of negroes. The modest Sambo was taking his ease in the Buckra house.[12] As the Colonel walked up—Sambo called to Philip who was with him. 'Who is that old white headed gentleman you have got there Philip?' The white headed gentleman forgot his age and weakness— he sprang toward Sambo—who jumped through a window and was off. Poor old man it was the last time he left his Cabin."

"I wonder he ventured on a violent ejection—in such a black mob."

"The Divinity that doth hedge a King—rough hew them as we will,"[13] replied Susan with dignity.

Her Mother bestowed a withering glance—but said nothing.

"The remains of plantation manners," suggested Emily, "but a rash proceeding all the same."

10. In James Kirke Paulding's *The Lion of the West,* Nimrod Wildfire declares to Mrs. Wollope that one of his old sweethearts can "whip her weight in wild cats" (Tidwell ed., 35).

11. Catchphrase describing a promise of compensatory property owed the Negro voiced by freedmen immediately after the war. The "promise" had as its basis the Confiscation Act of 1862, unenforced by Lincoln, which provided for confiscation of rebel land. At the end of the war, Thaddeus Stevens suggested confiscation of lands of those Confederates owning more than two hundred acres, to be distributed in forty-acre lots to freedmen. Stevens introduced such a bill in Congress in 1867, but it was rejected.

12. Plantation home of the white owners.

13. Susan here conflates two passages from Shakespeare's *Hamlet,* act 4, scene 5, line 123, and act 5, scene 2, line 10.

"I was thinking," said the Captain. "When things settle down—we will be very comfortable—I will have a long rent roll. I am going to divide my upland into farms and rent to my negroes. I have no body now to support but my wife."

"Ah foolish boy! Do you think they will be satisfied until you are ruined? They mean to punish you, not to relieve you of your burden. Rest assured of that."

Emily laughed at the sudden collapse of the Captain's Alnaschan visions.[14] She asked him, "Have you heard of a disrespectful, or even an unkind word from any of these poor creatures in all the madness of their saturnalia?"

"If he has not—I can tell him one," said Susan. "You will acknowledge Binky Anne's last fond farewell of Mamma was neither kind nor respectful. Was it 'Ole Missis'?" asked Susan. Mrs. Effingham disdained a reply.

"She dressed herself," said Emily laughing heartily, "in a gold colored satin, which formerly belonged to my father's grand mother. It was always the object of her profoundest admiration. She took possession of my Brussels lace shawl—and Susie's English hat with the Pheasant's wing. She held Margaret's Flamingo fan daintily in her hand. When she saw me at the foot of the stairs—she blushed blue black, and flew by like a Whirlwind. Mamma was at the bay window, as Binky Anne passed lolling back in our Landau. She raised herself languidly—and she cried, 'Good bye fat Joanna—you'll never ride in this fine carriage again.' Now Binky Anne was a good riddance. She tattled so—But Oh to see those horses go! Dawson stood sorrowfully at the gate as they drove off with Binky Anne in state."

"I see Scipio here still. The best butler in the world. Scipio Africanus is rather out of place before that side board."

"He left us however—for about ten minutes. He got himself up gorgeously and went to meet John Brown's ghost as it came marching on. They took his watch[15] which his master had given him with its resplendent gold chain. He came back a sadder and a wiser man."

"Why not?" asked the Captain. "Rob a fellow of his watch—but give him his freedom. Scipio ought not to have resented that trifle."

"But he did—he has not enlarged views—yet. In a wonderfully short time he was at his knife board and in his shirt sleeves."

14. In "The Barber's Fifth Brother," a tale in *The Arabian Nights,* Alnaschar, a beggar, inherits a hundred pieces of silver. With the money, he buys a basket of glassware. He dreams of all the riches he will accrue by making profitable trades, beginning with the glassware. Eventually, he imagines that he will be wealthy enough to spurn the Vizier's daughter. To punctuate the imaginary scene, he kicks the basket, breaking all the glass.

15. Cf. *MCCW,* 823.

"We had such a laugh at Mamma!"

"Is there worse to come than the shower of black babies—or Binky Anne's exit in a coach and four? Does any one dare laugh at this August lady?"

"You don't know! She is a darling now. Mamma has succumbed to circumstances. Things are so revolting in this world. After the Collingwood imbroglio, Emily revolted. That shook Regina from turret to foundation stone. She was defied—for the first time in her life. After Emily's little rebellion came the grand revolt of the southern lands—and disaster after disaster."

Mrs. Effingham made a slight motion of her hand as if annoyed by the buzzing of a gnat.

"Uncle Von Enden says Mamma differs from other people here—because she knows a fact when she sees one. We who are to the manor born—we can always fool ourselves with words."

Mrs. Effingham smiled grimly.

"I never can forget Mamma's face when Atlanta fell. She sat with a shawl over her head the picture of dumb misery. Then she told us to pack up— we must come home. She looks the same way—when she sees those paragraphs in the northern papers—about Uncle Von Enden."[16]

"Silence!"

"Well—I did not mean to offend. We left a city full of generals.[17] From a full general down to the very emptiest. No commands—all gone. Where? Dead on the battlefield—poor fellows. The generals were in full uniform and gallantly rode about on their fine horses. They were comfortable and hopeful to the last. They had maps and showed where Sherman would be stopped by rivers and swamps and imaginary armies; half a dozen stooping over a map—at a time. Each had a plan and they argued earnestly over it. They rode around with their maps until Sherman's cannon dissipated the fog of words in which they were lost. An army and no general may be

16. This is the first reference to a scandal involving Mr. Von Enden, further discussed in the following chapter. The novel never makes clear the nature of the Von Enden scandal, though it seems to have involved sexual misconduct on the part of Von Enden. The character Von Enden may be based in part on Horace Binney (1780–1875), a noted Philadelphia lawyer and brother-in-law of Mary Cox Chesnut, MBC's mother-in-law. Binney was a firm supporter of the Lincoln administration, and a critic of slavery, and MBC found his views offensive (see *MCCW*, 73). No evidence exists that Binney was involved in any scandal immediately after the war.

17. Joanna is referring to Richmond, presumably, since there is no hint in the novel that she has been in Columbia. In her revised Civil War journal, however, MBC repeatedly refers to the "horde of Generals without troops" in Columbia in January and February 1865. See, for example, *MCCW*, 716, where she uses words similar to these in *The Captain and the Colonel*.

bad—but we saw no end of generals—with no army. That is the worst thing of all."

"Whose conversation is she repeating?"

"We had to give it up. The pillar of fire in front of us—and the black cloud—at our backs.[18] The other side are awfully proud that we gave in. The few that were left of us—I expect the Persians made just such a row and honored and feted the generals who killed the three hundred at Thermopylae?[19]

"I tell Emily to send for *him*. Who is Mamma? Can she pretend to hold out after Lee has surrendered. But after all—"

"She need not send!" said Johnny. "I will answer for him. She is twenty one—that was her ultimatum; freedom's come to her too."

"She has been talking sensibly—in Mamma's style. When she does that, I always know Collingwood is in the air. And she is afraid her foolishness will come to the surface."

"As I pose for a family laughing stock," said Mrs. Effingham, "I would like to hear what caused your mirth."

"I am coming to you. When I have finished with Emily. Long time ago somebody said there would always be slaves—white and black—men and women continuing in the world. Blacks are free in these Reunited States; but Emily—will she be free long? Let us get up a Joanna Brown's spirit to stir up the women—or to lead them out of bondage.

"As I came across—I stopped to look at a black girl, twirling herself round until she resembled a balloon. She was yelling at the top of her voice to some one behind me. It was delightful to see her ecstacy. She said, 'Look here—see me—I am free as a bird.' I foresaw a husband for whom she must bake and brew—wash and sew—she will only exchange masters."

"Now for Mrs. Effingham!—she was seated just where she is now darning stockings at that table. When they came surging in—You know her Dutch blood has been heated already in two rebellions. The original Hartkopf came from Motley's Dutch republic—now Mamma is laughing at me!—You know he did—and your forefathers defied Philip and Alva[20]— they cut dykes and died in the last ditch. That was grand! And they came

18. Probably Susan's confused reference to Exod. 13:21.

19. See chap. 15, n. 4.

20. John Lothrop Motley (1814–77), a U.S. diplomat and historian, wrote *The Rise of the Dutch Republic* (London, 1856), a history much admired by MBC that stressed characterization and drama. Philip II of Spain (1527–98) was king of Spain from 1556. Fernando Álvarez de Toledo, Duque de Alba (or "Alva"; 1507–82), was governor general of the Netherlands. Noted for his tyranny, he was one of Philip II's leading ministers, and was sent to the Netherlands to put down a popular revolt in 1567.

over here just in time to lend a hand in Washington's rebellion. Well!—
This crowd of hungry soldiers rushed in—Yankees!

"'Hello there—you rebel woman git up—and git us something to eat.'

"'A rebel woman am I—and who do I rebel against? Such as you?' Think
of Mrs. Siddons.[21]

"Alas a heroic attitude was hard to sustain in the presence of Sherman's
bummers. Tony was there—he had bandaged his leg—he had no idea of
being taken away and made into a free black soldier; so he shammed lame.
He begged Mamma to keep silent—not to answer. To give them no fresh
cause for impertinence to her. He said he knew how 'to get along' with
them. Mamma adopted his suggestion."

"And Maum Elinor all this while?"

"We saw her go forth 'to see—for herself.' She dressed herself in her
Sunday clothes. She was radiant. 'No sea bounds like the bosom of a man
set free.'[22] She was sooner satisfied than Scipio. She came back she said to
look after her children—Emily and me."

"You see," said Mrs. Effingham, "these are brave girls. I am proud of my
daughters. They did not add to my trouble by any folly or weakness. What
I suffered—and what my thoughts were. That is between me and my
God—only—

"Emily keeps steadily to the ludicrous side in her descriptions of our trials during the raid. She will never let friend or foe see her break down.

"Our old people, as you see—are all here—except that jade Binky Anne.
As soon as they saw that the house was to be over run by soldiers, they constituted themselves body guard. We remained in this room—dressed—and
sitting up—night and day—while the army was here. And these people did
not leave us. No—not for a moment that could be avoided. You know old
Aneke is Emily's particular Maumer. At one time, I think she loved her
Maumer more than she did her Mother. Tony was wiser in his generation
than the children of light.[23] And I took his advice. After the first few words.
The scene became one of dumb show on our part, while parties of soldiers
charged in and out night and day. Occasionally the patience of one of these
old women gave way; as the soldiers jeered and taunted us.

"'Now you lean for protection on these poor creatures you ill treated.'

"Aneke kept Emily under her wing—her huge, bulky form was a shield.
'I look ill treated?' she said. 'I always thought white people had sense.'

21. Sarah Kemble Siddons, 1755–1831, English tragic actress.

22. William Wordsworth, "Liberty. Sequel to The Thorn. Addressed to a Friend," lines
30–31, in *Yarrow Revisited and Other Poems* (London, 1835).

23. Luke 16:8.

"'Sit down,' they shouted to Tony. 'You need not be afraid of them now.'

"Aneke was terribly taken aback by this. The idea that they expected 'a kinky headed, black negro boy to set down with ladies in the buckra house.' She informed them that Tony had been brought up with a gentleman who was dead in Virginia. She asked them—if they forgot their manners—and sat down when they went to see the queen. I told Tony to take a seat. He went down like a shot flat on the floor, with his back to the wall. Day and night—without food and without rest. It was hard work. And then the terrible tension of the nerves. Emily was white as a sheet—almost fainting. Aneke took her up in her lap. 'She looks like some thing that would ill treat her old Maumer—now, don't she?'

"Elinor had gone out to forage for us. She came back with a tin cup of coffee. The most delicious drop I have ever tasted. Elinor held out her treasure trove to Aneke. The old woman waved her back. 'You going to wake my chile—poor thing—she is dropt to sleep.'"

Years after, Susan, visiting in that neighbourhood, strolled by Effhall, more beautiful than ever in the spring time of the year. Suddenly a carriage dashed by her. The splendidly dressed lady inside seemed looking too, at the grand old place—now in the hands of strangers. When she spied Susan humbly walking on the dusty high road, she drew back, but not before Binky Anne's dark face shaded by laces and furs, had caught Susan's eye.

Binky Anne was the wife of a high official, one of the most noted of the robber band, whose arms were up to the elbows in the State Treasury.

17

Friends I owe more tears
To this dead man, than you shall see me pay;
I shall find time Cassius—I shall find time.[1]

"I am glad you have brought Margaret to day—for we are going away to morrow; and our dear Mother is giving her self up to sad, importunate memories."

"No—not giving my self up. I was recalling my husband's manner; he treated all things half in earnest, half in jest. Strange to say, death was a subject his mind perpetually hovered around. Shakespeare, who is supposed to have read human nature, or the human heart, next best to him who created

1. Shakespeare, *Julius Caesar,* 5.3.100–102.

it, says, 'The weariest and most loathed earthly life, which age, ache, penury, and imprisonment can lay on nature, is a Paradise to what we fear of death.'[2] And yet, I saw two of my own household smile a welcome, in Death's face. God knows they met him half way, and with out a murmur in the Hospital. The memory of the constancy and courage of those men haunts me. Remember Blanco White's sonnet?[3] War's black night revealed virtues hidden, and unknown in the glaring sunshine of our prosperity. To me—fear of death is natural—and not half so tragic as this eagerness to go. There seems a life weariness—as the world grows old."

"No more woes! Mamma—we can not afford to be mournful."

"It is depressing," said Susan—petulantly—that was ever her nearest approach to bad temper. "Every body gone—or killed—or dead."

"Susan—feels the loss of her dear Mary Sebbes," said Mrs. Effingham kindly.

"John Wilson—his wife—and his child buried together.[4] That was hard lines," said the Captain. "Tell me all about it Susie?"

"Yes. I will," she answered eagerly. "The baby was tiny and weak. The doctor did not think it would live, but Mary did not know that. It was only three days old, and the battles around Richmond going on all the time. They brought a telegram that John Wilson was wounded. Mary said, 'Bring him here.' Dr. Sebbes said, 'No—he must go to the hospital. They had only two

2. Shakespeare, *Measure for Measure,* 3.1.129–32.

3. Joseph Blanco White (1775–1841), "Night and Death" (1828). Because the poem has seldom been reprinted and is difficult to find, it is given in full here:

> Mysterious night, when the first man but knew
> Thee by report, unseen, and heard thy name,
> Did he not tremble for this lovely frame,
> This glorious canopy of light and blue?
> Yet 'neath a curtain of translucent dew
> Bathed in the rays of the great setting flame,
> Hesperus, with the host of heaven, came,
> And lo! creation widened on his view!
> Who could have thought what darkness lay concealed
> Within thy beams, oh Sun? Or who could find,
> Whilst fly, and leaf, and insect stood revealed,
> That to such endless orbs thou mad'st us blind?
> Weak man! Why to shun death, this anxious strife?
> If *light* can thus deceive, wherefore not *life*?

The Bijou; or Annual of Literature and the Arts (London: William Pickering, 1828), 16.

4. The tragic events described in this chapter are fictional, but MBC described several such instances in her revised Civil War journal. In *MCCW,* see for example the death of Rebecca Haskell (397), the deaths of Mrs. Means, her daughter Emma, and Colonel Means (426), and Robert Barnwell's death, followed by his wife Mary's death in childbirth (452–53).

rooms'; but Mary seemed so distressed at the bare idea; the Doctor gave up. When the whistle blew we began to look for him—hour after hour went by. And the Doctor did not come. We could hear nothing. Mary was very faint from anxiety—but we gave her things. We told her the Doctor had obstinately held to his own way, and taken her husband to the Hospital. The Doctor came; he was awfully pale—only the body had come—I never can forget it," sobbed Susan. "Mary continued to stare at her father. And he did not say a word. She drew the sheet over her face. And the Doctor told us *all* in an under tone. The little baby began to cry feebly—I said, 'It has grown very cold.' Mrs. Sebbes went to take the baby. She called out, 'She is dead!' We tried every thing—but she did not revive. Mrs. Sebbes and I sat up all night trying to keep that poor little baby warm—with hot flannels—and as near as we could get to the stove. It was of no use. It died before day. And so they were all buried together—. These chairs are very hard and uncomfortable," cried Susan. "How I miss my rocking chair! And the room is so close." She went near a window—where every pane was broken.

"Dr. and Mrs. Sebbes are here with their younger children; but the Blockingtons are swept from the face of the Earth. That poor nervous Mrs. Blockington was sad and silent—but a devoted wife and Mother. When her son was killed—she astonished me; she took it so quietly. I thought it absurd that Mr. Blockington should enter the Army—his age and his size— exempted him."

"He did not think so," said Johnny, "but he was awfully conspicuous at the head of his regiment."

"The night her house was burned, she tried to bring Matilda here. The girl was always delicate—like her Mother. There came on a heavy rain, and they took shelter under some trees by the way side. Maum Lucy says that timid woman rushed out and begged an officer for a blanket to put over her daughter. He gave her two. Maum Lucy—Mrs. Blockington's own woman, caught sight of them then—they were lost; she took them to her cabin and made them comfortable. But Matilda had got her death in that cold—and fright."

"And well old Lucy might," said Susan. "She had stolen enough of the dear old lady's things. The Yankees told the negroes to take all they wanted before they burned the house. And they did—Lucy as well as the others."

Mrs. Effingham as usual disregarded Susan's interruption—and continued.

"Lucy was devoted to them—as kind as a creature could be."

"Mrs. Blockington was very good to her always," said the indomitable Susan.

"Emily was there every day—but the girl sank rapidly. The poor Mother bore that death—in the same manner—no outward sign; but she grew weaker. At last she took her bed. One afternoon Emily came home and re-ported her so feeble. I gave my permission for her return there—at once."

"I found her worse on my return," said Emily. "Some one had been there—telling her that Johnston had not surrendered. And that there was to be more fighting. I tried to persuade her it was a false alarm. But the Doctor came. He thought it his duty to break the news to her. Some negro might tell her too abruptly. Col. Blockington was reported among the killed."

"I did not see—I never could see—what business it was of his," said Susan in a low monotone.

"As he came up in to the fire light, I knew something dreadful had happened. He began slowly breaking it to her as he called it. She never took her eyes from his face—gradually she seemed—drowsy. She began feebly counting her fingers—'one—two—three'—over and over again. Every thing was done for her that we could devise—the Doctor staid. She sunk very rapidly. She died without ever speaking again before midnight."

"You remember—we used to call him 'the giant B.' That uproarious laugh of his—generally at his own jokes. Sitting in that huge arm chair of his—fondling the glass of Madeira he loved so well."

"He did not do much laughing after he came home—which was a few hours after her death. He came by Block House that night—the ghastly window holes staring and the bare walls—standing out in the moonlight! Lucy made him as comfortable as she could—and I went there still every day. His head was as white as snow—and he was bowed by age and grief. 'All gone,' he said. 'My dear girl—they are all gone.'"

"Every body, black and white—went to his funeral.[5] He was buried with his people on that high bluff over the river. After the coffin was lowered—Mr. Tame came to me—saying, 'Mr. Blockington's negroes wanted to show their old Master some respect.' Five or six—grey headed old men formed a half circle round the grave. They were a striking group—well dressed, dignified, and solemn. They opened their prayer books—and began one of those wild weird melodies—known only to themselves. A Methodist negro hymn sung by all those powerful, musical, voices. The whole scene and all its meaning. It was too much for me. I cried like a baby."

5. Colonel Blockington's funeral is probably based on that of Colonel James Chesnut Sr., MBC's father-in-law, who died in February 1866. James Chesnut Jr.'s funeral in February 1885, described in Isabella Martin's introduction to the 1905 edition of *A Diary From Dixie*, seems to have been similar, and was undoubtedly traditional among the Chesnuts. Such a funeral included the family house servants, who prayed and sang to show respect to the dead master.

"Did you Mamma?" said Emily. "I stood there like stone. I am cold and hard as steel now. I could not shed a tear—Oh! I am so tired of hearing the sound of weeping and wailing."

18[1]

Emily was in a brown study—and the Captain watched her face—as a faint smile—or a slight blush—or a shiver indicated the thought passing like a flash through her mind. "That lovely look of her eye that I remember so well has come back," was his thought.

Emily's eye fell upon the stately Margaret—she now Mrs. Johannis—as she sat in the bay window—haggard, care worn, old. Why is Margaret so discontented, she thought. Her husband is here—safe. Then she saw her as she rode up to the gate that fatal morning, with Collingwood by her side,[2] she was patting and soothing the fiery horse she rode that day. How handsome she was then. A faint blush suffused her cheek—for there was Collingwood, bending low to open the gate for her, bare headed—his face flooded with the light of our glorious southern sunshine. Again he bowed low as he caught her eye; but that was in Mrs. Davis' drawing room—and the Piano was between them. And again his face—so near her—as he leaned in the carriage door, standing in the snow—at their door—Susie screaming from the windows for them to come in. Here she laughed out right. Surely that was a situation romantic enough to satisfy Lydia Languish.[3] He was ankle deep in snow.

She had not shared Susan's tranquil security. She felt something in the air—wrong. And she put her hand on his shoulder and whispered, "For my sake—no quarrel with Johnny." How emphatically he reassured her—not by words however. The very next day—the duel—after all—

And now was she never to see him again?

1. Chapter 18 seems to be a late draft, hurriedly written, with which MBC was not yet satisfied, for she did not copy it over in good form, nor did she give it an epigraph, as was her usual practice. Several passages in this chapter are confusing; several references are obscure. From this point on, the manuscript of *The Captain and the Colonel* shows signs of hurried completion—with almost no effort made to punctuate carefully, to make certain speakers are clearly identified, or to expand or clarify new or unexplained elements in the plot.

2. MBC is here using the pronouns "she" and "he" without identifying the persons about whom Emily (or perhaps Johannis) is thinking, though the thoughts appear to be about Emily and Collingwood in happier days. Further, there is no scene in the novel corresponding to the sentence here that begins, "Then she saw her as she rode up to the gate that fatal morning."

3. Heroine of Richard Brinsley Sheridan's *The Rivals* (London, 1775).

"The tide of time flowed back"[4] once more.

She was a happy, careless girl. Those wild stories of young Blockington—who laughed louder than she did. Where was young Blockington. Dead—and his kind father—all gone. Who could laugh now. Since that morning how difficult her life had been—all against her—Mamma—Johnny—Margaret—even Susan—with her good intentions—was sometimes a trial. The self suppression, the agony of these last five years. Would she go back to that other self—that light hearted self—who was lost forever—from that day at the gate. Never—Did the fairies under the water—Nymphs—did they require Undine to give back her soul.[5]

Again—she thought—In all that dreadful time I had hope—hope was my life.

Now—why should I expect to be happy—who is? All the weary grief and desolation she had witnessed in these latter days came surging up before her. Those boys at the gate—Mary Sebbes too! Her lips began to tremble—She remembered the sharp pang which shot through her heart—as she saw him enter the door at Mrs. Davis' that night. A keen pain like the parting of soul and body.

That was joy—What would sorrow be!

"What is it my daughter?"

She turned to her Mother. "I believe"—then her voice broke—and she covered her face with her hands.

"Ah! Why my heart this sadness," cried Johnny. "Soft heart—have your cry out. Better days are before you now." And he put his arm lightly around her shoulder. She shoved her chair back hastily—it grated harshly on the bare floor.

"She will not let me touch her since I raised my hand against Colley." She looked up defiantly—her face glowing with indignant protest.

He caught her eye and laughed.

Margaret spoke at once. "We were never considered a sensational family—in the old time. Now, it is nervous work. These girls are never satisfied without a scene."

"Margaret you are too severe," said Susan—always ready to take up the cudgels for Emily. "I do think she was going to say her creed—You may

---

4. See chap. 1, n. 1.

5. In *Undine* (Berlin, 1811) by Friedrich Heinrich Karl Fouqué, Freiherr De La Motte (1777–1843), a water nymph, foster daughter of a poor fisherman, achieves a soul through the love of a knight. She is forced to leave the knight, and when he remarries, she is faced with the choice of giving up her soul or killing her beloved, who has betrayed her. To retain her soul, she drowns the knight in her tears.

say the Lord's prayer and the ten commandments—Nobody hinders your pious exercises."

Mrs. Johannis made a grimace of disgust.

"My good wife—what is the matter with *you*," said Johnny in a tone of despair.

"My good wife," she repeated with a sneer. "You get that from Uncle Von Enden. It is essential however to know what those words mean. They do not mean me.

"Aunt Annie is a good wife. She worships her own beautiful character. That goes first with her. Her amiability—her sweet temper. How proudly she looks up when her husband praises her, 'My angel wife. The very best woman in the world.' For this she calmly endures—in her own house—the worst insult a man can put upon his wife. And she stands by him—to screen him—in society from the consequences of his escapades."

"Margaret!" and Mrs. Effingham's voice was angry indeed.

"He says such a woman is more precious than rubies," said Susan the great interrupter. "I dare say she is—I know he is the handsomest man I ever saw."

"He has broken her heart."

"Stuff and nonsense! She is contented—the only perfectly happy woman I ever knew except Susan—and for the same reason."

"Why drag me in. What have I to do with it?"

"She regards her husband as a dark background to bring out her virtues. In that light her beautiful life shines brightly. And she has had all this world can give. And she means to have the best of Heaven too.

"She will not be such a fool as to lose Heaven by sinful fretting over his misdoings. His vanity is colossal. Her supreme indifference he calls—Love. If she cared for him—how unpleasant she would make his life." The Captain looked on in amazement while his wife declaimed.

"Well—what has Mrs. Von Enden done to bring down this tirade. I am a dull fellow. So stupid am I, that I believe her to be one of God's loveliest creatures. She is as beautiful as she is good."

His Mother in law rewarded him by a look of love—of admiration—of thanks—such as she vouchsafed to few. She was too angry—too uneasy to venture to scold Margaret as she longed to do.

"My Aunt, Mrs. Von Enden, is as beautiful as ever—and while the world continues to admire her, she will be therewith content. She luxuriates in the reputation she has earned for good nature—and kindred virtues; she is a philosopher. She does not look for the impossible. She knows him thoroughly: and her profound disregard for him enables her to stand by him when the world frowns on him. If she had any heart—it would be broken.

I was there, when the terrible scandal came out. It could not be kept out of the newspapers. She was as smiling and kind as ever. She gave me to understand that he possessed every Christian virtue. She went down Broadway with him—an unusual thing for her to do. That night as he stood before the fire—with perfect self approval—no shadow of shame or remorse came near him. Certainly I thought he is the most splendid specimen of physical man I ever saw, and I wondered if we were to have the usual scene. Yes—she went up to him—he put his arm round her waist—drew her to him—kissed her—calling her 'the best wife in New York.'"

"They say Mamma is partly responsible for that match," said Susan.

"Mrs. Johannis," said the Captain irate still—but with an air of calm politeness. "What course would you advise a woman to pursue under those difficult circumstances."

"To be as *she* is—deaf, dumb, blind. As for myself—I have a horrid temper. I would make myself disagreeable. Then his overweening vanity would be tickled anew. I can see him chuckle and wink. He would take my deep disgust—my unutterable loathing—for *jealousy.*"

19

Look with thine ears: See how yon Justice rails upon yon simple thief.
Hark in thine ear: Change places; and handy dandy, which is the
Justice—Which is the thief? Thou hast seen a Farmer's dog bark at
a beggar? And the creature run from the cur? Thou might'st behold
the great Image of Authority—A dog's obeyed in office.[1]

Look kindly upon me my sister.
You are beautiful and gay.
Your days will be long and happy
But I am going away.

On his visits South Mr. Von Enden had made Regina's life a burden to her. No words could depict his horror of African marital relations, and their conjugal infidelities. To hear him, you would think until he saw negroes he had never met a divorced wife or a profligate husband. And Regina had moved Heaven and Earth to rectify what was amiss—with indifferent success.

1. Shakespeare, *King Lear*, 4.6.147–50.

Fancy her revulsion of feeling. The censor himself arraigned—the hero of a dreadful scandal—written of in every paper—*illustrated* in not a few. A case to disgrace any decent plantation negro.

"They might for very shame, after being so loud mouthed against the evil here, set a better Example!"

Regina was at her wits' end. Margaret with morbid tenacity clung to the disagreeable side of things—and made the Von Enden scandal her eternal topic.

Regina's plan of life was one by which she might secure all the pleasant things of the world.

"I hate," she said, "to hang my head all at one side—like Maid Barbara."[2]

Philip flung open the door with a flourish.

"De tings—Guinea Sam tief."[3]

"Look, my green and gold Shakespeare!"

"And my Mrs. Hemans!"[4]

"Here is the black bag—past your mending madame," said the Captain coolly.

"Good heavens! give it to me," cried Margaret—springing to her feet. Emily's voice rung out joyously. She had it—in her hand.

"The long lost epistle to Robert."

"Ha! ha! This is the best joke in the world. The cat is out of the bag now. Margaret! You are fairly caught! Letter and bag went up together—and you have been hunting the bag from that day to this. Who wants any more proof than that."

"If I had found it," said Margaret pale as death, "I intended to restore it to its proper owner."

There was profound silence.

"Mother, would you care to hear how it happened? That day I went into the library to be out of every body's way—on the desk was lying a letter addressed to Mr. Collingwood. Until then I did not know things had gone so far. As I took up the letter a thin sheet dropt out. At that very moment my eye fell on Emily standing with her back to me at the fire place. Unseen I stepped quickly into the drawing room; this paper still in my hands. There

2. In Shakespeare's *Othello*, Desdemona tells Emilia about her mother's maid, Barbary, who was forsaken by a lover. Desdemona remarks, "I have much to do / But to go hang my head all at one side, / . . . like poor Barbary," 4.3.25–32.

3. "Guinea Sam is a thief."

4. This edition of Shakespeare might either have been privately bound or any one of several editions in cloth binding, stamped in gold. Felicia Dorothea Hemans (1793–1835) was a popular poet. Many collected editions of her work were available by 1860.

you and Johnny confronted me—I slipped it in the leather bag on the chair. My shame began then—for I had time to think.

"You know the rest. I have suffered awfully—for this one moment's aberration."

She looked around—her husband's eyes with a strange light in them, had never been taken from her face. He spoke with an effort.

"No doubt it was very unpleasant—even I—falsely accused—suffered the tortures of the damned. They called me a sneak thief—a mail robber—an opener of other gentlemen's letters—"

"Now Johnny that is ungrateful of you. If Collingwood had not shot you Margaret would never have nursed you—and so never have married you! Do you know?

"I believe I understand Johnny, better than any of you do. He would sooner kill a man—than be so shabby as to break the seal of the other man's letter!—Now—Emily—I am going to tell my story—look out! I'll make Johnny forget Collingwood's letter. Mamma—I was engaged only one night—and married only a minute and a half when my husband left on the train."

"Emily take her away. She raves. *She* is as mad as a March hare too. Her folly—at such a time is more than I can bear."

"Em—Do you wonder I did it? I was a wise girl to marry myself. My own Mother treats me cruelly. She never could understand me."

Later in the day, having shaken off Susan, Emily went out for a breath of fresh air. She wanted to be alone—and to think. In the cedar avenue she met Capt. Johannis—the gay, debonaire Johnny of Antebellum days. He laughed *aloud.* "I have news for you—I dashed down to the Telegraph office to send a word to Collingwood. There I found the gentleman himself!

"Judging from the telegram he sent his family—he thinks the shortest way from Appomattox to Louisville is via the Atlantic Coast.[5]

"I told him the letter was found. He need never know who hid it in that bag. He forgives me freely for what I did not do—and forgives himself for shooting me for it.

"To day our explanation was thorough. The bullet hole he made in my leg let in no light on the subject. That is one of the beauties of satisfaction at the mouth of a pistol.

5. Johannis's statement that Collingwood is just now returning from Appomattox places this incident in April or early May 1865. This presents a problem with Margaret's statement that she was at the Von Endens' in New York when the "scandal" broke. Margaret could not have traveled north until April or May, and would hardly have had time to return to South Carolina before Collingwood reaches there.

"Now Em when you see him abreast of that Pine struck by lightning, I'll be off.

"Mrs. Effingham's strong good sense must have revolted long ago against the folly of repelling so gallant a son in law. What a lucky fellow he is. Fortune intact. He has lost nor life nor limb. And, like the mantle of charity, his military reputation would hide many faults—*if he had any.*

"And his bride awaits—like a love lighted watch fire—all night at the gate."[6]

"You are unjust to my Mother. She fancied him a mercenary wretch because he left me so soon after she told him—she would not give me a stiver if I married him. And my role was bergere délaissée.[7] We declined to accept the parts assigned to us—that is all. And then came the War—our small love affairs were lost in the grand hurley burley. Johnny! listen. Do not make the mistake of a life time. Who are we?—you and I—to arraign such women as Mamma and Margaret. They are Saints and Martyrs—better still—Sisters of Charity. Never look behind these five years. I said to her, 'Dear sister never let us think of that blunder—or talk of it again—.'"

"Collingwood says he will be but a few days here—and he will take you with him when he goes."

She showed no surprise. "Her eyes were with her heart and that was far away"—down the Cedar aisle.

"You have been bored with our inordinate affection."

"Say misplaced," she smilingly interrupted him. "My dutch phlegmatic nature enables me to endure a great deal."

"Well good b'ye. Forgive and forget. Your happiness is coming to meet you. I think that Kentucky fellow wears seven league boots judging by the speed of his advance. Now dear, this is the last word of the last chapter of all our misunderstanding."

From Mrs. Collingwood:[8]

6. Thomas Campbell (1777–1844), "Lochiel's Warning," lines 11–12, in *Poems* (Edinburgh, 1803).

7. Fr., jilted shepherdess.

8. Curiously, the two letters that end the novel, apparently part of an earlier version of this last chapter, have not been revised to eliminate references to events (such as Margaret's baby or Susan's departure for Europe) that were never dealt with in the novel, or to reflect the events of chapter 19. On the verso of the last section of *The Captain and the Colonel* (MS 343), a note reads "Combination of Miss Middleton's letters." The note is canceled, and may have no reference to *The Captain and the Colonel* at all. Only two letters among MBC's papers may bear light on the note. Both are copies in MBC's hand in the letterbook owned by Katherine Glover Herbert. The first, from S[usan] M[atilda] Middleton, is dated Columbia, 28 August [1865], and contains the sentence, "My poor little sister has nearly given way, and begins to look wan and wasted. It is hard to be a constant witness of suffering which one can do

My dear Mother.

By this time you have heard it all—As soon as we went into our stateroom I said, "Stop Robert—that woman there is listening to you." The door was wide open. He went up on deck—and I was to follow in a few minutes. This woman continued to walk up and down the cabin—her veil closely drawn and she was muffled up in a shawl. It had been a very fatiguing day. One's wedding day always is I dare say; so I sat down to rest. The strange woman came in—then rushed out muttering that she had mistaken her stateroom. Hers was next to mine—and I could hear her talking to herself and fidgeting in there. Her manner was so excited—I began to be afraid to be left alone with her. Every one seemed to be on deck; Suddenly I heard her go out— and the next minute a great bundle came tumbling down just outside of my window. I saw it was the same woman fallen over board. Screams—over head—and cries—"Man overboard"—another moment and a man did plunge over after her. I saw it was Collingwood. In one instant I was [on] deck. They were floating off. As soon as she struck the water, she put her hands under head; and so laid quietly on the top of the water. She did not sink, or alter her position in the slightest—until Collingwood caught her dress. He says—she tried to draw away from him—looking him full in the eye. Then she shut her eyes—and made no resistance.

On deck when I went up a frantic woman was showing how it all happened. The poor soul had stood still awhile vacantly drumming with her fingers on the guards. Then with a spring—like a flash she was over. Collingwood saw it all—came running from the opposite side where he was standing, tearing off his clothes as he ran. And he was in the water a minute after her. And yet she was a good way off, when he caught up with her—well for her poor thing—that he is so strong a swimmer.

I stood like a stock and a stone watching them.

A sailor jumped over board too—but he made little head way. They had tied a rope around his waist—the length of this rope dragged him too heavily. The boats were down in a wonderfully short time—they said—to me it seemed an eternity—and they picked Collingwood and Margaret up before they sunk.

---

nothing to relieve." Susan (1830–80), daughter of Oliver Hering Middleton and Susan Chisolm Middleton, had three younger sisters: Eleanor Maria, Olivia, and Emma. The second letter bears no signature, and is dated Saturday, 7 September 1865. It reads in part, "Mrs. Middleton continues in the most precarious state—distressing to her family. For weeks she has scarcely eaten anything they fear she is trying to starve herself."

The boat did not come back to the ship. As it passed us, he stood up and waved his hand to me—dripping like a water god. She was so draggled, and dreadful looking poor thing—with a shawl over her head and the blankets around her—they had been thrown in the boat as it went off. When Collingwood came back for the first time I knew it was Margaret who had done this thing.

They met her husband on the wharf. He was looking for her; but for an accident he would have been there in time to prevent her coming aboard ship. No one will guess who it really was.

The Captain said—"Dr. Jones and his wife." So did the newspapers—Johnny has written to us. She is so much better. He says no one need know any thing about it. It is so lucky Susan and her husband are in Europe. Though Susan can keep her own secrets well enough.

Collingwood said—Margaret's feat did not surprise him. Johnny can be a very disagreeable person to live with, when he chooses to be too coldly polite. She has not suffered physically. The Doctor told Johnny the shock had been of unspeakable service to her. Without this rough awakening it would have been worse with her—her mind was in a morbid unnatural state.

Dear Mamma—that terrible day I needed your strong minded self to sustain me—but we will try to forget it. All is well with me now—Collingwood sends you his kindest regards.

> Your daughter.
> Emily.

My dear Madame,

You saw by the daily paper that "Mrs. Jones" had attempted suicide. And on the very boat on board of which Emily and Collingwood had taken passage.

My poor misguided wife—was that Mrs. Jones—let that name pass—best for all parties that the truth should not be known.

You know she was never quite herself after her baby was born. She accused me of not caring for the child because it was hers. Then it died and things grew worse with her. She incessantly referred to ill advised words of mine during that carpet bag scene.

She thought I had gone to Emily's wedding—and she thought the bridal party were coming back to Effhall. To avoid them she determined to go north—and visit the Von Endens. When I got home after a worrying day on the plantation I found a note from her to that effect. I hastened after her without loss of a moment—but failed to get there in time. I received her from Collingwood's hands on the landing—and so let him go back to his bride.

When she found herself on board ship with the very people she was rushing off to avoid—and I believe she witnessed a Romeo and Juliet scene with stateroom door wide open—she could not face a voyage with these two happy people. And to her overstrained brain the only way out of it—was over board.

At last she and I understand one another. I am thoroughly ashamed of myself—and I hold myself strictly to account. I was too little at home. My out door work was very pressing. Things were—and are in a most distracted condition. But if it please God to tide me over this fatal quick sand—I hope never to trouble you again with my domestic difficulties. The Doctor advises change of scene—a summer in the Mountains—we will go. She remembers nothing after leaving home. For days her fever was very high. Then she told all that I have confided to you.

Affectionately as Ever—
Charles Johannis

The end.

Two Years—or The Way We Lived Then

1

A child in a nursery crying,
　　A boy in a cricket field "out"
A youth in a phantasy sighing,
　　A man with a fit of the gout.

"Why are you dragging me away? I don't want to be buried in a Mississippi swamp.[1] I do want so very much to stay here."

"Why ask? When you must see what a nice arrangement it is? The girls must have a Governess. Your father likes us all to be together. Besides it is economical. People are beginning to object to large boarding schools———. Then your father's mind is made up———."

---

1. MBC draws many of the details and most of the major events of *Two Years—or The Way We Lived Then* from her own childhood experiences. Her father, Stephen Decatur Miller, owned land in Mississippi and moved his family there from Camden, South Carolina, in 1835 or 1836. His eldest daughter, Mary Boykin Miller, was left in school in Charleston for several months, but in the fall of 1836, the family (who had returned east for the summer) took Mary back with them to the Mississippi plantation (*MBC*, 18–42).

Chesnut recalled her trip to Mississippi in a memoir she entitled "We Called Her Kitty," written to her nieces and nephews, children of her sister Kate (Catherine) following their mother's death on 17 April 1876:

　　We stopped at the roughest places—Some times had all to sleep in one room— ~~The night~~ Sally's principal pleasure as we passed a village was to sing at the top of her voice—a song called "The choctow nation pretty little wife & a big plantation" & as we were rather an unusual turn out . . . I think every living thing would come out to watch us pass—

　　We had then three plantations—& several hundred slaves—but it was hard to make ourselves more comfortable—it took ten oxen to haul up any thing from the river—& as we drove in the carrige we carried an axe to chop the hardened lime stone mud from the wheels—

"Really and truly? That is the amount of it? Why did he change his mind so suddenly? Yesterday, I was to be left as always before, with Madame;[2] to day—I must be carried off by force to the Grindstone! I wish you could hear Kitty[3] describe her."

"I wish you could see your own discontented face. You must learn to make the best of things. You will find this world does not arrange itself exactly to suit you. Now don't say another word. You must go with us."

Nobody had time to consider my feelings, so I dried my weeping eyes. Excitement and confusion pervaded the air. The horses were stamping impatiently at the door.

As every one hurried along, I stood apart, sullen and miserable.

My plans were all upset. This would have been the pleasantest winter of my life; that I knew. If they had only let me alone!

More over I felt in some inscrutable way that it was a punishment. A vague feeling rose within me. I had been gay and contented, hitherto, and I knew so many good people thought that wrong. I had noticed being too light hearted gave offense. And up to this time I had always been exasperatingly happy.

Our carriage held four inside, and a seat with the driver. The top was now thrown back but it could be made a very close carriage indeed, in bad weather.

We had four spanking bays now champing the bit; fiery and restless were they, but our coachmen hinted to them, they would be quiet enough before we reached our journey's end.

Our travelling party consisted of the Newtown family.[4] Let me present three of its members to whom I have not yet alluded. Frank, a boy just entering his teens, whose name had been changed to Dan in this wise, and by a gradual process. He was apt to put on his black cap and "pronounce sentences" upon us of the utmost severity. We cried, "A second Daniel come to judgment!" in scornful protest.[5] So from Daniel to Dan.

Constance—so called in vain by her sponsors in baptism, for her Maumer decided the matter, singing "Sweet Kitty Clover, you bother me

2. Ann Marson Talvande, born in San Domingo prior to 1800, died 15 November 1850. She ran a French School for Young Ladies in Charleston, S.C., to which Chesnut was sent at the age of twelve in 1836. See *MBC,* chapter 3.

3. Based on MBC's sister Kate, Catherine Miller Williams (1827–76), known in childhood as "Kitty."

4. Based on MBC's own family: her father, Stephen Decatur Miller (1788–1838); her mother, Mary Boykin Miller (1804–85); her sister Catherine; her brother Stephen Decatur Jr. (b. 1825); and her sister Sarah Amelia (b. 1831).

5. Shakespeare, *The Merchant of Venice,* 4.1.220, Shylock's allusion to the fifth chapter of Daniel, in which Daniel interprets the judgment of God on Belshazzar.

so."[6] And with its endless refrain of "Oh Oh Oh," she fastened Kitty upon her nursling forever. "My dear Catherine,"[7] began a prim play fellow. "Oh dear—pray don't say that. Kitty is only my nominal name," answered our sister. And that unlucky explanation we never allowed her to forget.

Harriet—or Tatty, a fair haired, soft and sweet, blue eyed beauty of four years old.

Fanny, our maid[8] was about my own age; she had always been with us in the nursery, since I could first remember. So we associated upon terms of perfect equality. Her business was to take care of Tatty—but this she turned over to Kitty and me at her convenience. My Mother was always on the side of the weak, and we were never allowed to complain of her. We were very fond of Fanny, who was very good natured and obliging, though of course we quarrelled sometimes. Fanny might very well have gone in the baggage wagon—but under pretense of "minding the baby" she resolutely kept her place in the carriage. Then there were two saddle horses.

Mr. and Mrs. Newtown rode a great deal; when they were tired of that, oh how joyfully Dan and I took their places. And then Kitty took mine. We loved to be in the open air—and fought for the place next the driver.

For my sins! for four or five weeks I was there pent up in close confinement, with my own family. While I was at school the others had twice before made the trip, and they luxuriated in the details of all the hardships I would have to encounter.

Day by day we saw less of our parents; the carriage they quietly resigned to the youngsters, as they grew more accustomed to the saddle and more impatient of our noise.

We were always making every possible change to alleviate our position. Shuffle the cards as we would the inevitable five remained.

The very first day (though I considered myself "a grown up" young lady and a possible heroine,) I contrived to get into trouble, and to be disgraced in the eyes of all, by a good scolding. The rule was to stop for our meals, if a house could be found. There also the luncheon baskets were always replenished; they never were to be touched if outside relief were possible; they were our reserved forces.

At the first dinner house the Landlady rushed forth to meet my father

6. Traditional English song cited in Sabine Baring-Gould, et al., *English Minstrelsie; A National Monument of English Song* (London, 1895–99).

7. Constance, based on MBC's sister Catherine, here asserts that her nickname "Kitty" is not short for Catherine.

8. Fanny seems to be fictional. The Millers took several servants with them to Mississippi, and at least one free black, a valet named Armstead (Richard Manning Boykin, *Captain Alexander Hamilton Boykin* [New York, 1942], 194).

with out stretched hands. So eager and joyous was her welcome I fancied they were old friends. She said, "Just in the nick of time! The very right minute! We killed a pig this morning."

On the plantation[9] I had seen them in wagons, so white and human with their gaping bloody throats. And now they expected me to eat one!

Every part of the animal so lately sacrificed was already on the table. I shuddered at the thought. The only alternative [was] a mound of turnip greens and huge pieces of corn bread called lick sides.

I slipped away, took a biscuit out of the basket, and made myself comfortable in the carriage, with my book, "Darnley or the Field of the Cloth of Gold,"[10] a book I then found perfectly charming. I have not seen it for forty years. And yet I remember it distinctly. *So* it must be good of its kind.

After dinner my Mother made Kitty take her place on horseback. Dan whispered, "She wants a fair chance at you. She is boiling over. Somebody will be scalded. You could not keep out of hot water for a single day."

My manners were pronounced atrocious. It was hoped under Mrs. Grindstone's care I would learn to respect the feelings of others. They all hoped my rudeness had escaped good old Mrs. Nab's attention. But after all, my dear Mother's reproofs never did amount to very much. She found it so hard to pretend to be angry with us.

Fanny always mingled freely in our conversation, and advised that I should be let alone. "She'd be bound" before we got to the plantation I would be glad enough for good corn bread, and I would think spare rib splendid. Tatty was on my side—she averred distinctly that for dinner she wanted "chicken and rice, not pig."

It was early in the Autumn, and we rarely had bad weather. If it rained we stopped at the nearest house, and waited for a clear sky.

So I became intimately acquainted with my own family. We read until our books gave out. We sang a good deal; and we slept a great deal. All the same the days seemed endless to the "young blood—blocked and chained up there," said Dan. There was nothing to divert the eye but monotonous Pine woods; and houses few and far between, each uglier, barer, squarer, more uninteresting than the last.

9. MBC does not say where in South Carolina the Newtown family lived before the move to Mississippi. Because the parallels between MBC and Helen Newtown are so close, however, Chesnut is almost certainly drawing on the Camden area. As a child, she lived at the Miller plantation, Plane Hill, seven miles southeast of Camden, and visited almost daily at the Boykin plantation, Mount Pleasant (sometimes called Pleasant Hill), a mile away.

10. Novel by George Payne Rainsford James (London, 1830).

As we approached the Creek Nation[11] one day, Dan and I had the luck to be on horseback. We discovered that a man on foot could keep up with a horse. A tall well dressed negro, black as the Ace of Spades, polite and affable, but devoured by curiosity, kept pace with us. Sometimes we galloped off, but a slough as they called those slushy watercourses, or a hill soon enabled him again to catch up with us. With pride he informed us that he too was a Carolinian. In his own words, "I'm fum de ole Sous State." His young missis had married, and moved to Georgia. Her maid was his wife, and they lived near the road. I suppose he was a slave, but he had a free and easy irresponsible way with him that was delightful. "I tole Nancy as I had her for a wife I'd come long too." But he did not like it, he sighed for Waccamaw[12]—he liked fish and rice better than bacon and hominy, sweet potatoes more than all. "Fish an pertater, What could be better," he sang.

"Sorter ticklish now, the way you goin, you got to cross the Creek Nation to git to Newerleens I reckon. Ingins can't be trusted now they tell me."

We rode back with our news and reported to Papa. "I have ascertained, that there is no danger. There have been disturbances,[13] but it is all over," said he.

We were wildly excited. Our sable friend winked at us. "Ticklish business—you'll see!" Dullness disappeared at the approach of danger. We were all life and animation now.

As we drew near a house after dark, Dan called out to the imprisoned females below, from the Coachman's seat. "Right ahead there is an Indian Ambush!"

We threw ourselves nearly out of the carriage to see. There were huge bonfires and dusky forms hovered around them in the red light. There was shouting and singing—a regular chorus at some points.

My father rode hastily up. Our cries had been heard. Tatty was yelling like a wild Indian.

11. The Newtowns were crossing the large Creek reservation in Alabama. Actually, treaties signed by the Creeks in 1832 had virtually ended the Creek Nation in Alabama. Most had begun the westward migration to the Indian Territory. The Creeks were a particularly frightening tribe to South Carolinians, for it was Creeks who had killed more than a dozen whites in what came to be known as the Long Cane massacre on Christmas Eve, 1763, in western South Carolina.

12. The area drained by the Waccamaw River in the northeastern part of South Carolina.

13. Indian raids were still common in the 1830s. For example, a letter from John Cantey in Columbia, Georgia, to Edward Kincaid Anderson dated 22 May 1836 gives an account of Creek raids (Kincaid-Anderson Family Papers, South Caroliniana Library, University of South Carolina).

"Stop that noise. There is no cause for alarm. This is what they call a log rolling—a neighbourhood gathering only. They are burning brush heaps."

And our Romance—was dissipated. Dan said, "Alas! for the Last of the Mohicans." I replied, "And the Wept of the Whisht on Whisht."[14] "You have too many *h*'s in that name," said Dan as usual putting us to rights.

The house as we drew near resolved itself into a few separate log cabins which approached each other very nearly with out touching. There lived a widow with several grown sons. They were pioneer relatives of my Mother.[15] They told us blood curdling tales of savage warfare; but they were not in the least afraid apparently.

Madame was an excellent shot. She might have had more useless accomplishments in her present situation.

She showed us her double barrelled guns on a rack at the head of her bed. And we saw numerous bear skins, trophies of her skill.

She was the most demonstratively affectionate woman I had ever met. And Dan with a boy's reluctance to be embraced—wiped his mouth and whimpered, "Her victims the bears taught her how to hug."

As for me, my family had given me up. They proclaimed me "an affected fine lady." They had been there before and knew how to behave. Fanny personifying public opinion said, "*Ef* we aint tired of your airs!"

In the course of our travel we passed several Indians, out on a War path, we thought, for they had on all their War paint and feathers. Not much clothes to speak of—principally brilliant coloured waist cloths—or rags.

One pair executed a pantomime, (we fancied afterwards) for our benefit. At the time it filled us with horror and dismay.

There was a mimic fight—and the conquering hero drew his knife several times round the head of the prostrate foe. Soon the downfallen one arose. And we saw his tuft of hair and a feather or two all safe.

How that knife gleamed around that man's head, in the sun! And how we stifled our cries our hearts standing still.

Gradually as we left the Creek Nation behind us we fell into our old apathy. At the beginning of our journey, the horses were only four handsome bays. Now they were as distinct and individual as any inmate of the carriage. We had each a horse favourite—whom we called by his name, and fed

14. Novels by James Fenimore Cooper, *The Last of the Mohicans* (Philadelphia, 1826) and *The Wept of Wish-Ton-Wish* (Philadelphia, 1829).

15. Possibly based on the family of Francis Boykin, half brother of MBC's mother. Francis (1785–1839) and Mary James Boykin lived in Portland, Alabama. Another brother of MBC's mother, William Whitaker Boykin (1813–89) was also in Alabama in the 1830s (Boykin, *A. H. Boykin,* 7).

with our own hands with scraps saved from our own meals. And they responded kindly to our petting—answering in the inarticulate horse fashion—a horse laugh.

I am sure we told each other every thing we knew. Even my Mother waxed confidential, and divulged the secret of my exile. "Old Mr. Meddlesome felt it his duty to tell us that he saw you on the battery one moonlight night with ———."[16]

"But his sister—Madelaine[17] was there. She was not ten steps off. Old Mr. Meddlesome is so near sighted," I interrupted with spirited self defence. "He is as blind as a bat and only sees what he wants to see."

"I dare say—he also told us you dined regularly with the same girl every Saturday. And there was always the same procession home by way of the battery. Moon light walks and all that."

"It is not always moonlight," said I doggedly.

"Your father did not like it; he said, 'You were so young. Not fifteen indeed. And that he deemed it expedient to bring you with me, and put you under my eye, and in Mrs. Grindstone's hands.'"

"Far from the madding crowd,"[18] I laughed hysterically.

"Your father said not one word to Old Meddlesome, who tried to reconcile him to his foolish revelations, by adding 'that we need not be alarmed—the whole family of ——— were going to Europe next Spring[19]—and would be absent several years.' Old Meddlesome hoped what he had said would not make mischief. 'Certainly not—but she had better be with her Mother,' said your father. 'So she had,' responded promptly that spiteful old thing, with his wrinkled, puckered up, smile."

My Mother owned that "she did not agree with them in that. She had gone through similar scenes in her youth, unscathed, in her own school days, in the same dear old place."— "'There are men every where,' I told them—and it seemed to me they were nicer in town than any we were likely to meet in the wilderness where we are going."

Then my Mother, as Fanny was happily for once with her charge, little Tatty in the baggage waggon, and Dan was on horseback with Papa, and the way being clear, delivered her honest opinion on the subject of neighbourly fault finding, mischief making, and unasked advice.

16. Based on MBC's own moonlight strolls with James Chesnut Jr., and her subsequent removal to Mississippi (*MBC* 28).

17. Madelaine Howard, the sister of Sydney Howard, Helen's suitor, seems to be based on Mary Serena Chesnut Williams (1821–87), niece of James Chesnut Jr., who spent most of her childhood with the latter, at Mulberry.

18. From Thomas Gray's *An Elegy Written in a Country Church Yard* (London, 1751), line 73.

19. James Chesnut Jr. accompanied his brother John to Europe in 1839 (see *MBC,* 37–40).

"No woman can get along with outsiders coming always with revelations of one's families' faults and failings. The head of the house knows of more than she can correct. Spies and tale bearers spoil every thing. Things come straight if you will only let them alone. There is often a judicious blindness worth all the clear sightedness in the world.

"While we lived in the country, things were as smooth as glass. But as soon as we came into town how different it was.

"On the plantation we were all a little lazy, but we got along admirably.

"Every body knows that I have the best servants in the world."

"And I know, they have the best mistress in the world," was my meek interruption.

"They do not exert themselves violently—but there are so many of them, nothing ever goes wrong. In town Mrs. Mac felt it her duty to call and let me know that Lydia—my cook, in collusion with her sister the poultry minder, gave her husband eggs and fried chicken for supper whenever he came. And the dairy woman's family had butter to eat with every thing and had been seen to give away milk.[20] What was I to do? What was I to say? You know I did not care, for there was enough for us all. These people are respectable members of the church. And I treat them with kindness and confidence. They never give me any trouble. Now if I make a row and let them know that I have found out they take my things without asking for them, they will feel degraded, and at last be as forlorn and disreputable as Mrs. Mac's own people. I was very polite, and got very comfortably out of it all. I did one wrong thing—I said I would see about it. And that is exactly what I did not do. I shut my eyes. I would not see any thing. I love peace. And resolutely I go in for a quiet life!"

"You do yourself injustice," I replied. "You are the most inquisitive person I ever knew. You see every thing. I defy any one to blind you. The smallest child in the house knows that. Then you are so energetic—so efficient—so all pervading as a housekeeper"—here I paused for a word—to express my intense appreciation of her in that capacity. "Perfection in short."

"Flattery—you are putting it on heavily. At any rate it is useless to tell me things—on my home people. I am so weak I dare not face the Mrs. Macs and order them to mind their own business. A sensible woman would do that. I did casually suggest to Lydia that when her husband came she ought to give him something extra and nice—and to the dairy maid to give skimmed milk always to those poor Mac negroes. And only give fresh milk

20. This passage corresponds closely to MBC's account of the Chesnuts' overseer, Adam Team, whose wife got fat from the butter taken from the Chesnut pantry (*MCCW,* 248). In her revised Civil War journal, MBC inserts this material into a tirade by her maid, Molly.

in case of sickness. I thought they looked a little foolish. If I have done any wrong to any one may God forgive me."

Here Kitty piped up, "Even Mrs. Grindstone makes Mamma miserable. She is a mischief making old hag."

"Kitty!"

"Helen, she was actually mad enough to begin that sort of thing with your father, the very first day he came home. She heard him, you know his way; intimating to us that we were all angels in human form.

"'And yet,' she began—I held up my hand to her warningly. 'Not a word before these children. It is always injudicious to discuss them in their presence.'

"'You are right—a most sensible remark,' she said patronizingly to me."

"Kitty, darling, what had you and Dan done to her?"

"I had only laughed—Dan will not get up—that boy has a genius for sleeping. Our Governess said, 'Let her try her hand. She could make him punctual.' So she called Fanny to hold a basin of water, and she went into his room, and began to flick water in his face. Dan waked in a rage. He seized the basin and let Fanny have it full in *her* face. And she squalled! Mrs. Grindstone tried to shake him; he pretended to think they were sky lark-ing; so he sprung us just as he was, and soused Mrs. G from head to foot with three buckets of water there for his bath. I did not see it of course—but he pursued them—across the passage pelting them with pillows and boots and—and—the last empty bucket came rattling against the door as they slammed it in his face. Mamma and I were standing before the fire—when these drowned rats came in. They were not only drenched, but from the rags and tatters, they had on—we saw there had been a real fight—but Dan had routed them—though they were two big ones to one little one. I was sorry for Mamma. You know she had to behave. She could not laugh—but I laughed for three days without stopping—."

"What did Mamma do to Dan?"

"She reproved Dan severely. She told him he had been 'guilty of conduct unworthy of a gentleman.' Dan said 'if he was a gentleman—they had no business in his room.' You know how grandly he talks when he knows he is wrong. 'They invaded my privacy,' he said."

Whereupon Kitty threw herself back and shouted with glee at the rec-ollection.

"You ought to have seen her face when I told her that nothing disagree-able was ever spoken of before Mr. Newtown. It was the rule of the house to keep unpleasant things to ourselves and never to annoy him in any way with our little tempests in a teapot.

"'Good heavens my dear Madam!' she cried. 'What do you do, when your children or servants misbehave.'

"'We do very well—indeed we are a model family—almost every thing comes right if you let it alone.'

"At any rate I do not mean to change my system. So much less is accomplished by harshness than people suppose. I have never said a word to worry my husband in my life, and I never will—he says his home is a heaven of peace and rest."

"When she tried to tell on me he took me up and smothered me with kisses. 'No tales out of school,' was all he said. He is a darling. She is an old cat."

That was Kitty's honest opinion of the Grindstone.

2

She never found fault with you:
        never implied
Your wrong by her right; and
        yet men at her side,
Grow nobler, girls purer, as
        through the whole town,
The children were gladder,
        that plucked at her gown.[1]

Unveil her mind and hide her face,
And love will need no fuel.
Alas that such an ugly case,
Should hide so rich a jewel.[2]

How light hearted I was! Now I understood it all. That very night I wrote a letter to my dearest friend, *his* sister, and told why I had been removed and suppressed—of course mentioning no names—putting all the blame *on the Battery.*

I thought of Madelaine's amazement and amusement, when she heard of people so infatuated, they did not trust Madame to be strict enough with us. Absolutely doubted the power and the will of the lynx-eyed Superior of

1. Elizabeth Barrett Browning (1806–61), "My Kate," lines 21–24 in *Last Poems* (London, 1862).

2. Joseph Rodman Drake, "Miss H. R.," in "Trifles in Rhyme," cited in Frank Lester Pleadwell, *The Life and Works of Joseph Rodman Drake (1795–1820): A Memoir and Complete Text of His Poems & Prose Including Much Never Before Printed* (Boston, 1935), 180.

our Convent in Legare St.!³ Did they know of her second in command Miss Anne? best of all Duennas—Queen of all detectives.

Once more our daily routine of travel lapsed back into its old monotonous dulness.

I had ceased to look out for beautiful scenery. My ideas on that subject were drawn from the "Lady of the Lake."⁴ I was prepared to go into raptures when confronted by a beautiful landscape; but in the mean time the wind moaned in the everlasting Pine Forests that we traversed day after day, at a slow cadenced trot.

We had "Corinne" with us—which I could translate with the aid of a dictionary.⁵ Then I would shut my eyes—for gorgeous day dreams, and arrange the fortunes of An American Sappho. At fifteen a girl is rather shy of such intense love as Phaon created—so I soon fell in with a more congenial style of heroine—Joan of Arc. With her for awhile I performed heroic and patriotic feats—always saving my Country at full speed on the most beautiful of horses.

But I have always found it easier to concentrate all the energy of my imagination on a hero—and to make him a military conqueror. As a heroine, I found myself a burden. For variety's sake, when I selected a civilian as my jeune premier,⁶ I had speedily to endow him with a gold mine, or a coal mine, in more difficult circumstances I did not shrink from diamond mines, so that I might enable him to strike at once a heroic attitude, as bridegroom and millionaire. If I had ample time given me—I made him a genius—or made him invent some miraculous thing for the benefit of humanity.

3. Madame Talvande's French School for Young Ladies, located in what is today called the Sword Gate House at 32 Legare Street in Charleston. Madame Talvande was Catholic, but many of the students were Protestant, and no religious instruction was offered. MBC identifies Miss Anne as Anne Eliza Johnson in "We Called Her Kitty." No records from the school have been found.

4. Helen Newtown refers to the dark, romantic, and wild scenery described in the first canto of Sir Walter Scott's *The Lady of the Lake* (Edinburgh, 1810).

5. Novel by Madame de Staël (Paris, 1807). Corinne, the heroine of Madame de Staël's novel, is a beautiful young Italian writer and poetess described as a latter-day Sappho. Sappho was a Greek lyric poetess, born in Lesbos in the mid-seventh century B.C.; Phaon was an old and ugly Lesbos boatman said to have received the gift of youth and beauty from Venus. He spurned the advances of Sappho when she fell madly in love with him. Desolate, she jumped into the sea. MBC could have learned the story from many sources. As she claimed to have no classical training, she may have learned it from *Sapho and Phao* (London, 1584) by John Lyly (1554?–1606), or more likely from Alexander Pope's *Sapho to Phaon* in *Tonson's Ovid's Epistles,* 8th edition (London, 1712). Joan of Arc was the subject of several works that MBC may well have read, including *La Pucelle d'Orléans* (Louvain, 1755) by Voltaire, and the epic poem *Joan of Arc* (Bristol, 1796) by Robert Southey (1774–1843).

6. Fr., romantic hero.

At first it was easier. I fell into the regular "Novel" plan of killing off more or less tragically all of his rich relations; but that seemed hard hearted. And as I held in my hand the wealth of the Earth and the sky and the water, I concluded to leave his fortune unstained by kindred gore.

Some times I went in for love in a cottage; but that was before I had seen or lived in the three room log house on the plantation.

Some times I left for Europe in a coach and six, where I had innumerable adventures with every body I had ever read of and equally thrilling ones, with purely imaginary characters. I rescued every body from suffering; and by my astounding sweetness and my persuasive tongue alone, I turned all wrong doers from their evil ways.

It has been intimated that all my friends were not boys—not quite. For a man who was graduated at Princeton,[7] and since then was studying Law, and had also been seen taking me home by way of the battery one beautiful moonlight night, always loomed up toward the winding up of the story. And whenever the song was "She stood beside the altar,"[8] he was standing there too, fumbling in his pocket for a wedding ring.

We had an infinite variety of experiences in night lodgings. At some houses, we were made thoroughly comfortable, and occasionally we struck a town.

From the Creek Nation to the Choctaws,[9] things steadily grew worse.

One night we were forced to stop at a house, which consisted of one room; and there we all had to sleep. There were the man of the house and his wife and a baby. And two men had arrived before us. We were piled on the carriage cushions, to sleep. And our parents nodded in the chairs beside us.

Once after plunging all day in mud and mire, limestone clay so stiff, it had to be chopped from the wheels with an axe; then suddenly sinking in sloughs, which seemed bottomless quick sands; long after night we saw the light of a solitary log house.

Outside [was] a traveller in the act of removing his saddle bags, and in it we found the inevitable man and his wife and baby.

7. Sydney Howard, based on MBC's husband, James Chesnut Jr., who graduated from Princeton in 1835 and was reading law in Charleston under noted jurist James Louis Petigru in 1836 when he was seen with Mary Miller strolling in the moonlight on the Battery.

8. Allusion to line 223 of Edmund Spenser's "Epithalamion" in *Amoretti and Epithalamion* (London, 1595).

9. The Choctaws inhabited large portions of Mississippi in the early part of the nineteenth century. Most moved west after the 1833 treaty of Dancing Rabbit Creek. In 1837, the year following the Newtowns' trip, there were only 750 heads of Choctaw families in Mississippi (Dunbar Roland, *History of Mississippi* [Chicago, 1925], 1:595).

These were painfully polite persons. They sprung out of bed and throwing back the bed clothes offered us their places. My parents declined with thanks the generous hospitality and we huddled together with our backs turned. By this time we were accustomed to sleep like cats on a pile of cushions barricaded by shawls and chairs.

But the woman, at day light next day, killed her last chicken before our very eyes, and picked it. We saw it in its death throes. She put it in a pot with two sweet potatoes. She said there was not another mouthful of food of any kind in the house.

The man with the saddle bags we left to share this last morsel of her food. My father as we left said, "Mount your horse. There is not enough there for the poor woman herself or her child."

The man hung his head—but remained to partake of this scanty repast. We could not eat what we saw die. Tatty had a bottle of milk. She did not suffer. We fasted. All appetite had departed at the sight of the chicken's death agonies—for awhile.

We did not find another house until noon. Dan said "now we knew what the starving poor felt." He tried to support us by stoical example—and words.

"Let Fanny howl, she is an untutored savage. We are civilized beings. We should know [how to] bear our pain in silence." Silence however did not suit Tatty's state of mind. She was singing at the highest pitch of her baby voice,

"Ah! ha! the Choctaw Nation—
Pretty little wife and a big plantation,"[10]

when we met the stage. It contained our precious Governess, Mrs. Grindstone.

Our Governess was tall and stout. I thought her old—I dare say she was fifty, but one's ideas of age vary so—perhaps she was younger. Of these facts I am certain; she had a brown leathery complexion—with large ears—so large indeed that Dan who had no respect for persons in authority—compared them to Peter Plummer's flying woman's—who slept upon one of hers—and covered with the other. Her eyes were deep black—and she had dark rings under them. Her shaggy eyebrows hung lowering. And yet the expression of her eye was kindly. She had a good straight nose. The black line of eyebrows, and the nose formed a perfect cross in the centre of her face. A broad, flat mouth and beautiful teeth. Her cheeks hung flabbily, and her hair was so thin, that she had it cut short like a man's, and parted at

10. Unidentified; see chap. 1, n. 1 above for transcription of corresponding passage in "We Called Her Kitty."

the side. Indeed she came near being that unusual creature a bald woman. Her upper lip, more than shaded, gave her a somewhat masculine appearance. And my young partners at the dancing school would have been too happy for such a moustache, those poor little fellows who had only of late mounted long tail coats.

I confess I stared—perhaps beyond the limit allowed by good manners; and when the children had gone to sleep, Fanny and I watched her evolutions with unabated curiosity. As she put on the grand mother of all night gowns, so vast was it—and tied up her head in a bandana—I sighed—awed—and she echoed my sigh.

She then proposed to begin our new acquaintance with a history of her journey. She was sure of a deeply interested listener. I had seen behind her in the stage a face, which sent quick tingles of pain, or pleasure, or surprise, I knew not which, through my heart. Strange to say chatterbox as I was—I had not even made an exclamation. I stood dumb with astonishment. Had Madelaine received my letter, and had the innocent cause of my punishment come to share it? The most loquacious woman in the world holds her tongue when her own affairs are in question.

Mrs. Grindstone seated herself—the chair creaked and groaned as if appealing loudly against the weight that was put upon it. She said gloomily, "Thank God—I am now under a man's protection. Women ought not to travel alone in these wilds. Poor helpless creatures that we are! Does your father go armed?"

"No! What put such an idea in your head? No body would dream of troubling us. We were a little afraid of the Indians—. At least the childish part of our family," I added with dignity.

"You might have been robbed?"

"They have travelled this road three times—and were never molested. After all it is an honest country."

"Well! up to yesterday—I had a delightful time."

Then it came out that her friends in New Orleans had warned her not to venture alone in these Savage regions. There had been horrible doings at Vicksburg. A Committee of Safety—had immolated a pack of Gamblers. She made my hair stand on end at the dreadful story.

After all—the men were very civil to her in the stage. At least—with one exception—a rude man who told tales of what he called fights—she thought murders were a better name for them. "Facing me there sat a nice young man, quiet, and well bred—he seemed vastly interested in these travellers' tales. He spoke always in the same low tone—indeed he had a very pleasant voice—evidently an utter stranger in these parts. The rough man seemed to single him out for his jokes. He said—a South Carolina

Colonel was all white starched shirt frill—and a Georgia Major was mostly shirt collar and spurs. That South Carolina was the 'chivalry'—'sayings' merely—and Georgia—'doings.' The man to whom this was addressed, passed his hand across his flat double breasted westcoat—and smiled but he did not say where he was from—in spite of taunts—he kept silent. The rough man drank occasionally from a flask he took from his coat pocket. Soon they all fell asleep; and as the stage rolled and pitched about on those bad roads, the rude creature nodded and fell forward, regularly striking me in the face with his head. Of course I uplifted my voice and complained bitterly. Then he would awake partially, with a snort—and then go right back to sleep and begin hammering me again. Finally he settled down to it regularly; he deliberately put his head on my shoulder going off into a steady snore. This was too much.

"'I am a lady—and alone,' I screamed. 'Will nobody protect me?'

"They tried to make him move but he only swore and kicked.

"'We must use force. We cannot let him insult a woman,' said the quiet gentleman. (Such a handsome man, my dear!)

"'I'll let you know I am a lady,' I cried. 'I am a Governess in Mr. Newtown's family—I have lived with them two years. And I am going there now.'

"'Ah! I see—I see. My dear lady, you shall be Duchess or Queen if you like. I am one of the chivalry—a mere Don Quixote—who mistakes every one of your sex for a—Dulcinea.'[11]

"'Not so dull either.' I screamed for my blood was up.

"'All right—forgive me. I had no time to cull my words. I did think a lady must be a woman.' He helped to drag the drunken brute away—and he took the place beside me. And I was free from all annoyance until next day. And then there came a cruel scene. I scarcely know how to tell it."

Here Mrs. Grindstone began to sniffle.

"Just after daylight the stage coach stopped to change horses. The men all got out, and I tried to smooth my rumpled hair and freshen up a little. I had a little cologne to dampen my handkerchief. When they were once more in their places—I found the rude man facing me with his face. Two gentlemen directly opposite to me—were between us, on the seat which occupies the middle of the coach—and crosses from door to door.

"It was awfully embarrassing to be faced in that way. How he stared! I was afraid some thing awkward had happened in the rough toilette I had attempted in their brief absence. I began to feel about my head and face—

---

11. Quixote's romantic ideal in Cervantes' romantic novel *Don Quixote de la Mancha* (1605, 1615).

and to pull things together—and to straighten up as well as I could—wondering what could be amiss. It made me wretchedly nervous."

3

Row gently here, my Gondolier,
   So softly wash the tide,
That not an ear, on Earth may hear
   But hers to whom we glide.
Had Heaven but tongues to speak as well
   As starry eyes to see,
Oh think what tales, 't would have to tell,
   Of wandering youths like me[1]

"With his eyes fixed on my face, he began his tale of frontier barbarities again—I could not bear it.

"'For shame!' I cried, 'remember you are in the presence of a lady.'

"The expression of his eye became intolerable as he glared at me. Slowly dropping word by word he described a family feud, which had ended most fatally." Here Mrs. Grindstone spoke with apparent effort. "I mean that unhappy affair in which poor old Mr. Hamlin was killed you know. He said the Hamlin boys were out still with horse and hound, and meant to shoot down Col. Blueskin at sight. Then he raised himself up and pointed at me.

"'That fellow Blueskin is escaping in disguise—he has been hiding for two years in woman's toggery. And I mean to let the Hamlins know. Can you deny it?' Here he shook his fist at me. My dear child—put your self in my place? fancy my feelings?"

The wretched woman was shaking like a jelly at the bare recollection.

"I burst out crying," she continued. "I fairly howled with terror—with tears of shame and mortification streaming from my eyes I begged them to protect me. He swore he would stick to what he had said unless they gagged him. That he never told a lie drunk or sober. Mr. Howard advised me to put up my veil and to put down my handkerchief—and not to try in any way to conceal my face.

"He soon forgot me, in his quarrel with those men. A Mr. Dickson who keeps that store at Choctaw a mile from your father's[2]—backed Mr.

1. Thomas Moore (1780–1852), "Row gently here," lines 1–8 in *National Airs* (London, 1827).

2. In "We Called Her Kitty," MBC mentions an incident that occurred on her 1838 trip to Mississippi with her mother to settle her father's estate:

Howard nobly; indeed every man in the stage was on my side. But it was bitter—one by one, he kept pointing out the unmistakable points of resemblance. Sometimes I laughed too—his drunken persistence was so absurd. They literally hauled him out by the driver. I could put Mr. Howard in my pocket—but he sat by me as my protector—he is so slight and slim— he was quiet—yet bold as a lion—I asked him if he was armed. 'No,' he answered. 'Never wore arms in my life.' 'Poor boy,' I said. 'You had better go home.' And in that row he was as rash and reckless as if he had cannons at his command.

"After all I could see the men eyed me curiously. My dear girl. It was a fearful ordeal for a delicate and refined person to go through. A lady born."

What could I say—I tried to look sympathetic. I was thinking—My friend Sydney Howard with that restless spirit has followed me. For the frolic of the thing doubtless. And already he is meeting with queer adventures.

A party of men came into the next room—making a great noise and clatter—and we were separated by only a board partition. They were all talking at once. One man was singing at the top of his voice—"A life on the ocean wave." Gradually the noise subsided. "The winds—the winds their revels keep"[3] grew fainter and fainter, and a partial quiet prevailed. Suddenly a hoarse voice sung out.

N. Orleans one night the man who drove our hack—& who took his meals at table with us—as at that time & place—the only line drawn was between negroes & white people all white people were supposed equal—and no second table possible—Several men joined this man & they talked bowie knives & revolvers—& murders—& wild western tales until I fancied they did it to frighten my Mother & myself—who shrunk close together & scarcely had any appetite under such conversation—the year before a man we knew very well—was shot dead in his little store—a negro woman of ours was hired there & was the only witness. . . Finally we retired—& our old friend dreamed or fancied he heard them plot to murder him—he came in our room white—& distraugh[t] We went up home in this condition—expecting to be robbed & murdered at every step—after a few hours I did not believe it—nobody troubled us but the agony of mind—indeed it amounted to monomania of our companion increased. We sat by him at night—he scarcely ever spoke—but now & then—he would lift up his hands & in a piteous voice—say—"Thou God seest me"—When we got home—we thought it was all over—but the second night I soon tired of the solemn talk of my elders & began to walk up & down the piazza—the boards of which not being nailed made a great noise—I heard a shriek & ran in—I was told the robbers & murderers had come & were in great force in the piazza—It was of no use to say *I* constituted the invading army—I was not listened to—the overseers were sent for—& the next morning our old friend left under their care—by another route home again.

The incident seems to have suggested the Hamlin-Blueskin feud story in *Two Years,* and certainly forms the basis for chapter 3.

3. "A Life on the Ocean Wave," by Epes Sargent, in *Songs of the Sea, with Other Poems,* 2d ed. (Boston, 1849), 50, lines 1 and 4.

"I am dead sure it is old Blueskin—I could swear to his ears. I mean to tell the Hamlins."

"Let him alone Mr. Dickson," said a voice which sent the blood in a shower to my face. "It is only his drunken pertinacity."

"Say another word like that and I'll rouse the country. We will soon scare up old Blueskin for he is in this house."

"Thou God seest me,"[4] cried Mrs. Grindstone on her knees—with her hands clasped piteously.

I put my finger on my lip—oh how cruel! I felt all this to be. And I was truly glad there was some one—near at hand that we could trust. She whimpered, "Where is Mr. Newtown?"

I pointed to the next room. At the door as I led her away, I whispered. "In my Mother's room there were two sofas drawn together—on which a mattrass had been placed for Tatty—who refused to leave me—and was now asleep in my bed." I told the grateful Grindstone that "if we were heard; it would not matter, they would think Fanny was bringing Tatty to her couch."

She said—"She would be less miserable if I led her softly to that haven of safety," under Papa's guns, so to speak. We crept in like mice. I placed a chair for her. The sofas were huge Mohair things, with high backs and arms, where she would be hid from sight as if in a curtained bed. But then she had to climb up and in it. Well! we came with cat like softness of tread. She stepped on the chair I had placed for her—she had one foot on the arm of the sofa—I was still holding her hand—as she felt about for a resting place for the other foot—down came the chair with a crash.

"Who is there! Speak? or I'll shoot," cried Papa, starting up in bed.

Men always say that, I believe.

"It is Helen!" I screamed. "Oh please don't shoot."

Constance hearing the row threw open the door at our backs. In an instant the whole scene was lighted up.

There stood this colossal figure draped in white—with her red bandana head gear nearly reaching to the ceiling—one huge foot in the air anxiously feeling around.

I flew from side to side.

"For Heaven's sake don't fire—they say she is a man. And they mean to murder her. Oh save her!" I cried in tragic accents.

"Stuff and nonsense! don't you see he has only a boot in his hand—fire indeed! but he would hurt her if he should fling that thing," said Mamma—always sensible and practical. She was already helping the Grindstone down

4. Genesis 16:13.

out of sight between the sofas. Constance was rolling over on the floor in convulsions of laughter. And Papa not nearly as bad. Mamma was bending over that mass of quivering flesh on the sofa bed and soothing the perturbed spirit.

Papa whispered to me—vainly trying to be calm, "Took her for a man—who did? She looked like one of the genii—forming into shape just vaporing up out of a jar—and you a little Sindbad looking on."[5]

"No—a white elephant at the circus trying to dance," tittered Constance.

I explained again and again.

"But what has my wife done with the danseuse? She has vanished."

We pointed to her retreat.

"Thou God seest me," came a pitiful cry near at hand marking the ill used creature's whereabouts.

"Go to bed—all of you," said Mamma in peremptory tones. "She is safe now."

Constance retired with me, leaving the door between the rooms wide open.

"Ah why did you not leave the child in Legare St.," said Mamma ruefully.

"Go to sleep wife—do not venture on a curtain lecture to night. We have too large an audience."

Before day break we heard the men in the next room talking and banging about. They left in the stage before we were up.

Between the Venetian blinds there was a rose—a paper attached, with an outline of silence—finger on lip—SH. So my romantic adventures had begun also.

No more dull days after that. Soon the children saw landmarks and recognized places which showed we were nearing our journey's end. We were following what they called "a blazed" road. They pointed out to me the blazes on the Pine trees.

I said, "I am glad to see one man has been here before us. And he has gone with a hatchet chopping out pieces of red pine bark, showing scraps of white wood underneath—making a path for himself out of this labyrinth of a Pine forest." We struck a fence. The coachman dismounted and pulled it down.

"Here we are!" they shouted.

There were no trees now, for we were in the centre of a cotton field. As we drew near the house, from the Bayou below came a powerful female voice, singing with wonderful sweetness.

5. Sinbad the Sailor, character in *The Arabian Nights* who tells the stories of his seven voyages.

"Let us haste to Kelvin Grove
Bonny lassie oh!"[6]

The home to which we dashed up in gallant style—Landau and four horses
—was a log cabin of two rooms—with a couple of clap board leantos.

We brought a little purple[7] and fine linen, silver, and china with us—to
this palatial residence, in which we found six chairs and a pine table. A huge
chimney—extended half way across the room. At first the only window
was closed by a heavy wooden shutter; but I complained of the open door,
from which came our only light, when the weather forced us to close the
window. And a man from a distance was sent for who glazed us a sash. All
then wondered why it was never done before.

A large four poster bed stead occupied one end of the room. It was
Pine—but its curtains and bed linen were worthy of Rosewood. They gave
me one of the clap board shed rooms. And The Grindstone, flabby, haggard, wild eyed still, took possession of the other log room, with Fanny and
the two little girls. She held her court there. It was their bedroom, their
school room, and their dining room.

From the first my father refused the restraint of a governess forever at
table with them. I was welcome in either room—and Dan who slept on a
pile of carriage cushions and pillows in the corner, often dined at both tables—as their hours were so different.

I forgot to tell the scene of wild excitement among the negroes when
they found we had come. Such a row and a rejoicing. My Mother's maid,
who had been left here on account of her large family, picked her mistress
up in her arms and ran around the room with her.

I had a French copy of "Arabian Nights"[8]—which had proved a Godsend
on the journey. My translations were not very accurate—but I knew enough
of French to glean the story and tell it to the children. And from what I read
there I drew this inference.

American Indians—are stoics—they scorn to laugh or to cry. And the
climate on this side of the Atlantic eliminates that weakness gradually from
all who are born here. But the African is Eastern pure and simple. For example—When ever the Sultan went away and returned unexpectedly, and
found his wife behaving dreadfully, for the men are all good and true, and

6. A song with words written by Thomas Lyle, sung to a traditional Scottish folk tune, "O
the shearin's no for you," cited in Minnie Earl Sears, ed., *Song Index* (New York, 1926).

7. Slang here used to mean elegant possessions, as in "befitting royalty."

8. MBC probably had a copy of a French translation by Antoine Galland (1646–1715)
which first appeared in 1704. The translation, *Les Mille et une nuits,* was published by several
French houses between 1704 and 1835 (seven editions by various publishers between 1820
and 1830 alone are cited in the *National Union Catalogue*).

are fearfully outraged by the women who are all bad—and that is one of the fabulous parts of the Arabian Nights—then, when he begins cutting off every body's head and throwing them out of the window; then the women begin to tear their hair, and strike themselves in the face, shrieking in the most pitiful manner. And the children scream and weep, making the very house re echo with their groans. Their fear or grief never takes a milder form. And their joy is even wilder, more vociferous and noisy—not to say stunning. This is a perfect description of our emotional blacks. They are perfectly portrayed in these eastern stories. I confess I grew tired of it; but my Mother was accustomed to it and liked it. And my father watched the affair with an amused face.

At tea he said, "Look at Helen. She is herself again. See, her color has come back, and her eye is as bright as ever. On the road I was afraid she would die of an over dose of her own family. She was growing paler—more listless every day."

"She came to life the night we met the stage! oh the night of the Grindstone tragedy you know," said Constance demurely.

As soon as Papa had settled us all comfortably as circumstances permitted; he decided to make a trip to New Orleans, and he hurried off that he might the sooner get back.

One night after I had prepared all my lessons for the next day I grew restless. For I was wondering why—oh why? this inexplicable silence. Did he come all this long way—to go without speaking to me?

Tramp—tramp—I went up and down the Piazza; which being laid with puncheons—and not nailed down—creaked and groaned and made noise enough to wake the dead, under my rapid tread.

I saw more heads than one peeping cautiously out. I advanced boldly to the Grindstone window, in time to see her throw herself on her knees and in an agony of terror—give her battle cry.

"Thou God seest me."

I flew round into her room to explain.

"They have come to murder an innocent woman. If I do look like him. It was not me."

We had a world of trouble in pacifying her. Mamma was as much offended with me as she could be with any body, for frightening her anew just as she began to leave off her nervous tremors. She called my romantic moonlight stroll "Such silly sentimental pretence—fresh air indeed!"

I thought that was hard. She sent for the overseer—and he marched as a sentinel up and down the open passage way, armed with his double barrelled gun all night. He would grin and snicker when ever anyone went near him—at this farce.

Quiet was once more restored; that is for a few days. Then a troop of wolves came.[9] I confess I feared them more than I did the Hamlins. Round and round the house they went—barking and howling, and roaring like a pack of hounds, knocking against every thing and sniffing as if resolved to get in somewhere. They would collect under the house; apparently hold a noisy council there; and then begin to prowl around and howl in chorus once more. We were nearly dead with fright and utterly cut off from the Grindstone contingent by that open passage way. How rejoiced we were that the heavy puncheon flooring was a safe barrier. They could not penetrate and storm.

Next day the children told us how admirably the Grindstone had behaved. She calmed their fears and showed them that they had no real cause for apprehension.

Mamma unfortunately hoped to strengthen her philosophic disregard for wolves. She said—we could easily guard against wolves—but our worst foe was the dreadful and insidious rattlesnake.

Last spring she saw one crawl through the holes of the floor, and coil—and spring his rattle near the foot of her bed. In vain we explained—they never came out of their holes in winter. Mrs. G knew more of snakes and their habits than we did. She declared she would not live "in the midst of alarms."

The rattlesnake anecdote finished the business. She first took to her bed, and then announced her determination to leave us. Mamma had lost her patience long ago and she "sped the parting guest." The overseer mounted the box with the driver. Mrs. Grindstone disguised to the utmost and doubly—nay trebly veiled, entered the carriage, bidding us farewell in muffled tones, evidently shaking the dust from her feet. All hands had joyously helped to pack her off.

When my father came home he heard with delight that she was gone. Then for the first time he allowed himself to laugh at his leisure.

"And I was about to fire a boot at her head, in default of a more deadly weapon. Kitty threw light on the subject. And Helen came pattering round barefooted in her little short night gown—with her hair streaming down her back. 'Ah papa dont shoot.' At any rate my little angel tried to stop the fray. If I could remember the Blueskin tragedy as you told it that night—what a screaming farce it would make.

9. This incident occurred during Chesnut's second trip to Mississippi in 1838, with her mother, to settle her father's estate. See "We Called Her Kitty": "We were then—only my Mother & my self in a Missippi Swamp along—with several hundred negroes—We were never frightened—except by gangs of wolves—who would go howling round the house at night like packs of hounds—& a huge rattle snake—came in sociably & was lying in a coil at Mothers feet—but did no harm beyond nearly taking her life with horror," MS p. 16.

"That poor old Governess in spite of her dark upper lip is womanly in the extreme. She is all nervous fidgits and hysterical fears. She had some cause of alarm that she kept to herself.

"The drunken fool whose very name she did not know, made too deep and abiding an impression."

[EDITORIAL NOTE: *Two chapters, 4 and 5, are missing here from the manuscript of* Two Years—or The Way We Lived Then. *References throughout the remainder of the novel suggest that these chapters may have detailed action relating to the Hamlin-Blueskin feud, the adventures of Helen's Charleston beau, Sydney Howard, a country dance at which Choctaws were present, and some interaction with a man named Dickson, a storekeeper. When the manuscript picks up again, Helen and her father are returning home.*]

6

Si l'on vous donne un soufflet—rendez en quatre. N'importe la joue.[1]

"My lord, the farther tidings are heavy for me to tell, and will be afflicting to you to hear. No aid of mine, or of living chivalry, could have availed the Excellent Prelate. William de la Marck has taken his Castle of Schonwaldt, and murdered him in his own hall."
"*Murdered him!*" repeated the Duke, in a deep and low tone, but which never the less was heard from the one end of the hall to the other. "Thou has been imposed upon Crevecoeur, by some wild report—it is impossible."

When about half way home we heard a shot—then another. "That was a rifle shot," said my father. Those young men are emptying their guns to have them cleaned."

We had barely taken our seats. I was still in my riding dress—when we heard shouts from a distance—and then loud talking. A crowd of negroes seemed [to be] following some one who intermixed her story with hysterical screams.

Dan dashed in. "They've killed him!"
"My God! Who is killed? Who?" cried my mother.
"It is the enemy—the enemy—he has shot Dickson."[2]

1. Fr. If someone gives you a slap in the face, slap him back four times. On either cheek.
2. Dickson is identified in chapter 2 as the shopkeeper of the nearest store, about a mile from the Newtowns' plantation. It is not clear who "the enemy" is, though he or they are likely Hamlins.

"We heard the shot," said my father reaching up for his gun which was on a rack at the head of his bed. "Wife—look to your daughter. She is fainting."

But I was not. Never in my life had my senses been so keenly alive.

Maum Sylla came in with blood upon her apron. She was weeping and wailing at the top of her voice and the noise made by the other negroes was deafening.

"Master—dey killed him. Shot him down on his own door sill. I couldn't lift him up. But Mr. Howard he come, and I run for you.

"As soon as we left the store," she said, "the same three men came back." She heard them talking and she saw the shooting. After firing twice, the strange men rode away as fast as they could gallop.

Upon being cross-examined she told the same story, with tears and lamentations and wringing of hands. She was going from the kitchen to the wood pile, when the first gun went off; she ran to the house as the men were mounting their horses. She found Dickson lying on his face, his head outside of the door. She tried to lift him; the blood spouted all over her.

Mr. Howard said he was dead. Old Choctow was there; she met him going for his mail, and when she told him he went hurrying to the spot.

She saw Mr. Howard meet the three men and she thought they would kill him too. He was on foot and they on horseback; then they were three to one; and he had no gun. How could he stop them?

My father had mounted his horse and was gone, long before we half understood it all.

Maum Sylla went off with some other old crones "to help her lay him out," she said.

A man I had shaken hands with not an hour ago!

When my father returned he pronounced it an atrocious and uncalled for murder. He was accompanied by the ex Indian Chief—who was more angry and excited than we thought an Indian ever allowed himself to be. But then he was half French.[3]

"You are civilized—eh? We are savages. And you are Christians. You may well hang your heads!"

---

3. Greenwood LaFlore (1800–1865), son of a Frenchman, Louis LeFleur, and an Indian woman, Rebecca Cravat, was chief of the Choctaws, and remained in Mississippi after the treaty of Dancing Rabbit Creek (1833), when most Choctaws moved west to Indian Territory, and established himself as a planter. He was the nearest neighbor of MBC's father, Stephen Decatur Miller, in Mississippi. By 1860, LeFlore was one of the largest slave owners in Mississippi, indeed in the entire South, having amassed more than fifteen thousand acres and some four hundred slaves, and remained loyal to the Union throughout the Civil War (*MBC,* 29–30). According to Chesnut, LeFlore's son-in-law administered the Miller estate ("We Called Her Kitty," MS p. 22).

"Young Howard met the enemy saying, 'Oh come ye in peace or come in war—or dance but one measure—oh young Lochinvar,'[4] as he smilingly stretched out his hand.

"'I can't do that—you will be sorry if you shake hands with me. See Dickson first. May be I have killed the wrong man. You began it. You insulted me for the sake of old Blue Skin.' The other men here interfered. They had enough of it for one day," they said.

The enemy announced that he was off for Texas. Old Choctow would make it too hot for him. The old chief took every advantage—he fought Ingin—he would be sure to get on his trail. "He aint like you—a greenhorn who goes about in new country without your shooting irons. After all— may be that saved your life today. Buy a pair of pistols and a bowie knife. And take off your gloves. Then you won't look so like a fool when you meet a man you insulted out on a war path. Good b'ye," he cried as he put spurs to his horse. The other two covered him with their guns all the time the enemy was speaking. Sidney Howard hastened to the house—sore at heart, for he dreaded what he should see there.

"It was all over. Old Choctow was dragging in the body. Young Howard told me this," said my father.

Then the country arose in the night. But the murderer kept his word; he was never heard of more.

A few days after this a strange man asked to be permitted to stay all night. I did not see him, for the murder had completely upset me. But at the breakfast table next morning he proclaimed himself a Morman Saint and a propagandist.[5] He was shown the door not too politely.

Then the Goliath of Gath—sent me a love letter. He had been persistent in his attention. He bribed Willis to bring me the letter; and Willis though bribed was not corrupted, for he took it straight to his master. I was not told a word of this. Indeed it was several years after that I heard of the suppression of my huge lover's, small love letter; and I have always resented it.

I was told to pack up without delay. "Madame's was the best place for me, after all."

They had built me, for my own separate apartment, such a nice clapboard shed room; with a spick and span new bed stead of such white pine;

4. Sir Walter Scott, *Marmion*, canto 5, line 12.

5. The Church of Jesus Christ of Latter Day Saints was founded in New York by Joseph Smith (1805–44), who published *The Book of Mormon* in 1830 as having been received from the angel Moroni in 1827. Although they engendered fear and anger, the followers of Smith, thought to be religious fanatics and abolitionists, and rumored to practice polygamy, made many converts, and the new religion spread quickly.

tables and shelves to match. I was busy with the white bed curtains when my marching orders came.

Mamma with tears in her eyes, folded my best dresses—saying, "I told you so. There are men every where—out here they frighten me. Murders—and Mormans. Next thing we might have a man try and runaway with you."

I tried not to let them see how glad I was to go. But Kitty[6] jumped for joy that she was to fall heir to my sweet little room—smelling so of new Pine.

As we drove through the village Mr. Howard joined us. He carried a rifle since the warning given him by the enemy; or to be strictly accurate since he had joined the party, the hue and cry who were in full pursuit of the enemy.

It was the first time I had seen him since the Ball.

And he bowed gravely; more embarrassed than I had ever supposed his serene highness could be.

"Do you intend to buy the track of land—formerly owned by Dickson, Mr. Newtown?"

"Certainly. It is too near me. I do not wish another store to be kept there."

"That ends my little affair. Old Sylla and I had arranged, when I bought the store, she would keep house for me. She says she is free. You told her when she had twelve children in the field she should be free—and her youngest is married."

"A woman who has twelve children in less than twenty years—has been to all intents and purposes, their slave," answered my father, "but her husband, who is our blacksmith, says the house is haunted. He will not let her stay there. I am afraid your housekeeper had failed you even if you had secured the land."

So it was settled. Mr. Howard was told he could not buy the land. And then my father suggested that we were taking him out of his way.

"No. I sail from New York in a month. Until then I scarcely know what to do with myself."

We had not exchanged a word. He heard our route—New Orleans Mobile–Pensacola–Augusta. He shook hands with my father; and bowing low to me—he rode off.

"My lad," thinks I to myself, "that means I will see you again before you put the Atlantic between us."

6. Throughout the next three chapters, the name "Constance" is carefully crossed out and "Kitty," the childhood nickname of her younger sister Kate, substituted—further evidence that this version of the novel was written after MBC's sister Kate's death.

Papa chuckled awhile. "You and the Englishman—who has a very pleasant low country accent, are not as cordial as you were the night the Albino
so often interrupted you—he said—'talking French.'"[7]

"Yes," I replied blushing scarlet, "his French was worse than mine. I asked
him if he had been taught at a boarding school—but he proudly answered
'No—in Paris.'

"We were just from the halls of dazzling light—though tallow candles illumined the festive scene. But now—I dare say he has never had a friend
murdered in the house with him before; and it has sobered him. It was
enough to make—his hair 'turn white in a single night,'"[8] said I warming
up to the gravity of the occasion.

"He did feel it. You know he walked home with me that night. We had
a long talk—almost a confidential one." My father suppressed a smile. "For
the life of me, I can't see any thing English about him—but his name. His
forefathers doubtless came from England."

"Why not himself?" I asked looking the other way.

"He did not speak of Habeas Corpus or Magna Charta or trial by Jury,
or even the Bill of rights.[9] But old Choctow blazed away after his kind;[10] he
suggested trailing the murderer and shooting him down at sight.

"You know you had the Albino as your lantern; next day he told queer
stories. He said the stranger picked you up out of a mud puddle. And instead of thanking him—you drew away from him 'like he was pizen.' When
the Patagonian tried to shoulder Howard away from you—Albino said you
begged the latter 'to go and walk with Mamma' but he would not. You promised him if he would be quiet you would freeze the blood of the Giraffe's—

7. See *The Captain and the Colonel*, chap. 6, n. 1. Chesnut and her set often spoke French
when they wished to prevent servants from understanding them. "The Albino" is a nickname
for a local hotel-keeper's son, playmate to Kitty, who must first have appeared in the missing chapters.

8. Byron's *The Prisoner of Chillon* (1816) begins, "My hair is grey, but not with years, / Nor
grew it white / In a single night."

9. Basic tenets of English common law; *habeas corpus,* an ancient principle that now pro-
tects personal liberty, is a writ issued by a court or judge directing that someone in the cus-
tody of another be produced in person before the court; the Magna Carta was a charter
granted by King John in 1215 to his barons, guaranteeing against abuses to freemen; trial by
jury is an ancient English practice antedating the Norman Conquest whereby crimes and
offenses are adjudicated based on evidence by a group of the defendant's peers; the Bill of
Rights here refers to the British 1689 "Act Declaring the Rights and Liberties of the Subject
and Settling the Succession of the Crown," which spelled out a number of individual rights,
including religious tolerance.

10. In the manner of. According to Mr. Newton, Mr. Howard does not respond like an
Englishman, whereas the Choctaw reacts like a member of the Choctaw tribe.

and something or other of 'all the blood of all the Howards'—he knew by your being scared lest he and the Giraffe should quarrel that you counted him *your beau*. Also because he tried so hard to get a word with you unbeknown to the Albino. And he was all the time sending him off to the front."

I had retired from this extraordinary conversation, leaving my father to tell me as much or as little as he pleased of the Albino's revelations.

The morning after the Ball thanks to their walls and windows that did not fit, my father according to his own showing was waked by the sound of the squeaking voice of the free born American Albino, so near his head, that he thought at first he was in the room; but he soon found where the sounds came from. Kitty was in the Piazza wrangling with the Albino in shrill and piercing tones.

She replied to a remark of the free and easy youth in this wise. "No gentleman sat with his chair tilted back, and his hat on his head—and his feet on the banister, and his back to a lady."

"You are a stuck up gang. No wonder nobody likes you. You are a great lady to be sure!"

"Now," said papa, "that took me aback. I am accustomed to every body liking me. You know as a lawyer, and as a politician my success in life has been complete; and in a great measure owing to the fact of my being wonderfully popular."

"Why don't they like us?" said Kitty in great disgust.

"Ladies and gentlemen are words forever in your mouths."

This Kitty strenuously denied. "But what's the harm if they were?"

The Albino illustrated. "When Dan shoved you so rudely last night, my Mother would have administered promptly a sharp box on my ear. And I would have gone off howling. Not so the superborn Mrs. Newtown.

"'Fie! Fie! on you—No gentleman is ever rude to a lady.' And Dan certainly hung his head as if he had been soundly slapped. Then again while you were all waiting for shawls—you lost your patience and flew out at Fanny. Mrs. Newtown—was down on you.

"'Chambermaids quarrel; little ladies never. A lady should never raise her voice nor show her temper.'" The Albino did us the honor to mimic us all perfectly.

"But my dear Helen, your airs—and your not shaking hands with every body—seems to have settled our fate, if the coach and four had not accomplished our destruction in public opinion from the very first."

"Until you drawed yourself up like a queen," the clear-sighted-in-the-dark youth replied, "just because he tetched you—and he only wanted to haul you out of the mud, he was pretty sure you were took with him. You had all the symptoms, but when you did that then he saw you thought yourself too good for any body. I think you had better cultivate that frame of mind—because you are to be at school three years longer."

The Albino still taking his ease of his Sun sat with his feet up and his back turned. He continued to torment Kitty. "The man with the gloves is soft on Helen."

"Miss Newtown if you please" said Kitty waxing indignant.

"Well! Any thing to please the children. But Goliath as Dan calls him and the lawyer who is death on poetry—they are going to make him show his hand." Receiving no answer—the precocious youth whistled a reel.

"The entire stranger means to keep store with Dickson; he told Helen so. Helen—Helen—you hear. And he means to sell on the wriggles—that's the ticket."

"She will never marry any body but a planter," said Kitty—coolly.

The boy changed his tune—to a mournful Methodist Hymn. "Though I am a hotel keeper's son—*I* mean to keep store someday. My people came from a free state. We never owned niggers and we never will."

I came out to Kitty's assistance; she was dumb with wonder.

"I thought the more negroes one had the better, Papa?"

"For you maybe—I was thinking of them."

"Papa—let's go away. He is a bad boy—he has no manners and he tells stories."

I petted my little darling—and suggested that in the matter of home affairs she must know better than outsiders. So never to take the word of people against herself—particularly when her knowledge was practical—and theirs theoretical—or worse, hearsay. I do not suppose she understood the drift of my remarks—but she felt strong with my arms around her.

The boy seemed delighted with the little love scene between Kitty and me—and he said in a patronizing way, "She is a smart little thing. She bangs us all out at our books. She is always head in her classes.

"As for Dan—we turn up our noses at him. A boy as big as he and a black man have to ride in to see them safe home." He testified that the "Englishman was always dawdling on their Piazza—with his horses ready hitched to a post. So when you came for the children—he could be your beau."

"Now what did he mean by selling on the wriggles?"

"Let me think." I recalled every word of that conversation—I have a good memory.

"Oh papa. He said—we must do things selon les règles."[11]

Never did a heartier laugh wake the echoes. We made the Pine woods ring.

11. Fr., according to the rules.

"Helen—who applied to you—or your name—which made such a quotation—inevitable.

> 'Oh thou art fairer than the evening air,
> Clad in the beauty of a thousand stars.'"[12]

"Nobody."

"Come now. I am an old lawyer. And I can read a witness's face."

"Well then—some one wondered why, the man who gave me Childe Harold unabridged did not—'try that awhile.'[13] The Albino mangled it awfully—but I made it out."

"Perfidious Albino!"

7

> One pang of remorse at a man's heart is of more avail
> than stripes applied to him.
>
> Talmud[1]

Après la découverte du Meschacebé par le père Marquette et l'infortuné La Salle. . . . Les deux rives du Meschacebé presentent le tableau le plus extraordinaire. . . . Ce fleuve, dans un cours de plus de mille lieues, arrose une delicieuse contrée que les habitants des Etats-Unis appellent le Nouvel Eden.

> Atala[2]

La Montagne quand on l'approche n'est tout que sable—pierre et roche.[3]

12. Christopher Marlowe (1564–93), *The Tragicall History of Doctor Faustus* (London, 1604), line 1297.

13. Byron, *Childe Harold's Pilgrimage* (1812–18).

1. The Talmud is a compilation of ancient teachings in Jewish law, and particularly commentaries upon them, dating from the 3rd to 6th centuries A.D.. This is MBC's only reference to the Talmud, likely gathered not from the Talmud itself, but from a quotation she saw elsewhere.

2. Fr. After the discovery of the Mississippi by Father Marquette and the ill-fated La Salle. . . . The two banks of the Mississippi present a most extraordinary scene. This river, running its course of more than a thousand leagues, waters a charming region called the New Eden by the inhabitants of the United States. François-René de Chateaubriand (1768–1848), *Atala* (1801), prologue.

3. Fr. The mountain, when you grow close to it, is nothing but sand, stone, and rock.

How could I be glad to leave my western home? every body had been so very kind there. And my mother so very indulgent; she tried to save me from every thing unpleasant, and to make all the world within her reach happy. It was the law of our house that the queen could do no wrong. So if any complication arose likely to lead to trouble she had only to say, "It is all my fault," and justice was disarmed. Mr. Newtown at that time was under fifty years, and he had begun life with no capital but that of brains— supplemented by energy and industry. That and nothing more. By his law practice he had amassed an ample fortune; and as a politician he had mounted the ladder as high as his state could send him. Such a career leaves small leisure for loitering around home. His own family had never palled upon him from too great familiarity. At that time I thought Mr. and Mrs. N an ordinary sample of conjugal felicity all over the world. With a wider experience has come a very different opinion. I think now that the late Mr. Newtown was the worst in love man I have ever known. Even without that weakness, he had a winning way of his own with all feminine things. He in- variably addressed a woman in language of high flown compliment. His wife lived in an atmosphere of adulation. He had a heathenish admiration for physical beauty and he avowed it, as if it were a credit to him. When he was pleased with us, he flattered us audaciously; when we did wrong, he frowned and stared; but he said not a word. To illustrate my meaning, I will describe a scene between Dan the head strong and his parents in my room the afternoon before I left the plantation.

"Why are you here Dan? You were sent to the Post office," said his Mother in reproachful accents.

"Yes—Papa did send me. But why did he not send one of his lazy negroes? Can you answer me that? It is so bitter cold," said Dan hovering over the fire.

"You unnatural cub. How disappointed he will be not to get his letters and papers."

"Not at all! I told Jim to go, and to bring me the letters and papers, that I might take them to him."

"Deception is worse than disobedience. It is all my own fault I have spoiled my children—Solomon is right."[4]

"At breakfast the other day the Mormon claimed Solomon in all his glory—he said the wise king had three hundred wives.[5] If he is not authority on the wife why is he on the rod? Do you give it up? Papa lost his temper

---

4. Prov. 13:24: "Spare the rod and spoil the child."

5. Mormons were rumored to practice polygamy, though according to Joseph Smith, this doctrine was not received from the angel Moroni until 1843, after the events of the novel take place.

with the Mormon, and just about that time the sacred rites of hospitality went up—didn't they?" snickered Dan.

"My dear boy—you shock me. Such speeches are flat blasphemies. Never touch your bible but with respectful hands."

"Well—well!" said Dan standing squarely in front of the fire, with his hands in his pockets. "*I* do not think whipping is what it is cracked up to be. These old negro women now. I say 'Maumer, your Jim is a bad boy.'

"'Yes—little master—he is,' Maumer replies curtseying down to the ground with mock deference, 'but it is none of my fault. God knows I beat him enough.' 'You nasty old beast—I hate you.' shouted Dan. 'Spare de rod—an spile de chile,' whimpered Maumer. Now Mama are you satisfied?"

"No—your behavior to that old woman was disgraceful. It was rude. You hurt her feelings."

"Nothing like she hurts Jim," Dan began to strut about. "Fighting is all right. We fight at our school, that I allow. Hit a fellow of your own size. But to beat babies! It sickens me. If you switch Tatty now, by the time she is my size I suppose you will need a horse whip—Eh? One of our boys says what he looks at—is that—grown people make a joke of thrashing us— they seem to think there is fun in it. Worse than that. Thanks to Solomon it is considered a sacred Christian duty. And if you think it a joke and not a cruelty to beat your poor little helpless children, my dear Mother, what must you do to the erring man servant and maid servant, the cattle and the stranger within your gates?"

"I do hope your teacher will give the boy who says all that a good thrashing. I see how it will end; you will all be infidels—see if you don't turn out badly."

The altercation grew so unguarded in its tones that the head of the house entered to find out what could the matter be. As he entered my Mother went up to him—putting a hand on each of his shoulders. "My dear—Dan suffers so from cold. Jim was sent for your mail in his place."

This ought to have been a bad lesson; and such a system ought to have worked injuriously; but it did not. Dan is a good man; and my sisters are the best women in the world. And I am no worse than my well disciplined contemporaries.

My proud spirit had been effectually quenched by the sight of that log cabin the night of our arrival at home. The only pleasant memory connected with that afternoon was the sweet clear voice rising from the Bayou—and ringing forth, "Will you come lassie come—To the Braes of Balquidder."[6]

6. Traditional Scottish song. See also "The Braes of Balquither" by William Glen (1787–1826) in *Heath Flowers* (Glasgow, 1817).

Soon I met our washerwoman face to face. She was a stout, hard working, good humored black woman—and no further sentiment or romance
could be wrung from that quarter. She was clean and comfortable—but she
did not understand my aesthetic needs. I determined for the sake of change
to seek the shades below. The Bayou was really something to see. It ran
through a deep ravine back of the house. The trees were very large, and the
water was not so muddy as had been the water of all streams which I had
passed since I left the Atlantic coast.

Then I was so charmed I resolved to create a bower down there, and to
take my books whenever I could manage to escape Mrs. Grindstone's vig-
ilance.

Next day it rained heavily, and it continued to rain for a week. I be-
moaned my fate, that this weather prevented me from making good my
plans of a retreat on the banks of the Bayou.

"Really it is the first bit of scenery I have encountered, so far."

"Keep near the beating of the washerwoman's paddle then—and in full
sound of her everlasting "Banks and Braes,"[7] for she scares the bears and the
wolves and the panthers that prowl up from the swamp. You'll have to vacate in the Spring. There's no end of rattlesnakes down there."

"Runaways—or people straying from the River—are always on that
road, I hear."

"At any rate she will be safe for awhile unless she means to ride the horses
to water—for to day Mamma had a raised walk made to the kitchen; the
yard is impassible—from the very door step."

"Ah! that awful sticky limestone mud."

So I was disappointed in the Bayou. My Mother took my arm as we went
into the other room. "What possessed you to tell your father you had been
to the Bayou?"

And now I was to see the River! On the Yazoo we were to take a small
boat—and at Vicksburg we were to go on board one of those floating
palaces which ply between Cincinnati and New Orleans.

After a day's journey in the carriage we arrived at a town on the river
in the usual earlier stages of building.

People all living in unfinished houses. The hotel was a huge skeleton—
very few rooms were absolutely completed. Most of them had only floor
and ceiling, with walls boarded up as high as one's head.

They were busy as bees, and happy as the day is long, preparing for a ball
that night.

7. Allusion to Robert Burns, "The Banks o' Doon," in *Johnson's Musical Museum* (Edinburgh,
1787–96). See *The Captain and the Colonel,* chap. 5, n. 10.

"I intend to play Mrs. Grindstone to night. I will sleep in your room, Papa—look there," I said pointing to the walls of my chamber. Whenever I mentioned that ill fated lady, he was sure to laugh heartily.

But they came to say a Boat was at the landing and I begged to go.

"What—and a ball to be, this very night?"

"Oh! I am tired of balls."

"Already! And you have been to but a singular number—and such a remarkable one!" said my father smiling. I answered. "Since he has taken to keep company with me, the grave and preoccupied Mr. Newtown has absolutely got into a way of laughing on the slightest provocation." And I retired with what dignity I could muster.

Once on the Boat we made ourselves very comfortable.

I was out on the guards[8]—watching the muddy waters of the Yazoo— and reading "Atala"; having made up my mind to await the Mississippi, for a sensation—Chateaubriand assuring me; I should find there the long expected gorgeous scenery of the South.

As we left home—my Mother called out to Dick, "Take care of Missy." He was obeying orders, for he rarely lost sight of me. Whenever I looked out of my own room, I was sure to find good old bronze hued Dick, grave, dignified, simple, and silent, seated where no one could approach me without his knowledge. This being the case—I was not surprised that he continued to hover around me out on the guards.

At last he said, "Did you ever hear of a boat race?"

"Yes—I have heard they are awfully risky."

"My Missis, you can only pray to the heavenly father. See that Boat yonder! We are racing now with that boat. You can sit here and pray. Shut your eyes and lift up your heart. You need not worry your pa." Dick was true to the prevailing sentiment of our house. The excitement soon became outrageous and contagious. I was nearly wild myself. My father sat by me, but perfectly still. He did not say so—but he acquiesced in Dick's philosophy, I dare say. Dick continued to beseech me furtively—"Pray God. There is no help in Man. They are all crazy." And he shook his head—adding, "When the steamboat Captain's blood's up—look out!"

The river was narrow and very winding just there. And at one of our sudden turns we ran into the other boat. Our men stormed and swore, and cursed; and accused the others of getting in our way when they saw we were sure to pass them. Such noise, confusion, shouting, threats, steam whistles blowing—steam letting off—snorting of engines, screaming of women. It was bedlam broke loose. My father held my hand—but we were motion-

8. At the guardrails.

less—and silent. I was terrified at the furious manner of some armed men who I thought meant to board us with their drawn swords. Dick explained.

"Never mind them, Missy—they have only their cotton hooks. They aint going to hurt any body. It's the biler!—the biler, that will bust. That's our danger."

The other Boat had its wheel crushed. And we dreaded an explosion.

However we escaped. The passengers came from the other boat to ours—and we went on our way rejoicing. My father relieved his feeling by emphatically declaring, "If there were any law in that part of the world—our Captain would suffer for that day's work."

That night we were transferred to a Mississippi steamer at Vicksburg. The lights of that town were all I saw of it.

Our Boat was the "Brian Borohme." As it was the first boat on the River that I ever went on board—I remember it. I was out bright and early next day. The Mississippi was wider and muddier—more desolate and mournful. Otherwise the "scenery" was unchanged. An enlarged specimen, deeper, wider and muddier, of all the rivers I had crossed in coming from the Atlantic.

We had only one lady on board. A Philadelphian married to a Southern Ex Senator. She was very nice, and very kind to me.

We had two chamber maids. A tall black woman, and a very short and stout yellow one. The latter had a beautiful child with her—about five or six years old—a few shades darker than herself.

As I sat near the guards with my "Atala," these two women drew near. Soon they were affably showing me every thing, and telling me the names of the places we passed.

They seemed desirous of enlightening my ignorance in every particular and soon called me as Dick did—"Little Missy."

They were very proud of the fact that they were born free. St. Louis or Cincinnati was their home.

They soon began to harrow my soul with tales of escaped slaves. At last I could stand it no longer—so horrible were their anecdotes—I burst out crying.

Dick interposed. "Miss Helen—go in with the other lady. Your Ma wouldn't like you settin out here talking to these negro women."

Of course after that—I went into my state room. I could hear the combined attack upon Dick. They abused him roundly, a creature so base as to live in contented slavery.

"I suppose you will send your husbands to beat me?" said Dick tauntingly.

They answered, "No indeed—we are not married. We can take care of ourselves. We despise men." Then Dick in his slowest style inquired, "How bout that little gal you got by the hand?"

The Ex Senator's wife described my tears—at dinner. She feared I was too excitable; and that I would take the world too bitterly in earnest.

The old steamboat Captain had been all over the world, as skipper of a sailing vessel. He encouraged me with a smile. "Rough men—no doubt in the valley of the Mississippi. I found such every where I have been. Bad people—are not confined to any one place. Before you die young lady—I dare say you will meet some sin and sorrow—where ever you go."

My father said. "This child was the lightest hearted creature—a few months ago. Everything has conspired to depress her lately. A man that we knew was killed within a mile of us. She took to her bed for a week. Then came anxiety for the party who were out on the war path hunting the murderer." Here he absolutely gave me a sly glance.

I blushed scarlet—and giggled like a school girl—as I was. But I forgot for a season to be so down hearted and despairing.

As we neared New Orleans, a man described the Battle. "Brave Jackson That the British turned their backs on," said somebody else not given to Hero worship. And then we heard of Aunt Rachel, how as she danced at some grand Ball, she held her dress—and set to some distinguished person—crying, "Rip Roan the bridle's broke."[9]

Those canoes and little boats filled with fruit—waked me up to the fact that I was in a new world. Then the Creole French of the negroes was a different language from Dédé's St. Domingon dialect.[10]

We met friends in the City, and they took us to see William Tell.[11] That night I made his acquaintance, apple and all.

9. The Battle of New Orleans was fought on 8 January 1815; although the War of 1812 had been ended by treaty on 24 December 1814, word had not yet reached the combatants. American troops commanded by Andrew Jackson repulsed the British in a decisive battle that took less than an hour. The British suffered more than two thousand casualties, the Americans only 71. Andrew Jackson's wife Rachel (1767–1828) was an unpretentious frontier woman who did not fit in well with the elegant Creole ladies of New Orleans. The source of this particular quotation is unknown, but stories of her uncouth manner were rife in the first half of the nineteenth century. One account is preserved in Geraldine Brooks, *Dames and Daughters of the Young Republic* (New York, 1901): "After supper . . . we were treated to a most delicious *pas de deux* by the conqueror and his spouse. To see these two figures—the General, a long haggard man with limbs like a skeleton, and Madame la Generale, a short fat dumpling—bobbing opposite each other, to the wild melody of 'Possum up de Gum Tree' and endeavoring to make a spring into the air was very remarkable and far more edifying a spectacle than any European ballet could possibly have furnished."

10. Dédé, a slave from Santo Domingo, is one of the servants at Helen Newton's Charleston boarding school, described in chapter 11.

11. Probably the popular play by James Sheridan Knowles (1784–1862), *William Tell; a Play in Five Acts* (London, 1825). The American actor Edwin Forrest (1806–72) performed in a revival of the play in the 1840s.

Sydney told the Enemy, no true born American was ever rude to a woman; there are exceptions to all rules it seems.

A splendid creature came out and sang, "Give me back my Arab Steed." In my simplicity, knowing no better I was delighted— with words—song, and songstress.

The poor soul had huge feet and a very short dress, very broad flat slippers with black ribbon tied about legs. She was not pretty, and she was not young—but she leered at us, and flapped up and down the stage; with her sword drawn lunging and parrying. Suddenly she would strike an attitude & break out,

> "A sword and falchion bright
> And I will to the battle field.
> And save him in the fight."

For a while her brave intentions were borne without a murmur. But when it came to his "noble crest I'll proudly bear"—the pit rose to man—howling, "Take that thing off!"

I was so sorry for her and I treasured up the memory of this disgusting row. At some future day I would prove to Mr. Howard, "Even in America a woman had better not be old or ugly." My father's only comment was, "She had boxed ankles."

Which evidently was a crime, not easily forgiven.

8

A man only attains to easy circumstances by his own labors;
if he gains wealth it must be by making others labor for him.

Taine[1]

Il est bon d'être sûr de soi dans ce monde.
Prenons vous et moi le temp de reflécher—
    Ce siècle a inventé une grande chose. Voila! La femme
camarade, c'est la femme de l'Avenir.[2]

1. Hippolyte-Adolphe Taine (1828–93), dominant French critic and historian of his era. MBC carefully read his *Histoire de la littérature anglaise* (3 vols., 1863; trans. H. Van Laun, 1871). The source of this passage is unidentified.

2. Fr. It is good to be self-assured in this world. Let's you and I take time to reflect. This century has invented a great thing. Here it is: woman as friend. It's the woman of the future. (Unidentified.)

In Mobile we stayed with friends, exiles like our selves. In our old home, they were the most charming people we knew in the city. In their adopted city, they had been already found out, and were as highly appreciated. Indeed they were already leaders of society as distinctly in the new place as in the old.

There I met young people of my own age; and my father commended my good sense, in dining with the children.

But we dined early every night that we might go to the Play. Fancy my feelings when I saw "Lydia Languish" on the bill. My youthful friends told me I was in luck. "The Rivals" was "perfectly splendid."[3]

I listened in rapt attention for a cause best known to my self. I hung my head as the lovely Lydia went on making a fool of herself (without a pause). I reached the acme of my disgust and shame when Mrs. Malaprop gave her a pinch while she denounced her as "You intricate little huzzy!"[4]

I did not comprehend then, a general likeness with all the details left out. I did not loose a word. Not even the doleful and tiresome Faulkland. One of the boys said. "Helen why don't you laugh? every body else does—at Bob Acres—and Sir Lucius. It is not a tragedy."

"What do you think of Lydia?"

"Oh Lydia! She is a silly, sentimental, romantic little fool."

"There the tragedy comes in," cried I laughing. "This is the wittiest crowd I ever met before. You need not bow. I mean on the stage."

"I have seen better "Lydia's" than this woman's."

"To me—it is all delightful."

The sting of the insulting comparison—was drowned in my enjoyment of the play.

And now the real troubles of our trip began.

Again it was the night that we landed, at Pensacola. I did not even see a black shadow of that old Spanish town.

We took the stage. It was filled with naval officers and merchants going North for goods.

3. Lydia Languish is a character in *The Rivals,* 1775, first play of Richard Brinsley Sheridan (1751–1816).

4. Sheridan, *The Rivals,* act 1, scene 2. Helen has apparently been compared to Lydia in the missing chapters. MBC here refers to Lydia Languish, a romantic, rich ingenue (and she reads novels!) determined to marry without her aunt's permission so she will be cut off without a penny, thereby insuring that no one marries her for her money; her aunt Mrs. Malaprop, whose hilarious confusion of vocabulary has given rise to the term "malapropism"; Sir Lucius O'Trigger, with whom Mrs. Malaprop is smitten; Bob Acres, cheerful country innocent; and Faulkland, so jealous of his Julia, and so fearful of all potential mishaps, that he postpones marriage perpetually.

A very pleasant party. These men were very attentive—and very considerate in their kindness to me. My father told me to be as polite as I knew how—but to say nothing whatever. Hard lines!

A very good looking and agreeable navy man was telling an interesting story, the scene laid in the Mediterranean, when there came a crash—a careen—we seemed wallowing in a trough of the sea—it recalled the short chopping waves of the Gulf, the night before. Every one sprung up—and were at once jostled down. There came a great sway from side to side, and, we turned over.

"Helen—are you hurt?"

"No—but a man is kicking me in the face."

We were dragged out through the window. Nobody was seriously injured—and every body knocked to pieces and badly bruised.

Our disaster came about in this wise. A wheel had come to grief—it flew about wildly for a while and then smashed up.

They put me on a stage horse covered with harness; not a bed of roses. And the Mediterranean Sea led the horse—a stranger—as nice as he could be walked by my side & my father on the other—so that I could not well fall off.

We arrived at the Stage Stand—no coach there. And no horses. Our luggage was left with Dick and the stage driver.

The greatest freshet ever known in the country was up. The creeks were booming, the bridges all broken. If there had been any way of accomplishing it, our wisest course would have been to return to Pensacola. But not a soul was willing to turn back.

An ox wagon was dispatched for our trunks. We were told, that the chances were good, for a week's detention at this road side Inn.

We could hear the roaring and splashing of the water; the creek near the house was a mile beyond its banks.

My father was floored, at his wits' end—despairing. Already we were behind time. We had been delayed all along the line. And finding it so pleasant in Mobile we had over stayed time there too.

That night at supper, we were a dismal party; but I took it coolly—and accidentally raised their spirits somewhat. For in the midst of all that night mare of pork, I asked the naval officer to finish his Mediterranean narrative.

Soon we had the excitement of the loud crack of the whip, and the whooping and swearing as the poor oxen came blundering on with the luggage. The calm, impassible Dick stalking along on escort duty.

Then there was a lull. Afar off, again a shouting was heard. The ox wagon approached us from the side of the silent woods.

But gradually this sound seemed to come from the opposite direction. It was faint—and far away. Some what like calling the Ferryman. The man of the house arose, saying, "it was beyond him. There was nothing but the creek on that side. And the bridge had been blown up. And the creek was swelled to the size of a sea." One after another they dropped away, to see what it all could mean.

My father and I were left in profound solitude. Soon we heard them coming back; cheerful voices now; louder and louder; torches waving, laughter—negro songs. A man seemed to have risked his life crossing in a canoe from the other side.

"Good evening Miss Newtown".

"God bless my soul! Howard is it you?" said my father. Miss Newtown said nothing; for once in her life she was speechless.

Our friend had waited for us at Macon; but growing restless, he came down to meet us. On the other side of this second flood his course was arrested. A negro from our side had his family on the other side, and unknown to any one paddled over in his canoe. He told of the crowd at the stage stand, including the young lady. So the dugout was hired, and the negro returned with a passenger.

Next morning—before day, I heard a tap at my door. I was told to arise and make ready to depart—and to be quiet about it. At the front door we found a carriage and pair awaiting us. So while our friends in misfortune slept, we deserted them.

The black paddling friend of Mr. Howard made known to him the existence of a carriage five miles off, which was returning after having taken a judge to his court. He walked off, secured it, came back in it, and we struck our tents and moved off without tap of drum.

I openly regretted that they had not allowed me the privilege of a last farewell to my Mediterranean hero. For indeed those men had been good to me. Attentive, kind, and considerate.

"You certainly dropped from the clouds at the right moment Mr. Howard. Pardon the question, but what brought you to this out of the way part of the world?"

"Oh! The same spirit of adventure which led me to take a look at the Choctaws. The Creeks are threatening a disturbance."

"I see. We came by Pensacola to avoid the Red skin Creeks. The creeks here have avenged their namesakes."

Never was there more heavenly day, bluer skies or balmier breezes. The road was fine, neither clay nor sand. And a happier party it would be hard to find.

Mr. Howard mapped out a plan of life—and intimated that he had no reason to doubt his power to carry out his idea.

First you were to go every where; after that you would know where it was best to go.

To our delightful home climate, with its flowers, fruit and easy going, dolce farniente[5] ways—give October, November and December.

Then brace yourself with the cold north for three months. Make that your working term. Business then. But he painted only the fun fast and furious, the excitement, and the keen enjoyment of skating, sleighing—snow-balling, and all the delights of his Princeton life.

"Three months bracing work. Where will the other six be spent?"

"April and May. At home—our coast is perfect then. And afterwards town life all we could wish for awhile. Then when stung by heat and mus-quitoes, off to the mountains, or the sea breezes—on either side of the Atlantic. Seek only cool shades—which are not enervating."

"Nine months holiday!"

"Even so. That is if I can arrange my life to my own taste," coolly answered the Youth. "And I think I can. I am not bitten with this American mania for work—for its own sake."

"Your father is a planter?"

"Yes—and so will be, my eldest brother. I have been reading Law. I do not know yet what my profession will be. If I touch cotton, it will not be near its source. I will go in for a cotton factory—or be a cotton bro-ker. They are always rich. Planters are apt to be poor. The black cloud only turns its silver lining—at a distance, from the field in which it rises. In spite of my nine months of the year in pleasant places—I do not mean to be al-together idle, or a vagabond. I seem to find it hard to fit into my place in this country. Suppose we had left the African in his native jungle—a savage?"

"We could not be three days together and not attack that subject. I have felt it in the air for some time. Helen—there—she never speaks—to me—or to you apparently—but some how I find out what she thinks. She was made a rabid abolitionist on the Mississippi by two worthless black women, who told her blood curdling tales. I saw she was seized with a horror of me as a slave owner. She nearly cried her eyes out—for a day. But a theatrical mania relieved her. I find from eavesdropping that she boldly pronounces William Tell a better man than Richard the Third. She has her doubts as to the morality of risking the boy's head, in the apple business—but then there

5. Italian, sweet idleness.

is no doubt as to the murder of the little Princes.[6] She loathes Lydia Languish—and I believe has a vain desire to be likened to Beatrice, in preference."[7]

"Never mind me. Answer Mr. Howard on the African question."

"So I will—in good time. But you—follow your mother and your grand mother in their relations with the poor African. And when you come to the great day, of Judgment—your mind need not be uneasy."

"Have you many native born Africans still alive with you? Think of them—and then look at Dick; talk with him; he is a very sensible fellow. Though he has never spoken five words to me in his life—I know it. 'Little Missy' taught him to read as soon as she could do so herself."

"I am so glad—I see we will agree. They are in a transition state, when the time comes—and it is coming like the man with the seven league boots, it will go. It will be cast off as the snake shakes off its last year's skin. Are we unwittingly sacrificing ourselves to the African's civilization?"

"If it be unprofitable to hold them in bondage we have not yet found it out. I am beginning to doubt the profit of it—to the Master. I made a handsome fortune by my law practice—and it seems that I am burying it in a Mississippi Swamp. But I hope to make it pay. I never fool myself with words. If I thought this thing wrong I would not do it. They could never induce me to say nullification[8] was a peaceful remedy—nor secession—I call it the right to fight. I have given up politics. And I am devoting myself to that good old gentlemanlike vice—avarice. I must make money, for the four youngsters I have to provide for in this world. To be candid—I did not exactly leave public life for that—I do not track well. I said—Let sleeping dogs lie. The great Southern leader is going too fast for me. He is precipitating the Explosion as madly as his antagonists. A handful—of people can not force their peculiar views on the Universe."

Here Sydney Howard handed a sketch he had made of himself—with a broad brimmed Panama hat. A bible in one hand and Calhoun's works in the other.

"The bible will get the best of it in the long run. The doctrines of Christ

6. Chesnut knows the story of the murder of the princes from Shakespeare's tragedy, Richard III (performed 1592–93, published 1597). Richard, duke of Gloucester, determines to obliterate everyone who stands in the way of the throne. He orders his two young nephews, Edward, prince of Wales, and Richard, duke of York, imprisoned in the Tower and then assassinated.

7. Beatrice, a character in Shakespeare's comedy *Much Ado About Nothing* (c. 1598), is witty and teasing, constantly engaging Benedick in verbal warfare.

8. Nullification: doctrine associated with John Caldwell Calhoun (1782–1850) and other Southern conservatives in the 1820s and '30s that contended that individual states had the right to nullify federal statutes.

must eliminate slavery (and many other things which the world clings to; and has done so for nearly 1900 years), if they ever prevail?"

This dialogue, I never forgot. And have often repeated it.

I learned many things not in my school books, while I was away from innocent slumberous old Charleston, where like the other inhabitants, I saw no wrong, and I am sure I would never have questioned any existing institution to my dying day.

Apropos of Howard's Christian outburst, the elder gentleman told of his father in law's pious joke—the prayer of the *Christian* old lady. "O Lord, let all the rain fall on Sunday, so that the poor negroes may not be kept from their daily labour."

We had an ample supply of provisions for man and beast. And we asked our way diligently of all that we met. Night overtook us; we feared we had lost our way, for the house to which we had been directed seemed to recede before us. Still we jogged slowly on by moonlight.

"I hope you are armed Mr. Howard. "The enemy" taught you that lesson."

"I have pistols. I left them in my trunk," said Mr. Howard looking rather foolish. "You know I could not bring it across in the canoe. I see myself going about, with a bowie knife in my boot—and one down my back, and a pair of pistols slung round my waist."

"And yet, just now—in these lone woods, I would not object to that arsenale ambulante[9] style of a companion. Where is your rifle?"

"Maum Sylla promised to take it to your house. She and I grew very intimate. She loved to talk of the family. And seated on a log—at a respectful distance we had some notable interviews.

"In all her life before, she had only known one man killed. And that was a 'jewel.' White men were as plenty as peas where she came from—too thick to thrive. And they did not kill one another. Out there in that lonesome, lonesome place, they came and killed the only white man there was for miles.

"Her everlasting lamentations were very painful to me. So I inquired as to the 'jewel.'

"She said it was to kill a young man. And they all went out in carriages. She saw them, laughing and talking—parsons, doctors and lawyers. I questioned the presence of parsons. She said,'Oh yes—they went to see it done fair and square. That's the way they did it there, not steal up on a man by himself and shoot him.'

"Well they killed him. Only one carriage load came back, her way. The

9. Fr., walking arsenal.

others took themselves off in a different direction. But the body of the dead man came by her house—stiff and stark—laid on a board. She pitied the friend sitting by it. And all of them that stood by and saw it done."

But this could not go on forever—so we agreed to stop for the night, by a running stream. To feed the horses, and tie them—and try to sleep as best we might.

Dick went with Mr. Howard to see after the horses and we saw neither of them again. My father and I occupied the back seat—leaving the front for our friend, who did not come to take possession of it.

Early next morning I was waked by the feeling that some one was staring at me. I was not mistaken, and a painful sight I must have been after that tumbled up night.

Mr. Howard helped me out of the carriage and pointed to where I could find water in abundance, for a refreshing toilette.

We had tea, and many other things. My Mother was an old traveler and provided for the contingencies.

It was a gypsy breakfast, and charming. Never were two young people who cared less for the privations and discomforts of a night in the woods.

We examined Dick's bed under the carriage—he had dug up a fine pillow of sand.

This day, we determined to let the horses take their own way, for it was toward their home we wished to go.

During this pleasant journey Mr. Howard's attentions to me were by no means "marked": they were, to my father, however.

The two men were in an earnest discussion of Homer. And I had not then, even, read Pope's translation[10]; I am sure I had never heard of it. But something they said fired my ambition. I began a sentimental verse from Mrs. Hemans.[11]

At this interruption, my father annihilated me with the old home frown, and the look he always adopted when things were amiss.

I stopped in the midst of a word; and I saw the young gentleman found it hard not to laugh.

Soon after we were left alone in the carriage. My father was stretching his legs for awhile and Dick was walking with him.

Most unexpectedly I heard that I was not to be asked any thing. And then I was told that two years hence I would still be at Madame Bince's in New York. I had not spoken since the Hemans fiasco—and I did not now. On my seventeenth birthday this young man proposed to ask his question—and

10. Alexander Pope (1688–1744) published his translation of Homer's *Iliad* between 1715 and 1720, and his *Odyssey* in 1725–26.

11. Felicia Dorothea Hemans (1793–1835), a popular poet.

until then he would listen to nothing; because he had promised to wait until then—before speaking to me.

Suddenly I became interested. "Who did you promise?"

"That does not matter. The promise is the thing. It is not more binding to one person than to another."

Then came a confused declaration; "if he were told, that I was engaged—married—dead. If he was not dead too—he would appear—and claim—"

"What?"

"Oh! You know—the right to ask—no matter what. Only from your own lips will I take my answer."

Here he begged for a ring I wore. I handed it to him promptly.

"It is not mine. It belongs to your sister Madelaine."

He gave a queer little smile, and threw the reins over his arm, as he took it, and fastened it on his watch chain. What he would have said next, or how much longer he would have respected the spirit of his promise, who knows.

Bang! Went a gun.

9

The Mature Syren—

En vieillissant le diable se fait
ermite, et la femme se fait diable.[1]

By heaven I'll tell her boldly that
'tis she;
Why should she ashamed or angry be,
To be beloved by me?[2]

I am my Mammy's ain bairn
Nor of my hame am weary yet,
So I would hae ye learn lads,
That ye for me maun tarry yet.
For I'm ower young, I'm ower young.
I'm ower young to marry yet.
I'm ower young 'twould be a sin
To take me frae my Mammy yet.[3]

1. Fr. In growing old, the devil turns himself into a hermit, and the woman turns herself into a devil.

2. Abraham Cowley (1618–67), "The Discovery," lines 1–3, in *The Works,* ed. A. R. Waller (Cambridge, 1905–6), 1:98.

3. Robert Burns adapted one version of this old Scottish song, but MBC probably learned

And away dashed the horses. Mr. Howard regained the reins and braced himself against the dash board. He pulled for his life. But for a moment's fooling with the reins over his arm—fastening that ring, the horses might not have gotten off.

We were near the top of a hill—I could see my father and Dick[4] walking slowly at its foot. I was perfectly cool. We jolted over some obstruction in the road—the rotten old dash board gave way, and Mr. Howard was down among the horses' feet.

I saw we were making for the Pine Forest for the road curved then and the horses kept on straight into the woods. I was saying to myself, "Now Helen you had better say your prayers." I was thinking, "I wonder if he is killed?" But I did not feel any thing. Neither grief nor fear. I was stupid. I saw a man spring to the horses' heads as they wound about among the pines—their pace very much slackened. I could hear a horse galloping up behind us. The wheel struck a tree, and we were upset once more.

Papa lifted me up. I had been thrown quite out of the carriage—which was an open one.

"Her head was not an inch from this great pine tree! What a God's mercy she did not strike it."

"Are you hurt darling?"

"No, papa—but my knees give way. I can't stand."

"That is only fright."

"I have not been frightened," I said beginning to sob bitterly.

There was Mr. Howard still clinging to those brutes of horses. Unhurt apparently.

The man who had done all this mischief was off his horse and helping Dick and Mr. Howard. The horses were trembling and prancing. The carriage was a hopeless wreck. The man with the gun informed us we were still four miles from the stage stand.

Again was poor Dick to be left in charge of the luggage. He said to me, "When I saw the young gentleman go down between the horses, I prayed to the Heavenly father for you—little Missy."

---

this version by ear as a child. I have consulted several standard collections of English and Scottish ballads recorded in the United States (including Francis James Child, *English and Scottish Popular Ballads* [Boston, 1904] and Cecil James Sharp, *English Folk Songs from the Southern Appalachians* [London, 1932]), but can find no reference to this song in the United States.

4. Stephen Decatur Miller's personal servant was named Dick; MBC claims to have taught him to read when she was a girl. In "We Called Her Kitty," MBC writes "One old fashioned trait of antique fidelity in Dick—my fathers man—who never left him—traveling or at home—Dick was the fiddl[e]r for the county—for the year after my father's death he refused to play—as a want of respect for Masters memory—When one thinks of the five dollars a night he sacrificed the *respect* assumes large proportions in our eyes."

"You ought to have prayed for him too—you good old soul."

The man on horseback said his horse would carry double and offered to take me behind him.

Mr. Howard requested him to give his saddle to Mr. Newtown and to lend him his horse, as he could ride as well without a saddle as with one; he had not been allowed to use a saddle until he was thirteen years old. He asked me for my long red scarf; this he tied round his waist; then he said, "Now give me your hand—now put your foot upon mine"; with help from all I was soon seated behind him. "Now take hold of my red sash."

The dismal cavalcade was soon in motion. The man with the gun rode off to send a cart for the trunks. Slowly my senses began to come back to me. My father was beguiling the way, by telling of the homely scenes of his youth, how pretty girls rode behind him from church, and how he jumped his horse over every thing, that they might squeal and hold hard.[5] Mr. Howard laughed; but I rode demurely—soberly and without a word.

Next day we were to take the stage again. Mr. Howard was obliged to go back and hunt up his traps. As I stood by my father's side, he shook hands with him. To me he said, "Good b'ye for two years." I held out my hand which he took and seemed uncertain what to do with it for awhile.

Suddenly he kissed it—and was gone.

At that time people were never in a hurry. And we found within a day of our journey's end, we were to be detained twenty four hours in Augusta.

Sunday intervened.

At Macon two men that we had in a measure run away from in New Orleans over took us. They were persons well known to Mr. Newtown but whose company he liked best when without me. They proposed to join our party going East, and we could not refuse to say something polite on the occasion. Then instead of waiting until afternoon as we had agreed, we fled by an early train. No reference was made to our unexpected disappearance, and our friends were as cordial and affable as ever. And we shipped a new cargo so to speak—and one which cost me dear. These last, were a kind of far 'awa cousins, as the Scotch have it.[6] Great admirers of mine, from the West.

One of them brought me a pearl necklace. Sent by an Aunt of mine, in feeble health, with an only son; it was a family heirloom and she thought the eldest girl ought to have it.

5. In the revised Civil War journal, MBC records an anecdote about her father's ability to charm women (see *MCCW,* 187).

6. Stephen Decatur Miller, MBC's father, had a number of relatives who had moved away from South Carolina to Alabama and Mississippi, any one of whom could have been the source for this incident. See letter from SDM to his daughter, copied in MBC's hand, dated 23 July 1835, in which he lists his relatives (Williams-Chesnut-Manning Collection).

We had but a few minutes. While I was waiting for my trunk to lock it up safely, my curiosity induced me to open the case, and my vanity to try on the necklace, there in the broad day light before a hotel mirror. Remember I was only fifteen. The necklace was restored to its case, as I thought and carefully placed in my trunk. And we were off for the Station.

At Madame's after a glowing description of my Pearls I opened the case to exhibit them. Lo! it was empty. Twenty years after, I met for the first time the Pearl man. With pride he narrated to what lengths his former infatuation carried him. "Why! I wore those wax beads of yours in my westcoat pocket until they were only white dust. I had seen them around your neck—and I put them near my heart." Comment is useless.

At Augusta Dick informed me that his Master would remain in bed all day—to rest—he was so broken down by the journey—and he advised me to do likewise.

I was young, and in perfect health—neither fatigued nor dispirited. To have stayed in bed would have been absolute torture. So as I needed no rest—and I could not get out—I sat down by a window, to watch the crowds returning from church.

Among them, making her way directly for our house, I saw a very short, stout woman with so little neck that her chin and bonnet strings seemed to rest on her magnificent bust. I could see her distinctly through the window glass; her face was very red; redder were her lips. Her teeth were beautifully white and regular as she seemed to be showing every one. Her hair was glossy black and in a thousand ringlets. There were two men with her, upon whom she was bestowing nods and becks and wreathed smiles, accompanied by taps of a gorgeous fan. One of them appeared to be earnestly entreating some favour. Finally she yielded, she took off her glove, and held out to him, the fattest little hand I ever saw, covered, nay, smothered in rings.

They shook hands upon their bargain; but the other man was shaking his head in grave disapprobation of it all, that was plain.

This scene diverted me in my enforced solitude. And I was trying to imagine a meaning for it. The man was so young and so handsome, and the woman—she was old enough to be my mother.

A card was brought to me, "Mrs. Mynherr." And below was scribbled, "an old friend of your family desires to see you."

In a moment I was on my feet. My prison gates were opened; and I followed the man into the drawing room.

Near the centre table stood the heroine of the street scene, surrounded by men. She was radiant, and smiling; as she saw me, she extended the plump little hand, beaming on me graciously.

"You are the image of your mother," she exclaimed turning to the crowd of her admirers. "Her mother is a celebrated beauty." At the expense of truth one polite individual mumbled, "That he could well believe it."

She described a magnificent ball, one of a series of such, which she had attended at Mrs. Newtown's when Mr. Newtown held a position which involved entertaining the public.

She descanted on the high aristocratic circles, "her familiar circle—for she had been raised in Figinia"—and her horror of the "mixed multitude among whom she had been called upon to mix still further, in these new states." She paused for a reply. Seeing me silent and confounded, she affably tried to reassure me.

"My dear young friend—you know it is so."

I found courage to say, "I have seen no multitude any where. The county is a mere wilderness yet. We have liked extremely the few people we have met." Here I was overwhelmed with confusion at my own audacity. But I could not bear to hear my kind neighbours maligned.

"Bravo!" cried the lady clapping her hands. "Let me introduce a western gentleman. He was anxious to know you before. What will it be now!"

I sat down to enjoy the situation, it was so comfortable to be properly chaperoned once more. I went to dinner with them, Dick standing grimly behind my chair. And as he handed the rice—he groaned, "Your Ma wouldn't like you to do this er way."

My handsome new acquaintance monopolised my attention. The New Orleans party stared in surprise. After dinner, "Will you attend after noon church?" said Mrs. Mynherr. And I was quite ready to do so. As she advanced upon the Piazza with a liberal allowance of men, she made herself very conspicuous by a playful and noisy altercation with them, she was "selecting a beau," she said. "It did not look well to take too many men to church with you."

The western man offered me his arm and we followed her, to confront my father at the door.

"Where are you going?"

"To church with your old friend Mrs. Mynherr," said I ignoring the tall youth at my side. "You must have seen her as she passed you just now."

"Yes—and I heard her too. I am sorry to disappoint you. We leave for Aiken in an hour." He took my hand and with a bow to the dumb struck man he led me to my room.

"Papa she knew Mamma—so well. She says she was at our house—at all of our balls."

"Tut—tut—tut. Never saw the woman before in my life. She is not a creature one is likely to forget. I am sure that I have never heard her name before. The New Orleans chap says those young men induced her to trump up that tale to inveigle you into the drawing room; and he led me where I could prevent this latest escapade. Do not speak to any one, unless I introduce you—until you are safe under Madame's wing." Suddenly he began to laugh nervously.

"It was all my fault. My poor wife. She knew the world better than I do."

In 1835, when I was first taken to Madame's, we made the journey in the carriage. We were three days getting to Inabinet's and then we met the train.[7]

The cars were then built some what like an elongated omnibus; the seats were placed as they are still, in the omnibuses.

Facing me sat a very stout man with a large moon face—fat, flabby cheeks, and a very woe begone expression.

At that time the cars ran very roughly—jolting and jarring abominably. The rails were laid unevenly—and the skeleton piling, so high we seemed to be gliding or bumping rather in mid air. This motion communicated itself to the heavy cheeks of the stout man. The effect was comic beyond measure. I wondered he did not tie up his face in his handkerchief to steady it. I was nearly suffocated with an attack of fou rire[8]—as the French have it, that kind of feeling that comes over one at church, or any where, else, when one would rather die than laugh. I tried not to look at the fat man's quivering cheeks; but there was no where else to look; he was directly in front of me. A fit of the giggles! at last!

My father and the jelly fish were old acquaintances; to correspond with his face, his voice was whining and melancholy. He said the first engine had terrified the country people.

"That day Calhoun and McDuffie[9] had piled on the agony—to an enlightened audience. The crisis, and the Tariff, you know," he said ruefully.

"At night some of the citizens were unhitching their horses—down came Engine No. 1. snorting, shrieking, roaring, whistling, with its glaring red eye to the fore.

---

7. According to Charles Fraser, *Reminiscences of Charleston* (Charleston, 1854), 114, the South Carolina Rail Road began offering public travel on 7 November 1832, for a distance of sixty-two miles, from Charleston to Branchville. By 1835, the train ran "136 miles, performed in daylight, from 6 A.M. to 6 P.M." from Charleston to Hamburg, opposite Augusta. Inabinet's was a regular stop thirty-two miles from Charleston (1835 advertisement in *Miller's Planters and Merchants Almanac* [Charleston, 1835], reproduced between pages 84 and 85 in Samuel Melanchthon Derrick, *Centennial History of South Carolina Railroad* [Columbia, S.C., 1930]).

8. A fit of hysterical laughter.

9. George McDuffie (c. 1788–1851), U.S. congressman. MBC here refers to the Nullification Crisis of 1833, brought about by South Carolina's decision to nullify the federally imposed tariffs of 1828 and 1832, and President Andrew Jackson's threats of military intervention to uphold the law. Both Calhoun and McDuffie attended mass meetings in Charleston in January and February of 1833 to discuss the crisis.

"'My God,' they cried—huddling together.

"'Pshaw! dont be scared—it is the tariff—I knew it as soon as I saw it,' said the leader of the party."

Heavens! how glad I was to have something to laugh at. And I took advantage of the opportunity whenever I caught his eye. Someone else said it had been called—"Hell in harness"—by a back woodsman.

In two years the change had been very great. The cars were comfortable. But I had a schoolgirl's horror of a tale bearer.[10] And I would not look at the New Orleans man—much less speak to him.

10

A Boarding School Fifty Years Ago

> Ah me! full sore is my heart forlorn,
> To think how modest worth neglected lies;
> While partial fame doth with her blasts adorn,
> Such deeds alone as pride and pomp disguise;
> Lend me thy Clarion Goddess! Let me try
> To sound the praise of merit ere it dies;
> Such as I oft have chanced to espy,
> Lost in the shades of dull obscurity.
> In every village marked with little Spire,
> Embowered in trees and hardly known to fame,
> There dwells in lowly shed, and mean attire,
> A matron old, whom we school mistress name.[1]

I prevailed upon my father, without difficulty, to take me from the depôt to Legare Street.

We parted at the narrow Green Gate.[2] And I walked straight down the broad avenue paved with marble. Beautiful evergreen trees waved and rustled a welcome over my head.

10. The "tale bearer" from whom Helen shrinks on this train ride is the "New Orleans man" who accompanies them. The "jelly fish" episode occurred on a train ride two years earlier.

1. William Shenstone (1714–63), "The Schoolmistress," lines 1–12, in *The Poetical Works of William Shenstone* (Edinburgh, 1857).

2. In the 1830s, the famous Sword Gates for which the house at 32 Legare Street is now known had not yet been installed. According to Robert Molloy, the gates were originally cast for the Guard House at Meeting and Broad Streets that was destroyed in an earthquake in

On the marble steps at the Front door Monkey[3] was sitting as usual studying her catechism—more assiduously than ever, just then, for she was soon to make her first communion.

"Girls! Come and see. Helen Newtown is here. She's come! if I can believe my eyes? She's dropt down from the clouds!" You could hear the cry taken up from room to room as it rolled up to the third story front—and back toward the brick building which opened by a Porte Cochère on Tradd St.[4]

My friends came trooping down the various stairs—and gave me a warm reception—kissing, shrieking, chattering like magpies.

Monkey had darted away to tell Nenaine,[5] as we called Madame in our hours of ease; i.e. when she was in a good humor—with all of us.

Many of these girls were the daughters of Madame's former pupils.

The first old friend who rushed into my arms, had come to Nenaine an infant. Such had been the wish of her dying mother, and the Surviving Parent, a wealthy planter, had acquiesced.

No school mistress could desire a stronger proof of the faith and love of her scholar.

Miss Anne, our second in command, still showed the desk which had been the baby's cradle. And she told queer stories of how the volunteer nurses fought over her. For this tribe of school girls played with and petted her as a doll and not as a young immortal.

It is almost a miracle that she was no worse. This fairy, had glorious brown eyes, and an experience of life as varied as a sensation novel. After all—when her ships came home, when all her troubles were buried in the grave of husband number one, and with husband number two she had every inducement to be happy ever after—she died. Still young, beautiful, and beloved.

September, 1886 (*Charleston: A Gracious Heritage* [New York, 1947], 227). The *National Register of Historic Places,* ed. Ronald M. Greenberg (Washington: U.S. Department of the Interior, 1976) states that the gates were added to the Legare Street house in 1849.

3. Monkey will subsequently be identified in the text as a young black girl whom Madame Talvande, the headmistress of the school, has agreed to raise and educate.

4. As the author describes, Madame Talvande's school consisted of two homes that had been joined by a walkway and gardens. One, which housed the school rooms, is known today as the Sword Gates House, at 32 Legare Street. The other, 109 Tradd Street, was used as living quarters for boarding students. In 1835, these houses were numbered 24 Legare and 98 Tradd (*Charleston Directory,* 1835).

5. Nickname for Madame Talvande. A letter from Sophia Springs quoted in Katherine Wooten Springs, *The Squires of Springfield* (Charlotte, N.C., 1965) confirms that other students used the name "Nenaine" (French, meaning nursemaid or "nanny") to refer to Madame.

The school was a very large one, both in boarders and day scholars.

For the girls who began with her "from the beginning" Madame seemed to feel the deepest interest. For those who were sent her for a few months "to finish" she felt very slight responsibility. "Hard cases" to polish off— she called some of these. And they thereby escaped the agonies of terror which consumed the greater part of us.

These grown, young ladies, who came in January and departed in April, took lessons from every Master; Painting—Music, dancing, and any thing whatsoever there was any body on the spot to teach. She did not expect this top dressing to amount to much, and she left them to an easy and pleasant life.

If they were handsome, well mannered, graceful and a credit to her establishment, she adored them. But her French soul revolted from awkwardness, ugliness and stupidity. The priest to whom she confessed ought to have arranged a heavy penance for her sins of unjust discrimination.

Boarding schools have in the Progress of the World, developed into something so very different from all this, that I will venture to tell the girls of the present day, by way of contrast, how their grand mothers were treated, trained, and taught.

Madame's House and Grounds formed the very beau ideal of a "select school for young ladies"; and yet the House was built, and the Yard walled in, laid out, and planted by a selfish old bachelor[6] for his own personal gratification, and for nothing else. It was a Convent in its seclusion, and the high brick walls were surmounted by rows of broken glass bottles. The small door in the wall on Legare St. suggested a Nunnery. There had been an extensive hot house, which was now in a neglected condition. But the orchard and flower garden were in beautiful order. So we had ample play ground, and there was no need of leaving the safe guardianship of those protecting walls for fresh air, or exercise.

6. The property on which both houses are built was sold by Isaac Holmes to James Simons in 1803, and when Mr. Simons divided the property into several lots and registered his plat, both houses were shown on the plat (Emma B. Richardson, *Charleston Garden Plats,* Charleston Museum Leaflet No. 19 [Charleston, 1943], 16, 19). Therefore, both houses may have been built by Isaac Holmes. Although MBC says the house was built by a bachelor, if Holmes was indeed the builder, her information was incorrect. Holmes, one of the prominent citizens of Charleston who was seized and imprisoned at St. Augustine during British occupation of the city in 1780–82, married Rebecca Bee and was the father of at least one son, John Bee Holmes (Reynolds and Faunt, *Biographical Directory of the Senate of the State of South Carolina* [Columbia, S.C., 1964], 238). Nothing is known about James Simons. *The National Register of Historic Places* states that the house was built in about 1803. Madame Talvande operated her school in these houses from 1819 to 1849 (*Historic Charleston Guidebook,* 60). Tradition holds that the high wall surrounding the property was built by Madame Talvande herself, to separate her charges from their suitors (Molloy, *Charleston,* 84).

The house consisted of two distinct buildings welded together. The one of brick, which opened on Tradd Street, by a Porte Cochère, must have been a grand establishment in its day; so thick were the walls and so fine the wood carving,[7] not to speak of the sculptured white marble mantle pieces. The other [was] a wooden building, with its three tiers of Piazzas open to the breezes from East, South and West. The whole formed a U— the two arms of which were our school room and our dining room. The space between the two was made beautiful by flowering trees—in the Spring. We had a private parlor and a State drawing room; the latter finely furnished in French style with mirrors, to the superfluous point. The walls were papered with the story of Paul and Virginia.[8] To the last day of my three years at Madame's, there never was man, woman, or child, sufficiently interesting to me, to divert my attention wholly from the sad fortunes of these lovers, depicted in every color of the rainbow on a back ground of gorgeous tropical scenery.

Here also stood our grand Piano.

Of Pianos more or less ill-used there were one or two in every room in the house. From "morn till dewy eve"[9] the sound of their drumming and strumming abated not. Singing, taking lessons, practicing.

As you entered the Hall door—every imaginable sound of *Musique man-quée*[10] burst forth or was shut off, by the opening or shutting of doors, dominated generally by the deep, gruff, growling voice of the old man, who gave singing and guitar lessons in the small parlor; round the corner of the brick house passage, came portentous sounds, for there a younger and more energetic Frenchman strenuously battered to his heart's content a loud Piano—if one may be allowed such a contradiction in terms. We were perfectly accustomed to this Babel—and cared as little for it as a Miller does for the racket of his Mill.

Madame's chamber was over the large drawing room. And her beautiful chapel formed part of the Piazza opening west from her room.

There was one ghostly peculiarity of this room, and one to which I never

7. The *Historic Charleston Guidebook* describes the Tradd Street house as containing "a beautiful Adam ballroom with woodwork still decorated in the original gold leaf" (60).

8. Bernardin de Saint-Pierre (1737–1814), *Paul et Virginie* (Paris, 1789). Paul and Virginia, both fatherless, are raised in a pastoral setting and love one another. Virginia is called away, and in her attempt to return, she is drowned before Paul's eyes. Brokenhearted, Paul dies soon after.

9. John Milton, *Paradise Lost* (London, 1667), book 1, lines 742–43, "From morn / To noon he fell, from noon to dewy eve."

10. Fr., music in name only; music which badly misses the mark.

became reconciled. The half of the room devoted to *feu* Monsieur remained exactly as he left it, the night he was brought home on a shutter—dead.[11]

There stood his hat—his dressing gown, his slippers, every thing of his, dusty and depressing. No living girl was ever bold enough to go into that room by night or by day—alone.

Poor man, in his life, they said, to indemnify himself for the severity of good behavior required of him in a girls' school, he repaired nightly to scenes better suited to his taste, and amid a circle of congenial spirits, it ended as we have said.

His wife then began a series of Masses for his soul; to which pious work she devoted a large part of her income. The girls were sure he had gone no further down than Purgatory; and were surprised at the difficulty of rescuing him thence. Those who did not love Madame, thought he had served out a part of his sentence here, above ground.

He died without a will, and she was entitled by law to only one third of the money she had herself accumulated by her own industry. I believe he taught Arithmetic, and that he also was the writing master of the school.

Our room was in the third story and had windows on three sides. We overlooked the river, the battery—and that melancholy group of Pines on James Island. From our Piazza we had a view of the bay and the Islands surrounding it.[12]

There were beds for twelve of us in that large room. One side of it was given up to wash-hand stands and dressing tables, and one side to a Piano—and the stairs which led to the observatory above.

We secured a modicum of privacy by bed curtains formed of our frocks and petticoats—which served as screens also.

On bright nights the telescope was taken to the Cupola above us—and there the astronomy class looked out upon the moon and stars—and I hope we learned something about them.

As I said before twelve young barbarians camped in this room, and never under one ceiling rioted a lighter hearted more joyous band.

While we dressed some early bird, of a conscientious turn of mind, was always practicing; oftenest with wide stretched mouth singing her solfeggios. We heeded her not, the roar of our chatter would have drowned the ocean.

11. Andrew Talvande (1787–1834); a contemporary diary, in an entry dated 15 October 1834, records, "A. Talvande fell down in a fit in a Billiard room, taken home & died" ("The Schirmer Diary," *South Carolina Historical and Genealogical Magazine* 68 [1967]: 99).

12. The islands surrounding Charleston Bay include James Island and Morris Island on the southwest, Haddrill's Island, just east of Charleston across the mouth of the Cooper River, and Sullivan's Island, site of Fort Moultrie, at the east side of the mouth of the bay.

Madame kept an excellent table, every thing was served with neatness and propriety. There was spread before us, all things, wholesome, dainty, and prepared to tempt the capricious youthful appetite. Every thing admirable of its kind.

On Wednesdays Bishop England[13] dined with us. And Miss Anne boasted that no alteration was visible in our bill of fare on that day. Still after we had adjourned to the school room—in spite of the intervening trees, through the windows that faced each other, we could see a slow procession of dishes wending their way, toward the end of the table where Madame and the Bishop and a few Catholic teachers worthy of the honor, sat for an hour or so longer, plainly "having a good time."

Happily for me my seat was at Nenaine's right hand; so when the Bishop came I moved down one, and was then next to him at table. In that education without books of which one is ever insensibly secreting a grain, I look upon those Wednesday dinners with benefit of Clergy, as no mean part. The Bishop doubtless never forgot the peculiar atmosphere in which he then breathed and dined; he found however an immense number of interesting topics by which he could enliven our monotonous girlish babble. Then he was never without an Irish story, told with the richest of brogues. We waited for it anxiously, knowing the fun that was sure to come with it.

He hinted a fear, not without foundation, that he had "the least taste in the world of the brogue" at all times.

There were other Priests who came; agreeable and accomplished gentlemen, but there was but one Bishop England.

Some of the Priests read aloud admirably; they were all kind, and ready to aid in amusing us.

The Irish Priest who sang Moore's Melodies would wind us up to agony with the "Harp that once Through Tara's Halls," and "She is far from the Land where her Young Hero Sleeps," and then quench our tears—with "Rory O'Moore courted Kathleen Baun."[14]

Once we broke bounds and crowded round this handsome young Christian—for it was against rules to leave our seats "tumultuously" in the Drawing room. He gave us for the first time—"The low backed car":

13. John England (1786–1842), Roman Catholic Bishop of Charleston from 1820, when he arrived from Ireland, until his death.

14. Thomas Moore (1779–1852), *Irish Melodies* (irregularly published, London, 1807–34). "Harp That Once through Tara's Halls" and "She Is Far from the Land Where Her Young Hero Sleeps" were both published in Moore's *Irish Melodies*. "Rory O'More, or, Good Omens" sometimes entitled "Young Rory O'More," by Samuel Lover (1797–1868), *Songs and Ballads* (London, 1839), cited in Sears, ed., *Song Index.*

Of the lovers who came near and far
And envied the chicken
Peggy was pickin
As she sat in her low back car.[15]

A greater part of the up country girls went home for the summer; and the day scholars, at least those who were planter's daughters, disappeared regularly for a month or so at Christmas and again at Easter. They went "into the Country," that is to say to their plantations.

These planter's daughters were models of propriety in dress and in conduct; absolutely blameless in every respect. Noblesse oblige? They were prim, precise, self poised, exclusive, good scholars, and they had withal the sweetest voices; which they have still.

We had two or three distinct cliques. To begin with, the refugees from St. Domingo,[16] of whom Madame was a distinguished representative. There were wonderfully handsome girls among these: they were gayer and less studious than Charleston proper. They were excellent musicians and excelled in all graceful accomplishments. Like Monkey they seemed always studying their catechism, and always preparing for their first communion. One of them, (whose forefathers were doubtless French nobles of the purest water—but their descendants after a course of St. Domingo did their duty to God and their families, by being the best French bakers) said, she hated books, she wanted "to stay home an bake little breads." They spoke French habitually; now and then for the pleasure of breaking a rule they interchanged a few words with us in broken English, which after all was far better than our mangled French. Remember this was a French boarding school, par excellence, and English was a forbidden tongue except to those who "did not study French."

And now for the "Juggernauts and Cavillers" so called by Ker Boyce twenty years before the "Bigelow papers."[17]

15. "When First I Saw Sweet Peggy," usually called "The Jolly Ploughboy" or "Jolly Ploughman," words by Samuel Lover, *Songs and Ballads* (London, 1839).

16. San Domingo, the Caribbean island whose western portion became French in 1695 and was renamed Saint-Domingue; a slave revolt in 1791 preceded ten years of war and unrest, before the colony gained independence as Haiti in 1802.

17. James Russell Lowell (1819–91), *The Biglow Papers* (first series, 1848; second series, 1867). One passage in the second series describes "Miss S. (her maiden name wuz Higgs, o' the fus' fem'ly here) / On her Ma's side 'a all Juggernot [Huguenot], on her Pa's all Cavileer" (Boston, 1867), 93. Ker Boyce (1787–1854) of Newberry, S.C., was a factor in Charleston, a state senator, and president of the Charleston Bank (John Belton O'Neall, *Annals of Newberry* [Charleston, 1859], 117–20).

Every Friday some girl was sure to give us, with feeble voice, and misplaced emphasis, Mrs. Hemans, and the Mayflower.[18]

The Huguenots were not ashamed then to be both Americans and protestants. They had not learned to look wistfully across the water, and gibe at Christopher Columbus as the author of all their woes. They even bore no ill will to the Edict of Nantes,[19] for had it not sent them over to this pleasant land, to possess it.

And they loved to dwell upon the heroic virtues of the noble colony who had planted them here. These ancestors of theirs were brave and manly fellows; and they brought to these shores, beside the piety, which was indeed their *raison d'être ici,*[20] a little more thrift, industry, energy and worldly wisdom than usually falls to the lot of those born in our sunny clime.

They were also more stiff necked, with somewhat of a hard narrowness. Perhaps like their contemporary Pilgrims, on "the Rock bound shore,"[21] they were more embued with the stern spirit of the Old Testament than with that of the New. To this the "Christian names" of the most distinguished Huguenots bear witness. These girls of Huguenot descent were bright brunettes; graceful and vivacious, with an ease of manner and motion recalling their French extraction.

(I will not say more of them. One tires of self laudation, Boston style "Freedom to worship God"—and Mammon, and above all our noble selves! Mind, body, and Estate—ad nauseam. Let us Laud and magnify our selves, and every thing that is ours! We have Freedom above all to believe the worst of every body else. There is the grandest of all Earthly organs in Boston which unceasingly sings loud anthems of praise to those within sound of its own noise. We cannot deny, we do not deny the truth of this Chorus of Compliment. Sometimes—we would be glad of a respite from the *Hub*-bub. No matter how good a thing may be—prose or poetry—indeed some one says of bad poetry even—that it is better than the best criticism made on it.)

But we will modestly return to our own Geographical limits. And tell of our English girls—those of the Cavalier stock. We can understand how

18. Felicia Dorothea (Browne) Hemans (1793–1835), "The Landing of the Pilgrim Fathers," stanza 10, in *Records of Women: With Other Poems* (Edinburgh, 1828).

19. The Edict of Nantes, signed into law in April 1598 by Henry IV of France, granted religious liberty to Huguenots, or French Protestants. Prior to its complete revocation by Louis XIV in October 1685, Cardinal de Richelieu had revoked portions of the edict because certain political clauses were considered threats to the state. Anticipating and following the revocation in 1685, more than 400,000 French Protestants left France and emigrated to other countries. The first Huguenot immigrants to South Carolina came from England in 1680. By 1700, more than four hundred French Huguenots had settled in South Carolina.

20. Fr., reason for being here.

21. Hemans, "The Landing of the Pilgrim Fathers," stanza 1, line 2. See n. 18 above.

they kept those lovely complexions, for the winds of heaven were not allowed to touch them, they were carefully screened from the glare which tans. But the men of this race, tall, fine looking with an unmistakable air of distinction, they had braved this burning sun for more than a hundred years. They were thorough planters, and lived in the open air, they were hardy hunters, and consummate riders. In Washington once, a scion of the English stock bore the red and white roses of the home of his forefathers, so conspicuously in his face, as to be remarked for the Apple Blossom hue of his perfect complexion, in that gathering of all nationalities.

Fancy how the pure, fair faces of this group stood out, amidst our sallow paleness. For to that our climate tends.

This party were also noted, as dignified, reticent creatures, self poised, and high bred, with a calm and cool resolution to keep every body at arm's length, who was not so happy as to be of their own Brahmin Caste.[22]

The Sea Islanders—Long Staple heiresses.[23] They were a race apart. A distinct dialect too marked them.

A lovely little thing too young to have left home, said, "No use for me to larn—I've plenty nigger an lan." This small Islander's sister was less horrified at the sentiment of the speech than at its vulgar use of the word nigger. I am sure the first time I ever heard "nigger" for "Negro" was in London at the American Minister's.[24]

"You know yourself to be rich—*raison de plus,*"[25] and Madame made this the text for a sermon on the duty of making the most of one's advantages, royally.

Our little beauty married a Frenchman with an honored and historical name. The Bonny bird's nest was built in the clefts of the Vieille Roche.[26] I heard Monsieur once plead as an excuse, "The head pain that I have here." Belle Isle replied—plaintively, "And it is your English that aches me."

22. The most exclusive of the upper classes; term coined by Oliver Wendell Holmes (1809–94) in the first chapter of his novel *Elsie Venner* (Boston, 1861), "The Brahmin Caste of New England."

23. Daughters of planters of black seed or long staple sea island cotton, grown on the sea islands and in the low country of South Carolina and Georgia after the Revolution.

24. MBC was in London in 1845, where she met Louis McLane (1786–1857), minister to Great Britain. McLane had received a letter of introduction to MBC and James Chesnut Jr. from James Buchanan, then Secretary of State (see *MBC,* 56, 234).

25. Fr., all the more reason.

26. Although positive identification is impossible with so little information, MBC may here be referring to Martha Washington Seabrook, daughter of William Seabrook, an Edisto Island cotton planter. Martha married Count Ferdinand de Lasteyrie, said to be a nephew of the Marquis de Lafayette. The de Lasteyrie plantation, named "The Rocks," was located on Wadmalaw Island south of Charleston (*Names in South Carolina,* ed. Claude Henry Neuffer [Columbia, S.C., 1967], 58, 115).

The nine Miss Banisters—were new girls who had made their appearance in Legare St. during my six months' Exile. I found them thoroughly at home and with nick names firmly affixed to every one of them. So I am not in the least to be censured for the girlish hardness of heart which named them. Some few got off easily, having come from places with odd Indian names, that sufficed to distinguish them. Others were duly branded by their personal peculiarities. They seemed to find the joke a good one, and endured their names meekly, and with laughter. Beauty Banister tried to look unconscious of her own loveliness. Cat and Pig Banister, require no explanation. There were their faces to speak for themselves. Beast Banister said gayly that she preferred the generic insult to the specific.

Another Banister had the sweetest face imaginable, when it was in repose. When she laughed it lost all shape, and stretched about vaguely, developing the strangest confusion of feature. She was India rubber B.

One poor thing was said to merit a name, but none was found to fit her case, until the school went in a body to a Menagerie. And there a sick ourang outang settled her fate. Henceforth she was, Miss Jane Ourang outang, from her likeness to this consumptive animal. She smiled good naturedly and said "girls would have their fun."

One alone revolted and reported us to Madame for conduct unbecoming ladies. We could hardly blame her. There are few persons philosophical enough to endure the name of Buzzard B. She said, "It was more than flesh and blood could bear."

We were ordered up for punishment, and we were cold with terror. Whatever should happen we admitted that we deserved it. The poor creature that had been blighted by a name was so forlorn, [that] later in life, when we had time to think and to feel, she would have been an object of our tenderest sympathy.

Madame was down upon us, fierce enough to daunt the stoutest heart. And the name of that obscene bird was forbidden in that house thenceforth and forever. We slipped away quaking in our shoes.

As soon as we had gained the safety of our own room, and were locked in, a spirit more rebellious than the rest began to sing audibly,

> "Turkey buzzard, Turkey buzzard
> Lend me your wing
> To fly over the river and see Sally King."

But we flew at her—and sternly ordered her to hold her tongue. "Madame is right," we voted. With us "bête" and "*sot*" had a meaning not in any dictionary.[27]

27. Fr., stupid; silly.

Madame, the Tyrant of Legare St. was of an excellent French family
driven in to Charleston by stress of weather, that is, driven out of San
Domingo by Toussaint l'Ouverture, Dessalines or Christophe.[28]

Like all refugees, in all times, of her nation, she wasted no time in vain
regrets, or in thoughts of what was due her by God and man—on account
of her social position—before the social earthquake; but she at once took
measures to utilize her rare accomplishments, and to make them pay, and
she succeeded as she deserved to do.

She was small, but beautifully formed, her hands and feet were models
both as to size and shape. We had opportunities of regarding her from various points of view. Different rooms in the house looked down upon her
dressing room. So in warm weather, when open windows were a necessity,
we saw her in absolute dishabille; her head tied up in a red bandana and her
torn and soiled dressing gown flying in the breeze, slippers down at the
heel, or kicked off.

At ten every day she descended upon us in the school room. She advanced with airy grace and rapid pace; smiling, bowing, curtsying, flirting
a gossamer handkerchief redolent of Cologne. The sombre widow's cap
strings floating at right angles did not disturb, the cheerfulness of the general effect. On cold days she wore a boa, a fur lined cloak and even her tiny
shoes were lined with fur.

She was quite regal in appearance seated on her throne; she took off her
gloves, waved her handkerchief aloft—and business began in earnest.

Once a dead hawk was brought in and thrown upon a table in the Hall.
Later in the evening, the hawk having come to life, to our amazement
walked into the drawing room. He was ruffled, and bloody, as he staggered
across, unsteadily on his feet. Heavens! how well I remember the keen and
bitter expression of that eye. Reproach, rage, indignation, hatred, scorn,
vengeance, it was all there.

Madame's eye was the counterpart of that broken winged Hawk's eye;
it was the fiercest I have ever seen in a mortal head. She had the faculty of
inspiring terror, and by that power she ruled us absolutely.

---

28. Toussaint l'Ouverture (1743–1803), born a slave, became one of the leaders of the
1791 slave revolt in San Domingo. A skilled military leader, he assumed rule of French Saint-
Domingue (San Domingo), and proclaimed himself governor general. He finally surrendered
to the French in 1802, and died in a French prison. Jean-Jacques Dessalines (c. 1748–1806)
was an illiterate slave who achieved rank in the war that followed the 1791 slave revolt. The
chief hero of the Haitian war for independence, he was proclaimed emperor in 1804, but was
killed in ambush two years later. Henri Christophe (1767–1820) served as a lieutenant of
Toussaint and, later, Dessalines. After the death of Dessalines, Christophe assumed rule, calling himself King Henry I after 1811.

Until she lost her temper Madame was a charming French woman, she loved dress, and she had a genius in that way. She was exceedingly polite, and her manners were very attractive. For all that—she was a cruel despot.

When things went wrong, she began to sneer a little with a most unmirthful smile, then the demoralized girl failed from pure fright. After that the snapping was persistent. They had no need to miss, the lessons were easy—in that particular she was not a hard task mistress. I often wondered—they knew what was to come; why would they not study?

Soon the storm was at its height; the small hand would wipe the stormy brow, and the screaming wildness of her tone sent a chill to every heart. She actually foamed at the mouth. Then the pale terror of those young faces!

After all what was the worst we need fear?

As we have said; you missed once—she frowned until you lost your senses. Twice—and you were ordered to the Idle Bench.

"Go! Miss! Go!"

"Where?" cried a new girl beside herself with fear.

"She thinks I am calling her to take a seat in my lap! For your insolence go and stand on the very centre of that Idle bench. Do you hear!"

Now this was the acme of horror. Nothing worse could happen in school hours. For several failings during the week, Saturday was lost to you as a holiday. To fail again on Saturday—doomed you to the Cabinet, our black hole of Calcutta. Like all human things it seemed worse than it was in reality. In this way the narrow dark space between the two houses had been utilized. It opened upon a passage by which two staircases led—some one was always passing, and nobody was so unsympathetic as to pass empty handed. In that way the solitude, and bread and water part of the sentence was rendered nugatory. The disgrace of the thing was left however in its unmitigated form.

Good Samaritans with stuffed pockets were the accidents to these victims of Justice. Maum Jute was their special Providence.

The Dunce Bench was semi circular and stood in the middle of the room. It was painted black with "Idleness" in huge white letters. It was capable of holding a dozen persons. It was rarely empty and held generally the same party. Of these very few were ever known to come back on Saturday, and during my three years' sojourn in Legare Street, not a half dozen were ever in the Cabinet. Those who went there once, grew hardened, and were apt to go very often.

The second French teacher was Mademoiselle Heloise, a niece of Madame. In spite of her tropical origin Mademoiselle was blessed with a soft pink and white complexion and very delicate features; in manners she was gentle, graceful, gracious. Toward her Aunt however she remained in a chronic state of abject fear, often in tears; she was blamed for the faults of her pupils—in her capacity of Governess for the smaller girls.

With us, she was careless, and spirited, often laughing gayly, when we who adored her surrounded her. When I returned, Madame said, she was too sweet, she had not been able to keep her. She had been proposed for, and had made an excellent marriage while I was away.

I have found more than once in my life, that it still means fascination, grace, and refinement, and a high heart, to have noble French blood in one's veins.

Over the mantle piece in our schoolroom we had a very suggestive picture, painted in glaring colors. Globes, books, Harp and Guitar, the last held by a long blue ribbon.

Legend:

> 'Tis education forms the youthful mind,
> Just as the twig is bent, the tree's inclined.[29]

As we entered this room from either door, we curtsied to the Presiding Genius on her throne; as we left it we turned and did the same. This gave an air of movement and life to the scene, almost a dancing gayety, for a young horde were trooping in and out incessantly.

Before Madame came down, that is between eight and ten, and after two when she left us, the din was deafening. During her presence silence reigned supreme.

Friday was "piece day." That is every one had a selected piece to recite or declaim. This thing every body prepared in an audible voice. I arrived on Thursday, and on Friday morning as I entered the smaller schoolroom— a splendid brunette, was standing on a desk in a striking attitude. She stretched out her right arm toward me.

> "The breath of submission I breathe not,
> The sword that I draw, I'll sheathe not"[30]—

a sudden break down—a spring on the floor and a search in the desk for her Campbell's poems.

A faint little voice at my elbow piped up.

> "And fire they cried
> And then *I cried* Oh Lord what shall I do!"

29. Paraphrase of Alexander Pope, "Epistle 1 To Sir Richard Temple, Lord Viscount Cobham," lines 101–2, in *Epistles to Several Persons* (London, 1733).

30. Thomas Campbell (1777–1844), "Song of the Greeks," lines 21–22, in *Theodoric: A Domestic Tale, and Other Poems* (London, 1824).

"Oh! Haggard Queen to Athens
Dost thou guide—[31]

"guide—thy chariot—steeped—steeped—in what? Kindred gore. What a dunder head I am." "Take the book and hear me." "Don't you see you don't know a word of it?"

"Around the shadowy brow of care
will hope and fancy twine her roses

"—their I I have—"

"A chieftain from the highlands bound
Cried Boatman do not tarry."[32]

"Hear me. I have it to a t."

"Arise fellow freeman and stretch the right hand
And swear to prevail in your dear native land."[33]

As the door was opened came in stentorian tones—from the private parlor—"Row, brothers row"[34]—with a ting, ting, of guitar and accompanying the deep voiced old man the shrill singing of a child.

"Oh for mercy sake let us get out of this row." And we go toward the drawing room to wait until Miss Anne's advent shall still the tempest. As we approach the door which is wide open—a mighty crash—four hands come down at once on the Piano in a stunning "duet."

"From Scylla into Charybdis."

"Do you suppose Bedlam is worse than this?"

"It is because you have just come—in a day or so you will not mind any more than we do."

Not many days ago a friend was speaking of the rules of an excellent school at which her daughters were placed. "Profound silence reigned throughout the building. Visitors were requested not to speak between the front door and the drawing room." This air of stillness, repose, refinement characterized the establishment.

---

31. Campbell, "Speech of the Chorus in the Same Tragedy [*Medea*]," lines 1–2, in *Poetical Works* (London, 1830).

32. Campbell, "Lord Ullin's Daughter," lines 1–2, in *Gertrude of Wyoming: A Pennsylvanian Tale, and Other Poems* (London, 1809).

33. Campbell, "Stanzas on the Threatened Invasion, 1803," lines 5–6, in *The Pleasures of Hope, with Other Poems,* 7th ed. (London, 1803).

34. Thomas Moore, "A Canadian Boat-Song," line 5, in *Epistles, Odes and Other Poems* (London, 1806).

One of the pupils when asked if this rule was never broken, answered with surprise, "It would be ill bred to stay in a lady's house and not conform to her wishes."

We were of a totally different opinion, and broke rules freely when we were certain of not being found out. After all we did nothing very heinous. And we were a wonderfully contented gang of young outlaws.

I have said that the "Cynthias of the minute," those who only came for a light top dressing, made their flitting peacefully. They had only to be gentle and ornamental, and Madame took them to her heart; but if by no fault of theirs poor things, they were ugly, awkward or stupid—they had a foretaste in Legare Street of what awaited them in the outside world.

Harriet was a perfect specimen of the successful sort. She had large grey eyes—and long black lashes. Her complexion was so brilliant, it took one's breath away. She was ready witted, airy, graceful, charming. Her most striking peculiarity in school hours was that she did not shake her lessons in her head longitudinally—with an up and down motion as the others did—but with a slow graceful movement, rhythmically—and from side to side, in parallels of latitude.

Envious of her perfections no doubt—it was said, she might be able to read a little—but that she could not write. If this were true, in spite of such unusual drawbacks, she was a prime favourite with Nenaine, and all the world outside.

During the late War I met Harriet in Richmond,[35] she was a distinguished person in Society; she had lived abroad a great deal. We may safely call her a married belle. She was a devoted wife and a good mother all the same.

Another of the old Legare St. set[36] was standing by me in my own drawing room, when I happened to mention that I had sent a note to Harriet; my object was to find out something about the house she had boarded at, in a neighbouring county.

"Oh! Oh!—I was there too. It won't suit you. The well has gone dry, the children have the whooping cough, the man of the house drinks and the servants have all runaway to the Yankees. But—I will take my seat once more. I mean to stay and see if she answers your note. We never did find out if she could write. I asked her, innocently, while she was engaged, 'if she wrote

35. An entry dated 22 March 1861 in MBC's Civil War journal relates this anecdote, and MBC identifies the woman in question as the wife of a man named Jack Hamilton (*TPMC*, 45).

36. In the Civil War journal entry mentioned above, this is identified as Sue Petigru King (1826–75), daughter of James Louis Petigru, one of South Carolina's most distinguished jurists. Sue King became a novelist; her works include *Busy Moments of an Idle Woman* (New York, 1854), *Lily* (New York, 1855), and *Sylvia's World* (New York, 1859).

to Henry?' She fired up, and said with some indignation, 'No. I promised my Mother never to write to a man until I had married him. Many a slip between the cup and the lip."

After a while a very respectable old woman came curtsying in.

"Our Miss Harriet sent me—she can't write."

It was impossible not to laugh.

"I told you so," said Susan, "I am satisfied—and I am off."

After she went out, the amazed maid continued her message.

"Miss Harriet say I mus tell you she has company—so she can't write—but I were there—and I knows all—and can tell you all you want to know."

How often have I sympathized with that bored, inert, easy going, hard to move, Roi fainéant[37] Hamlet. He only wanted to be let alone, to be allowed the peace of his life; and every thing dead and alive, up, and telling him *what he ought to do*. No wonder he said, "Man delights not me—no—nor woman neither."[38]

I am pervaded by the exact reverse of this sentiment of poor Hamlet—a wretch dogged and hunted to his doom by two meddlesome worlds.

Why did I then, why do I now prefer this city by the sea to the whole world?

I will state my case prosaically, and try to keep any thing "high toned" from creeping in. One always likes the best of its kind—be it cart horse or thorough bred. If the choice were given me to be a cat or a tiger, I should choose the tiger life, if I died for it.

Lord Byron said every body knew a gentleman when he saw one—and yet he had never met a person who could give a satisfactory description of one.[39] So I will not try.

But this indescribable thing is there still—and now found in the queerest places, and in the oddest employments. But the fine flavor lingers. They are strong men, they work with smiling faces, coûte qui coûte.[40] And they bear ridicule with a careless shrug.

No doubt Sancho had his homely joke at the Don's expense. The chivalry has been laughed out of court, and yet it lingered its last here. Gil Blas would turn over Bayard and Sir Philip Sydney to Nast,[41] who would make

37. Fr., lazy king.

38. Shakespeare, *Hamlet,* 2.2.310–11.

39. This comment attributed to Byron cannot be identified. So far as I can determine, it does not appear in any of his poetry or in his collected correspondence.

40. Fr., at any cost.

41. Sancho Panza, squire to Don Quixote in Cervantes' *Don Quixote de la Mancha.* Gil Blas is the main character in Alain-René le Sage (1668–1747), *Histoire de Gil Blas de Santillane* (Paris, 1715–35); this picaresque romance was translated into English by Tobias Smollett as *The*

Cartoons of them, for a laugh from the Groundlings. For alas they could never have been made useful republicans.

If John Brown and Lincoln had lived, I think they would have shared Horace Greeley's fate,[42] and have died a laughing stock in the house of their friends. *Hardily* thinking for themselves they would not shove the machine, and so Nast would impale them in Harper's Weekly.

But to return to my friends. In face of all difficulties when a race continues from father to son, perfect in manners, scrupulously correct in conduct, gentlemanlike in bearing even though they work like galley slaves, it is a thing to thank God for.

> Love thou thy land!
> Aye! Aye! And honor it too.[43]

11

> I own Earth's law, the conquered are the wrong,
> Why should I murmur? Why accuse the strong.

La liberalité consiste moins à donner beaucoup qu'à donner à propos.[1]

Madame was indeed an awe inspiring person. It was agreed on all hands that her temper was fiendish.

History and Adventures of Gil Blas of Santillane (Edinburgh, 1749). For Bayard, see *The Captain and the Colonel,* chap. 6, n. 8. English poet Sir Phillip Sydney was remembered for his romantic death: wounded in an attack on the Spanish in 1586, Sydney is said to have offered water to another sufferer, saying, "Thy necessity is greater than mine." Thomas Nast (1840–1902), illustrator and political cartoonist, joined the staff of *Harper's Weekly* in 1862.

42. Founder and editor of the New York *Tribune.* Greeley (1811–72), broke with the Radicals following the Civil War because he felt their policies toward the South were too harsh. He advocated amnesty and impartial suffrage for Southerners, and in 1867, in the face of public contempt, he signed Jefferson Davis's bail bond. Greeley ran against Ulysses S. Grant in 1872 on the Liberal Republican and Democratic ticket, on a platform of national unity. In July, August, and September 1872, Greeley was attacked by Nast in a series of cartoons in *Harper's Weekly.* One cartoon pictured Greeley reaching a hand to John Wilkes Booth over Lincoln's grave; another showed him stretching out his hand to the South in friendship across Andersonville prison. Greeley was roundly defeated by Grant.

43. Alfred, Lord Tennyson, "Love thou thy land," line 1, in *Poems* (London, 1842), vol. 1.

1. Jean de La Bruyère (1645–96), *Du Coeur,* line 4, "Liberality consists less in giving profusely than seasonably" (translation in W. Francis H. King, *Classical and Foreign Quotations* [New York, 1958], 161.

Upon mature reflection I have come to think there was method in her madness. She kept her tantrums as people keep a loud-barking dog, more to scare than to hurt—and to be untied only at regular hours. Dreadful as she was in the school room, in the drawing room, she was as pleasant tempered, as amiable, nay as fascinating a woman of the world as heart could wish. She was too well bred to unmuzzle the growler there. Even there however one look sufficed to conquer the recalcitrant.

The terror of her name brought about one unexpected and mortifying humiliation.

She bought a family of negroes, who were nearly white, husband, wife, and children. When they heard the name of their mistress, they filled the air with their cries and lamentations. This was immediately reported to her, by the person employed by her, to make the purchase.

She showed her temper, but after a fashion of her own, and it was neither mean nor cruel as had been feared. She sent them word never to let her see or hear of them again so greatly had their conduct disgusted her. And at the same time she sent them "free papers" legally made out.

After a while they ventured to go and thank her, taking with them their eldest child. This little girl struck her fancy, and she offered to educate her, making one stipulation.[2] The girl was never to sleep out of Madame's room. She was to expect some what of a separation from her own caste. Monkey (whose real name was Charlotte) could only visit her Mother occasionally by day. The parents joyfully accepted her terms. And Nenaine kept her word; Monkey slept in a cot near Nenaine's bed, and she was faithfully taught in her dressing room. We were very fond of her, and she was always with us, except at table, and in school hours. At that time she was a curly headed, black eyed, happy, round, roly poly, little thing.

I will give her whole history now. Years after, I was paying my respects to Madame in Legare St. as I always did when I went to town. I inquired, "Why do I not see the ubiquitous Monkey?"

I brought upon my self a torrent.

"L'Ingrrrate! Cette Vilaine moricaude!"[3]

It amounted to this. Monkey's father was vain of her beauty and wanted to exhibit it at Negro balls. In spite of Madame she did go to one, and further more broke the family compact by staying all night at her father's house. When she presented herself next day Madame refused to see her.

2. This statement cannot be verified. However, in the U.S. Census Records for Charleston County, 1830, the household of A. Talvande (Andrew Talvande, Madame's deceased husband) is noted as containing one free black female under ten years in age (vol. 25, p. 3).

3. Fr., ungrateful brown-skinned wretch!

Again a few years and I was in town. I found Madame in high glee over Monkey's Wedding. There had evidently been a reconciliation of so old a date that she had forgotten it. The bridegroom was a Portuguese. And the whole family had gone with him to South America. Madame had given Monkey her trousseau. And she remarked good humouredly, "The bridegroom though white was much darker than Monkey. My experiment was rather risky, raising her above the level of her own people. Thank God it has all ended well."

I must say a word for our first class.

It consisted of three girls. They were so far ahead of us all, that a great gulf intervened. At the head of this class was a brilliant brunette, tall, graceful, with soft and beautiful black eyes, so winning in manner withal, that I have no doubt the men would have forgiven her cleverness. But it was not to be—she died young.

The next was a tiny blond, who in addition to her scholarship was a miracle of goodness and piety. She was cool and quiet, prim, precise, self possessed, and a little old maidish in manner; a total change came over her face with its rare sweet smile. She married admirably, very soon after leaving school; and has kept the promise of her youth, she is now, as then, a model woman in all the relations of life—Wife, Mother, Widow, Grandmother.

> Let no face be kept in mind
> But the fair of Rosalind,
> Helen's cheek, but not her heart;
> Cleopatra's majesty:
> Atalanta's better part;
> Sad Lucretia's modesty.[4]

Our Rosalind had only been a short while with Madame, so she still laughed joyously; sometimes before Madame descended upon us, she would tell the two others a merry tale—at which they in their rôle of pinks of perfection would smile with an air of gentle tolerance. They were subdued and impassable, a course of Madame tended that way.

These three girls not only made brilliant recitations themselves, but they lent a helping hand to every one who needed it. Many a poor belated scholar they found struggling under difficulties—and left her rejoicing. Theirs was a most enviable position. We looked up to them. We even honored and obeyed them.

Our male teachers had experience on their side. None were under sixty,

4. Shakespeare, *As You Like It,* 3.2.92–98.

few over seventy. The youngest had that disadvantage removed; said a cruel girl, "because his face was like Vesuvius subject to fearful eruptions."

The most mummy like of all was our dancing master. If no longer active, he was gentle and graceful, with a sad and subdued, though highly polished manner. They were mostly of that dislocated St. Domingo colony. And no one could say, who, or what, our dancing master may have been before his misfortunes.

We danced cotillions, and when sufficiently advanced in our Art, we were taught to hop around in a Gavotte—or kick up our heels in a horn pipe: He insisted on teaching us the most difficult steps. We remonstrated, we knew they were no longer the fashion, but our venerable preceptor was obdurate. Strauss had set all the world a spinning;[5] but if we wished to glide or slide in waltz or galop it had to be some where away from Legare St. We generally wound up our lesson with a boulangère[6]—nearly as gay a romp as the Virginia Reel. Usually Madame came down awhile and looked on.

Once she smilingly laid aside her wraps and stood up to fill a vacant place in a Cotillion.

We saw dancing then. And we understood why Terpsichore was called the "Muse of the many twinkling feet."[7] She flew, barely touching the floor with the tips of her toes. She held her dress high, and her tiny foot was poised and pointed higher still in air, as she prepared to dart away.

Her face was radiant with delight, and self approval, as of a good thing well done.

"Why do you stare? Have you never seen a lady dance before?"

"No! Nenaine! not like you."

"You lazy, awkward, heavy footed clods—an old woman can shame you."

> Safe though fluttered and amazed
> We paused and on the strange scene gazed.[8]

French blood is likewise required for Loto. When she wished to be more than usually gracious she ordered the tables to be prepared for Loto.[9] And the dreary, weary, game dragged its slow length along.

She believed amusement absolutely essential for us. Our dancing mas-

---

5. Johann Strauss (1804–49), Austrian composer, wrote 150 waltzes. In 1835, he was appointed court dance music director in Vienna.

6. A dance similar to the Paul Jones.

7. Byron, *The Waltz* (London, 1813), line 1.

8. Adapted from Sir Walter Scott, *The Lady of the Lake* (Edinburgh, 1810), canto 1, stanza 20, lines 17–18: "Safe though fluttered and amazed / She paused and on the stranger gazed."

9. An early form of bingo.

ter gave a weekly ball at a place he called his Long-Room; and we were taken there, under strict chaperonage—guards doubled, so to speak. I doubt if I have ever enjoyed dancing in all my life, as I did in those Long Room days. There was a stage upon which the better sort danced, and below the million disported themselves. How each party found its proper level I never could guess. It was the inscrutable separation of upstairs and downstairs at the Choctaw Ball.[10] As the miners shake their pans until the pure gold is separated, I suppose we were hustled up on the stage.

I remember how we looked. Our dresses did not go much below the calf of the leg, so there was no hiding an ugly foot or ankle; these dresses were also scant and narrow; we wore with short waists large buckles and broad belts; and the eider down cushions in our huge sleeves made us look winged.

Our hair was plastered down on each cheek, leaving the ears standing out like handles to a jug or "walrus ears"; and then it was done up in what was called a "French twist" and on the top of the head it was arranged in one high puff. This does not sound very enticing. But if we were not lovely, the men did not find us out, and we were perfectly satisfied with ourselves.

We were taken to all concerts and to the Theatre[11] if Madame approved both play and actors. That is on Friday and Saturday nights. We continued to perform a travesty of the last play, every night in our rooms, (in all the freedom of night gowns and counterpane robes of state trailing behind, with most ingenious devices to simulate male attire) until we saw a new one.

We had an old menagerie of servants, ranging from our stately Thérèse whom we called Dédé to Maum Jute.

Dédé—if colored, was barely colored—handled ivory. She had followed her master's fortunes from St. Domingo. Her turban was white as snow and stiffly starched. And her gold ear rings were of the largest. On state occa-

10. Helen's reference here to the Choctaw Ball alludes to one of the events almost certainly included in the missing chapters. In "We Called Her Kitty," MBC mentions a ball in Mississippi, "Stephen & Kates school people gave a ball and we went to it—& all danced—father—Mother & all of us—& then there were mysterious whisperings—& I was packed up—& taken back to Charleston. Some of the men I met at the ball—& I do not in the least remember any of them—wrote to me—& were fool enough to give the letters to Willis—who did not think they were fit for Missy to wipe her shoes on. So the letters were answered—& I did not hear of it until several years after."

11. After the old Charleston Theatre was closed in 1833, theatricals were held in the Queen Street Theatre and in Seyle's Long Room through 1836. In December, 1837, the New Charleston Theatre opened, and introduced regular opera seasons. During the period when MBC would have been exposed to the Charleston theater, however, musical productions, pantomimes and circuses were more often produced than legitimate drama (Charles S. Watson, *Antebellum Charleston Dramatists* [University, Ala., 1976], 22).

sions, that is, when she meant to way lay the Bishop in the Hall and kneel down and be blessed, she wore an apron of muslin with pink bows on the pockets.

The children whose Bonne[12] she had been were our day scholars, and occasionally we surprised a rapturous meeting between Dédé and her nurslings. There was a heart of gold in that old woman's bosom. She adopted me from the first—and I responded with enthusiasm. I was forever jumping in her lap, and munching "bon bons" which were sure to come out of her pocket, when I might have been more profitably employed.

She watched over me with a mother's care and darned, and mended faithfully though that was no part of her duty. Of course I gave her all that she would take.

It was an understood thing, that when I left school I was to buy her. She proposed to follow me to the ends of the Earth. Alas! When that time came—I could not—It was a near thing to prevent being sold myself—but I am anticipating. She gave me a Pearl ring—as a keepsake. We parted with many tears—and she died before I was able to keep my promise. She was very happy in her home, and I doubt if she would have liked living in the country.

Maum Margaret and her son little Ben were a connecting link between our magnificent Dédé and the africans pûr sang[13] Maum Jute and Big Ben; they were Guinea Negroes, sooty black with skins tattooed like tanned alligators.

Old Ben used to slip slop about, in shoes down at the heel; his language was nearly unintelligible, but sufficed for the drudge of the Establishment which he was. At table he was an excellent waiter, regulated by signs from the intelligent "little Ben." Maum Jute, was called "Juliet" by Nenaine when she was in a good humour. When she was in one of her tantrums, it was— "Cette vilaine Négrrresse!"[14]

We took her own name for herself—Jute being her way of pronouncing Juliet. The servants were all our friends and made common cause with us against our tyrant. But Maum Jute above all. Why did she dress herself so? Who knows. They gave her the same clothes which enabled Maum Margaret to go so neat and trim.

Maum Jute was always slip shod, and you could hear her flip flop in regular cadences when she did not object to her whereabouts being known. When on any predatory expedition she went bare foot—and was noise-

12. Fr., maid.
13. Fr., pure-blooded.
14. Fr., this wretched black woman.

less as a cat. She wore a Linsey Woolsey gown, always sufficiently unbuttoned to reveal the absence of all undergarments—and so short as to show the entire contour of those old husky legs set in the middle of her feet. Her much soiled red handkerchief, which she wore as a turban, was always out of plumb. It hung over one ear—or over her forehead, or was pushed back as far as it would go; for when spoken to, her first movement was to scratch her head, and so shove her head gear out of place; it was always toppling, but never fell.

As I have said before—we were not put upon short rations. Our fare was excellent; ample in quantity, perfect in quality. In after years in conversation with Miss Anne memory hovered over those fine turkeys which graced our board on Wednesdays and Sundays.

"The turkey put in front of the Bishop was stuffed with truffles always," said Miss Anne with a faint smile. "You were a lucky girl to sit next to him." And so in this world even no secrets are hid. I had been idiot enough to think every turkey on table, for a hundred school girls, as good as the one put before the Bishop.

But to return to Maum Jute. Nearly every night as noiseless as a mouse she slipped into our room with a contraband supper. In winter oysters—sausages—and rice. In summer Ices. Nougat—and candy always: cocoa nut candy and pender candy[15] the best in the world I still think, [and] a style of confectionary called "Love kisses" all egg and sugar, a species of meringues.

Every Saturday we drew our allowance of fifty cents. That was not a dangerous quantity of pocket money; but all letters from home were apt to contain a bank bill. And Dédé and Maum Jute got it all.

When some of us fell ill of gastric fever, Miss Anne explained to the Doctor that it could not be our diet. She knew how plain and wholesome that was. They could not be more particular in that matter—she said. The Doctor said we had been living on unwholesome trash; and she could not understand it.

It was in that tedious illness and my family still on the Mississippi—far away—that I found how truly kind these people were.

To recruit our strength after this, they took us to Sullivan's Island. It was before the regular season; it was a desert and "we were monarchs of all we surveyed."[16]

15. Peanut candy.

16. Paraphrase of the first line of William Cowper, "Verses Supposed to Be Written by Alexander Selkirk" in *Poems* (London, 1782).

There was however the Garrison at Fort Moultrie[17]—and we listened to the drum—and occasionally got a peep at the Parade. It was a gay and romping holiday, bathing and sleeping our chief duties.

And now I must account for the many good novels that we were allowed to read, as part of our holiday: as we were lying for hours on the mattresses spread over the floor.

At Madame's every day scholar was followed by a servant bringing her basket of luncheon, and her books. These were hardly ever exactly punctual—and so there was a place where these things were put, to be at hand when the owner came for them. I have coolly watched many a basket of books sent there for me—many a smuggled basket of partridges and every imaginable sweet thing. The men that Mamma said would be every where certainly were in town—and continued to be my friends. Once or twice my contraband baskets were confiscated. I was not on the look out and they were left after all day scholars had gone.

Miss Anne went about holding them aloft, calling upon the owner to come forward and claim her property.

I dared not—of course.

At night she would ostentatiously seat herself at the centre table, and read my Pickwick,[18] and parade her laughter. I was raging furiously but I made no sign.

Just before my illness we had one of these scenes.

"Nenaine would you believe there was a girl here, so bold and so reckless, as to allow books to be sent to her without your knowledge?"

"No Anne—it is impossible. I will not believe it."

"Whose basket is this?"

Unbroken silence.

"I found it in the Hall." Then I drew near.

"Miss Anne lend us some of them to read?"

17. A United States fort built in 1811 near the original Fort Moultrie, site of a battle on 28 June 1776, in which a small Continental force successfully defended the city of Charleston against the British fleet. In the 1830s, Moultrie was held by a small garrison. It was from Fort Moultrie that Major Robert Anderson moved into Fort Sumter in December 1860, just prior to the outbreak of the Civil War.

18. Charles Dickens (1812–70), *The Posthumous Papers of the Pickwick Club. The Pickwick Papers* was issued in monthly parts from April 1836 through November 1837. When *The Pickwick Papers* is again mentioned later in *Two Years,* MBC implies that the students at Madame Talvande's were reading it as it came out in installments. Although *The Pickwick Papers* was not published in monthly parts in the United States, Madame Talvande's students may have read several installments in *The Albion,* a New York magazine that republished materials from British journals.

"No—the shepherd suspects all that comes in over the wall, and not at the gate. These may be wolves in disguise."

"Read the names of the books," said some girl—who rarely went beyond that herself.

"Sense and Sensibility. Pride and Prejudice. Marriage, and The Inheritance. Dunallen. Discipline. Jacob Faithful. Peter Simple."[19]

I was wild with delight, and seized "Peter."

Miss Anne darted after me to take it away. I held it aloft—and out dropt a card. Monkey picked it up; and after a glance threw it in the fire.

"What is that?" cried Madame.

"Rubbish," answered Monkey rising to the greatness of the occasion in a manner that left nothing to be desired. She turned her back to Nenaine and Miss Anne. And with her lips she said to me, "Yours."

This accounts for the amount of light Literature turned over to us on the Island. Miss Anne had no time to read them—but she called in an expert, a person of great analytical power, and he could find no trace of poison in all that basket. Indeed he pronounced its contents, "selected with great care." Which I could well believe, for, they came from England, by a sure hand and were sent by one more keenly interested in my maiden purity of thought, and freedom from contamination, than Miss Anne herself.

After this delightful holiday we returned to town in high health and spirits. Madame found it expedient to substitute Friday night parties at her own house, for our Long-Room privileges of amusement.

"Small and Earlies" we would call them now. We were told we would have the right to invite a few friends—and each of us sent up the names of our chosen few. It proved a delusion and a snare. The drawing room was always pleasantly filled, but our lists had been evidently lost or forgotten. A nice supper was always prepared for us before the fatal bell ring.

Our curfew.[20] Did every body go home when the bell rang? or the "Drum-beat?" We did, and moreover every body who came to see us did

19. *Sense and Sensibility* (London, 1811) and *Pride and Prejudice* (London, 1813), novels by Jane Austen; *Marriage* (London, 1818) and *The Inheritance* (London, 1824), novels by Susan Edmonstone Ferrier (1782–1854); *Dunallen; or Know What You Judge* (1st ed., n.p., n.d., 2nd ed., London, 1825), by Grace Kennedy (1782–1825); *Discipline,* novel (Edinburgh, 1814) by Mary Balfour Brunton (1778–1818); *Jacob Faithful* (Philadelphia, 1834) and *Peter Simple* (Philadelphia, 1834), novels by Frederick Marryat (1792–1848).

20. In accordance with an 1823 act, all blacks were to be off the streets after 9 P.M. from 20 September to 20 March, and after 10 P.M. from 20 March to 20 September. Free blacks found violating the curfew were treated as slaves (John Belton O'Neall, *The Negro Law of South Carolina* [Columbia, 1848], 41).

the same. In Summer—it did not seem very long after dark. It was a quaint old custom, gotten up for the benefit of the blacks, as witness their song.

> Bell done ring, drum done beat
> To keep dem darkies out de street—&c &c.

12

From Mrs. Willard's School at Troy[1]

> Stern daughter of the voice of God!
> Oh Duty! If that name we love
> Who art a light to guide, a rod
> To check the erring, and reprove:
> Thou, who art victory and law
> When empty terrors over awe;
> From vain temptations dost set free;
> And calmest the weary strife of frail humanity.[2]

Madame was in marked contrast to my two years' previous experience, in school mistresses.

In the up country our lonely school room[3] had two magnificent oaks— one at each door. They made the glory of the place. Under their wide spread shade our Queen of May was yearly crowned.

1. Emma Willard (1787–1870) began a boarding school in her home after her marriage in 1809 to Dr. John Willard. The citizens of Troy, New York, built her the Troy Female Seminary, which opened in 1821, where she trained young teachers.

2. William Wordsworth, "Ode to Duty," lines 1–9, in *Poems, in Two Volumes* (London, 1807).

3. According to Thomas J. Kirkland and Robert M. Kennedy, *Historic Camden,* vol. 2 (Columbia, S.C., 1926), 272, the school was located "in Mr. Niles' schoolroom on Lyttleton street just above York." On verso of the cover sheet for *Two Years of My Life,* section 5, is the following note: "The greater part of this is written from memory—Though I used my diary, of more than forty years ago, freely. But then no diary was possible in Legare St.
My sister when she read this MSS—asked—Why not discribe Miss Stella's school also. That prepared us for the hard lines at Madame Talvande. You see I have taken her advice." This note helps to date the MS, although not very precisely. An early version of the novel must have been completed (at least through chapter 11) before 1876, when Chesnut's sister Catherine Miller Williams (Kate) died. Her reference to a diary now lost of "more than forty years ago," which must have been kept during the trips to Mississippi, dates the last revisions of the MS to about 1877 or 1878.

We had appealed to Mrs. Willard for help—having arrived at an educational state of destitution. For her selection of teachers, we had cause to be grateful.

Our Principal—Miss Stella,[4] was tall and thin, with blue eyes, and a clear, straight forward look in them; dark hair, what there was of it; beautiful hard white teeth—a fair complexion—a fine face withal, from its honest, pure, expression. [She was] flat chested, awkward and ungainly with a certain unmistakable dignity of bearing, which commanded our respect.

A rigid Presbyterian, not a shadow of injustice or unfairness ever came near her.

Mrs. Willard afterwards made a tour of observation.[5] The townspeople fêted her to the best of their ability. She ought to have felt proud of her proconsuls.

We had huge fire places at each end of our school rooms. And I dare say our poor school mistress, accustomed to better behavior, was driven wild by our undisciplined conduct. We were in the first place hopelessly restless. And to go up and warm, or to go out and drink water presented two very convenient means of stretching our young legs.

Having drunk the bucket of water dry, or slopped it all over the floor, the next move was to ask permission to fill it at the well. Her patience was inexhaustible. Certainly my two years with this excellent woman were invaluable to me.

On Fridays, as my family lived seven miles from town, I was always sent for, to remain at home until Monday.

One Friday our teachers were invited to accompany me.

A conversation which I overheard while they were there, made a strong impression.

My father whose manner to women was always courteous, nay, flattering, was saying the most complimentary [things] to Miss Stella. She was cold, calm, unbending. She said "the governing principle of her life was Duty."

Finally they began to discuss the peculiar danger which environed our northern teachers. "They would marry the untutored natives." She coolly replied, "When I marry—I doubt if I ever shall know any thing of love as a passion; it will be from a sense of duty."

4. Stella Phelps (?-1876) studied at Emma Willard's Troy Female Seminary from 1832 to 1833, when she came to Camden to teach. Miss Phelps, the daughter of John Phelps, a U.S. congressman from Vermont, contributed prose and verse to periodicals (Kirkland and Kennedy, 2:272).

5. Mrs. A. W. Fairbanks records that "It was a favorite pastime for Mrs. Willard to visit her girls as they married and settled in new homes" (*Emma Willard and Her Pupils of Fifty Years of Troy Female Seminary* [New York, 1898], 19).

"God forbid any woman should marry me from a sense of duty," piously and fervently cried the padre. "I married from a sense of beauty. And you see. It was the wisest thing I ever did in my life."

Miss Stella did marry. From what sense—who knows.

She allied her life with that of a widower,[6] with many children, a native born—Male Academy teacher. And in all her new relations in life— Wife—Step Mother, Mother, she continued as before a model of all the virtues.

She took very womanly views of life sometimes. Years after my own marriage I met her at the wedding of one of her former pupils.

She was as kind as ever, but she astonished me by one of her admonitions.

"You were always very wrong in one thing—Helen. You never did yourself justice. A woman should care more for dress than you do. Your sister there dresses beautifully."

She too had an eye to the eternal fitness of things. And I was charmed that she still felt an interest in me—sufficient indeed to lead her to scold my old black velvet, grown shabby in service.

We never saw her fairly roused but once. Some unlucky girl was asked, what noted corps Vermont had furnished in our revolutionary war.

She said she had never heard of any.

"What—you have never heard of The Green Mountain boys,"[7] said our mild teacher with flaming eyes. "And now you may go to the foot of your class." She was from Vermont. And we found her patriotic weakness—the most natural thing in the world.

But this was mere child's play to Madame's angry black eye when a school text book attacked her church. She bit her lips and was silent. She was forced to keep faith with her protestant patrons. But she swelled and raged. Woe to the wight who missed a word then. One girl translated *culte* culture? cultivation? plowing? hoeing? harvesting?

"Will she stand there guessing forever?—Go—Next—Next—What not one of you? Will not some Catholic girl—tell them—the word means worship. They cannot comprehend it." The Thomas à Becket business tried her.

6. Stella Phelps married Henry P. Hatfield, principal of the Camden Academies for males and females, in 1841. Hatfield was a native of New Jersey, but his first wife, Abigail Reed, who had died two years earlier, was a native of Kershaw County. Stella Phelps Hatfield and Henry Hatfield ran the two brick academies until 1845, when they moved to Augusta (Fairbanks, 219; Kirkland and Kennedy, 2:267–68, 272).

7. Regiments of Vermont settlers raised by Ethan Allen in 1770 to prevent the colony of New York from regranting or reselling Vermont lands which New Hampshire had already granted. The Green Mountain Boys later fought in the Revolution.

And John Knox's way with Mary Queen of Scots. But Leo and Luther[8] and the indulgences were more than her patience could endure.

"The air of this room is stifling. Anne Eliza hear this class for me."

Do you fancy I have forgotten my dearest friend of last year? I am neither false nor fickle. For a time Madelaine wrote with surprising regularity. Her life was a very busy one. She was taking lessons in every thing; and at the same time going every where, to see every thing.

Going over, aboard ship, they encountered a family called Hamlin; concerning whom, it was hinted to her, she might write me as much as she pleased.

There was an elder brother whose mother was a southern woman. The father at her death had married a Philadelphian.

This elder brother was a handsome and interesting man—but a confirmed invalid. Madelaine was inclined to think, a very querulous one at times, and given to taxing his brother's patience to the utmost. The younger brother and sister; they were perfection. Their mother was also dead; and they had not been south for years. Their father had been killed. On that subject they acknowledged that Willie was scarcely sane. So that they were at the utmost pains to avoid not only that topic, but any other which might possibly lead their brother's mind back to his trouble. Letter by letter, I felt the intimacy growing before my very eyes.[9]

At one time I wrote, haughtily requesting her to take her ring—which her brother had taken from me. Fortunately I slept upon it. And next morning as the red disk of the sun peeped over the edge of the bay, and those tall Pines on James Island met my eye with all their mournful suggestion; I thanked my stars that the letter was still under my pillow. And I tore it up—into minute strips. Have a man think me jealous? Heavens! How near making a fool of myself I had been.

8. Thomas à Becket, (1118–70), Archbishop of Canterbury, was murdered in his cathedral by knights of Henry II after he had excommunicated the bishops who crowned Henry. He was canonized in 1173. John Knox (1514–72), a leader of the Scottish Reformation, was forced to flee England during the reign of Mary Tudor. He returned to Scotland in 1559, and preached throughout Scotland against Roman Catholicism and against Mary, Queen of Scots. Giovanni de' Medici, Pope Leo X (1475–1521), issued a papal bull in 1520 excommunicating Martin Luther (1483–1546), the father of the Reformation in Germany, who, in 1517, had attacked the Church's practice of selling indulgences by nailing ninety-five theses concerning the value of such indulgences to the door of the church in Wittenberg. Luther publicly burned the bull proclaiming his excommunication.

9. The sense of the following paragraph suggests that Helen fears an intimacy between Sydney Howard and the aforementioned Miss Hamlin.

So I continued to write occasionally, hoping they were enjoying life as I was.

I took good care not to show my strong feeling of disgust at Madelaine's taste. She who knew such charming people at home, to go abroad and get herself mixed up with Mrs. Grindstone's vulgar vendetta clan. Mysteries, and murders—and revenges, and that kind of melodramatic stuff. Of late I had been so contented, that my vivid western experiences were fading in the dim distance. Long since even the new girls yawned when I tried to lug in my hair breadth escapes apropos to nothing.

Now I went in for gloomy poetry. "O'Conner's child," I spouted on Fridays.

> "Spare him Desmond fierce! Oh God—Oh God!
> "His life blood oozing from the sod.
> "The flower of love lies bleeding."[10]

At that time the most prudish matron allowed her daughters to read James' novels which were pouring forth in a perennial stream. "Henrietta Temple"—ticketed—as the most perfect of love stories—and "Vivian Grey" Madelaine sent me. Also "Godolphin"[11] which was then not acknowledged by its author, and which all girls of sixteen thought fascinating. Bulwer's name on the title page would have rendered it contraband. Our books had to be like Caesar's wife, above suspicion. "Helen" and the "Lady of the Manor."[12] To one as reckless in skipping as I was then—this last also was delightful—for there are capital stories buried away in all that sermonizing.

We parsed Milton, and Cowper; we did not read them or commit them to memory. Campbell—and Mrs. Hemans[13] were the poets allowed. We

10. Assorted unconnected lines from Thomas Campbell, "O'Connor's Child" in *Gertrude of Wyoming,* 2nd ed. (London, 1810).

11. George Payne Rainsford James (1799–1860), author of numerous novels, including *Richelieu* (1829), *Attila, a Romance* (1837), *The Gipsy* (1835), *The Robber* (1838), and *Darnley; or the Field of the Cloth of Gold. Henrietta Temple* (London, 1837) and *Vivian Grey* (London, 1826–27) are by Benjamin Disraeli. *Godolphin* (1833) is by Edward George Earle Bulwer-Lytton. Bulwer's name did not appear on the 1833 London edition of *Godolphin,* but did appear in 1840 on a Paris edition (Baudry's European Library) and a New York edition (Harper and Brothers), and on English editions from 1850 on.

12. *Helen* is a novel (London, 1834) by Maria Edgeworth. "Lady of the Manor" is probably Mary Martha Sherwood, *The Lady of the Manor: Being a Series of Conversations on the Subject of Confirmation: Intended for the Use of the Middle and Higher Ranks of Young Women,* first published in London in 1823 and rapidly republished in several versions in the U.S., including a seven-volume edition in Tuscaloosa in 1833. (I am indebted to Michael O'Brien for this identification.)

13. See chap. 10, nn. 18, 21.

had contraband editions of Scott and Byron.[14] We loved Scott's poetry as we did his prose, and language can be no stronger than that.

Pickwick kept us all in a broad grin. Charley O'Malley was sent me in the Albion,[15] all the Hamlins to the contrary notwithstanding. Afterwards we took it regularly for twenty years—and it made me intensely English in all my sympathies.

They saw the girl Queen—Victoria—at the opera. And in the language of the slang of the day, a snob in the pit called, "Little Vic does your Mother know you are out."[16]

Sydney bragged that he took off his hat to the Queen in the Park. There was something interesting in the bright girl Queen, even to democratic Americans.

Finally they drifted away from the Hamlins. The Elder brother was ordered to try a winter in Egypt. Madelaine heard from them, that was certain, but she had ceased to sound their praises. That was a bad sign. When a woman feels it necessary to hold her tongue—.

Mr. Hamlin died in spite of the Nile. And after a great deal of trouble one way or another—Madelaine married the other brother. Sydney said— "his brother in law was a Quaker on the Mother's side. And he thought him the last man in the world to take up all that Mississippi row. He was a Man of the Period, and left vendettas to the stage."

The shadow of him, and his name will cause trouble once more in these pages—but in the flesh we will never see him more. He died, from the same disease as his brother, before he ever revisited America.

In some inscrutable way Old Mr. Hamlin (seeing Macbeth—and hearing the murder of King Duncan described,[17] made me understand the Hamlin story at last;) having left a beautiful daughter, knocking about the world in every body's way, made me a strong Blueskin partisan. Mrs. Grindstone wrote to my mother for a letter of recommendation. Mamma had scruples—but I urged her to send it.

---

14. Many pirated American editions of both authors were available by 1836, as well as numerous English and European editions, but Helen most likely uses "contraband" here to mean forbidden by school rules.

15. Charles James Lever (1806–72), *Charles O'Malley, the Irish Dragoon,* a best-seller generally listed as published in 1841 (in Dublin, Edinburgh, London, New York, and Philadelphia), though at least one edition was published in Philadelphia in 1840. A search of volumes 4–7 (1836–39) of the *Albion* fails to show publication in that periodical.

16. Victoria (1819–1901) succeeded to the throne in June, 1837, at the age of eighteen. An inveterate Anglophile, Chesnut followed the career of the girl queen closely, noting that she, like Chesnut herself, had married in the Spring of 1840.

17. Shakespeare, *Macbeth,* 2.3.

All this happened late in the Autumn when my parents were once more in town. My father fired by the ardent desire to make a large cotton crop, and to pay his debts therewith, for the first time in his life, stayed all summer on the plantation.[18] Every member of the family had fever. And my Mother was ill enough to frighten all thought of ever living in a malarious country out of his head.

The girls were left with me at school and my Mother comfortably settled in apartments at the "Planters."[19] She had Fanny with her—and Willis[20] with her carriage and horses. We were with her from Friday till Monday morning. She was very apt to walk round to see us when ever it was a pleasant afternoon. And she rarely came alone; so many of our friends were always at the Planters.

And then it takes so little to induce a man to risk a visit to a girls' school. It has an invincible attraction—almost as great as a Nunnery. It excites the imagination. They sympathise with the bright young things immured there.

Sometimes we were cut off effectually from the "rest of mankind" by a storm. In that antique world—gentle folk thought they ought to keep out

---

18. In "We Called Her Kitty," Chesnut writes: "Father was spending the winter alone on the plantation. He had brought them all away because of the fever. Mother had it first & as I intimated pretty plainly before she was his first care in the world—While he was devoting himself to her—for she was desperately ill—he failed to notice the children one by one taking the fever. . ." (*MBC*, 31).

19. Planter's Hotel, at the corner of Church and Queen streets (*Charleston Directory; and Register, for 1835–6* [Charleston: David J. Dowling, 1835]), now renovated as the Dock Street Theater. In "We Called Her Kitty," she writes:

The next year all came out—& Kitty & Sally were put at school with me—Kitty as a boarder Sally remained at the Planters Hotel with Mother—who had her own carrige & two servants & rooms there for the winter. Now began a delightful life—which I will hurry to shorten—for it its her life & not mine that I am writing—She & I went home every Friday night & remained with Mother (home meaning Mother) until Monday after breakfast—& Mother invented every manner every manner of excuse to come & see us—& to take us out walking with her. Mad Talvande's scholars were all taken to see whatever was worth seeing—& a good deal besides—& as soon as we were all seated in solid phalanx flanked by Miss Anne Johnson—& her deputies on every side would come some nice young man who had considerately gone for Mother & persuaded her to come too—& Mad T would be requested through him or them (for some times there were two of them)—to allow myself & my sister to sit with our Mother—if there was a box at the Theatre—it would be very nice. Madame thought our Mother very indiscreet—but she dared not refuse.

MBC is here following her own life precisely.

20. Another of Stephen Decatur Miller's servants. In *Two Years*, Willis goes with Helen's mother to Charleston; in "We Called Her Kitty," he is said to have been with Miller in Mississippi throughout Miller's last illness.

of the rain. And they did not like their horses and servants sent out in bad weather either.

The larger part of our school were day scholars, so when not a single one came, which sometimes happened, we had a holiday.

Now Mary Hatherway's father kept a livery stable. Horses and men were nothing to him. Until I led a party of free lances—we had school for Mary Hatherway! All that was soon changed. We watched for her and banged her back with our school bags filled with books.

One day as I flew down stairs with my ardent young troops at my heels, furious for the fray, I was surprised to see Miss Anne dodge into the Cabinet—but I had not a moment to spare and we dashed on. We drove Mary Hatherway down the avenue and into her hack with gaieté de coeur, worthy of Olivier.[21] And she was too happy to be driven. She liked a little gentle violence to be used, as an excuse at home.

Not long before her death Miss Anne said to me, "You nearly caught me once. I had barely time to get out of your way. I did not want to interfere or catch you—before you had cleared the house of Mary Hatherway. When I slipped into Nenaine's room, I told her that I had to run for it, and that I was so closely pursued I had to hide in the Cabinet.

"She answered solemnly, 'Anne if you had suffered yourself to be caught—I would have put you on bread and water for a week.'"

These were the people we thought filled with an intense hankering to teach us night and day.

It grew daily harder for me to leave that perfectly delightful "Planters," after my gay Saturdays and Sundays with the kindest and most indulgent society loving mother in the world—and—reluctant, melancholy, slow, return on Monday morning to reflexive verbs and indefinite articles.

It was race week[22] and the news papers said Carolina had gathered there her beauty and her chivalry.

On the Friday night in question our small parlor was crammed. I suppose I could scarcely mention a name which has not since made itself mem-

21. Émile Ollivier (1825–1913), French statesman and chief minister in Napoleon III's empire, was responsible for the declaration of war with Germany in 1870. His critics forced his resignation, charging that he had undertaken "with a light heart" a war which proved to be a national disaster. These accusations against Ollivier were made in 1873; *Two Years* could not, therefore, have been written prior to that date.

22. Annually in February, races were run on the New Market race course. Harriott Horry Ravenel described the event thus: "The whole low country joined in the sport, as the horses came down with their owners from the different plantations. The schools gave holiday, the law courts closed, the shops were shut, only the sick and the infirm stayed at home" (*Charleston: The Place and the People* [New York, 1906], 129).

orable in its Country's history. Langdon Cheves and Wade Hampton[23] were there.

One feels no scruple in following a woman who is called faultlessly beautiful.[24] Such occasions are rare in one's life. When this party got up to leave, I accompanied them to the Public drawing room door. Forgetful of the people I left behind in my Mother's parlor, I strayed in.

A friend of theirs from Philadelphia was at the Piano, making it hard for me to keep my feet still, with a new batch of Strauss waltzes. Another strikingly handsome young lady from Virginia was waltzing. As we stood near the Piano, she stopped, and presented a man. He wasted no time, but asked me in an out of breath kind of way, to waltz with him.

And I agreed readily.

But I had reckoned without my host. As we were in the act of moving off, Constance laid her restraining hand upon my shoulder—sharply.

"Helen!" in accents of deep disgust. "And you told Nenaine your head ached so—you could n't stay to her Friday night! Mamma says come back instantly. You are so rude to those people in there."

There was nothing to do—but to obey. And likewise to feel that you were found out; that you were playing grown young lady; and you were only a school girl; and every body was laughing at you.

"Mamma is very much offended with you. She told you never to come into these public rooms without her. And she ordered you not to waltz."

"I was with intimate friends of hers. Is that waltzing?" said I angrily, if not candidly.

"You are raving distracted child. Do you mean to say you were not going to waltz? I call that dreadful news. Who was it you were standing up with?"

23. Langdon Cheves (1776–1857), U.S. congressman, 1810–15, Speaker of the House, 1814–15, judge of the Court of Law of South Carolina, 1816–19, president of the United States Bank, 1819–22. Wade Hampton II (1791–1858), of "Millwood" plantation, owned large plantations in South Carolina and Mississippi; his racing stables were recognized for their excellence in sporting circles throughout the United States. MBC may be referring to his son, Wade Hampton III (1818–1902), who continued and enlarged his father's planting interests and, like his father, served in the South Carolina Senate. Wade Hampton III became a lieutenant general during the Civil War, and after the war, served as the first post-Reconstruction governor (1876–79) and as a U.S. senator. He was a friend and political ally of James Chesnut. Langdon Cheves Jr. (1814–63), served with James Chesnut in the Nashville Southern Rights convention of 1852, and in the Georgia secession convention. A captain of engineers during the Civil War, he designed and built the first observation balloon for military purposes.

24. This reference to the "faultlessly beautiful" woman is unclear, presumably one of the party in Mrs. Newtown's parlor.

"That's not grammar."

"Grammar can wait. Who is it?"

"I did not hear his name. You tormenting imp."

"You were standing with a man's arm around your waist! Dry. You were not going to waltz with him—and you do not know his name. Well. I never did! no never! hear a tale like that."

"Mamma if you don't make Constance let me alone—I will go mad."

She was an enfant terrible of twelve years old, clear, cold, logical—remorseless.

The next day we were watching the fine equipages—but more than all, the beautiful horses, as the people drove off.

I pointed to a small man whose turn out was simply perfection, and his horses as fine as any which came from the Hampton or Singleton stables.[25] Fanny had given us a queer story of him. His parlor was next to ours. And we were forced to pass each other so often in the narrow passage that a bowing acquaintance had sprung up—though it had stopped short of a smile on my part—until I could find out his name.

Lots of men were always crowding into his room. A scrupulous maiden lady had taken the room next to his. And the key of a door of communication between the rooms was lost. So Dame Punctiliozo sent for a carpenter and had her side barricaded and nailed. When he came to understand the cause of the hammering; he ordered two nails on his side for every one she had put in on hers. So they kept up for awhile such a rat-a-tat you would suppose they were shingling a house. The next day, this lady, who had been horribly outraged by the counternailing, for she had arrived at years of discretion; in the flurry of arriving from the race course, late for dinner, rushed into the wrong room—by mistake. He was standing with his back to the fire. She was fearfully taken aback. She gave one scream and stood still. He stared at her without moving. She screamed more piteously.

"*Then* why don't you go out!" he said with astonishment.

She fled as fast as a fainting woman may.

"I know her well," said Mamma. "She has never had an adventure before in her life, she will dilate upon, and relate this one to her dying day."

"You mean this approach to one," said one of the men of our party. "It is queer Miss Newtown has never heard his name. He is the best match south of the Potomac. They say his head is turned. The attentions of the demoiselles à marier[26] are so marked."

25. The stables of Wade Hampton at Millwood and those of Richard Singleton at Singleton Hall.

26. Fr., young ladies of marriageable age.

"That's a mistake. They can't turn his head—it is a cool one. Besides do not blame the girls. He is beset by their Mothers. I know the case you mean.

> She kept with care, her beauty rare,
> For the rich came not to woo.[27]

"That is what it amounts to—from all accounts."

13

Quand un Seminole me raconta cette histoire, je la trouvai fort instructive et parfaitement belle parce qu'il mit la fleur desért, la grâce de la cabane, et une simplicité à conter la douleur, que je ne me flatte pas d'avoir conservées.

Atala.[1]

Là sont les héros, les reines; ceux qui se sont acquis un nom; qui ont aspiré à quelque bût noble.

Goëthe.[2]

Man's ingress into the world is naked and bare.
His progress through life is trouble and care.
His egress out of the world, is nobody knows where.
If you do well here, you will do well there.
I can tell you no more if I preach for a year.[3]

The next day Miss Anne met me on King Street—followed by Fanny with a basket.

Out of school we were not only perfectly at ease with one another—we were "great friends."

"Who were those young men who fled when they saw me?"

27. Nathaniel Parker Willis (1806–67), "Unseen Spirits" in *Poems of Passion* (New York, 1843).

1. François-René de Chateaubriand (1768–1848), *Atala* (Paris, 1801), epilogue. "When a Seminole told me this story, I found it very instructive and flawlessly beautiful, because he revealed the bloom of the desert, the charm of the cabin, and a simplicity as he talked about his sorrow that I do not pretend to have preserved."

2. MBC attributes this to Johann Wolfgang von Goëthe, but the precise source of the quotation, certainly a French translation of one of Goëthe's works, has not been identified. "There are the heroes, the queens; those who acquired a name for themselves, who have aspired to some noble aim."

3. John Edwin (1749–90), *The Eccentricities of John Edwin,* 2d ed. (London, 1791), 1:74.

"Nobody in particular. Mamma knows them. They are nice enough."

"Satisfactory though vague! but if Mamma approves—it is no affair of mine. Amélie—says you give every body a name. You call her brother 'The Mediterranean Sea.'"[4]

"When that began I really did not know his name. He laid the scene of all his stories in the Mediterranean—none of us had been there—and it was a distinction."

"Don't you like him?"

"Most assuredly. Why should I not like him? He is nothing to me."

"Exactly. Now what do you think of that brother of Madelaine Howard?"

Never dreaming of such a facer I was looking innocently in her very eyes. I could not blink it. And the blood flooded my face, I felt as if it would never stop mounting into my very hair.

I said—valiantly, "I do not know him. He was on the plantation—he did not come to town."

"Those girls say you blush for nothing—now I know it is true. You are of a scarlet hue—because I spoke of a man you never saw. You do know Sydney Howard however—he was forever dawdling around Madelaine and you. And the 'Mediterranean' says he was out west and at your house last year. Come now. What do you think of him?"

"Why should I think of him?"

"I wonder if any man will ever make you confess that you like him—I doubt if you ever own it to yourself. You see I know you."

"Why do you think he went west last winter?

"And why—ah why? do you think it necessary to make a mystery of it. Why are you afraid to trust yourself to make a civil speech about him. You lavish so many—you throw them on the right hand and on the left when you do not care a fig for the person praised.

"Miss Anne still keeps her little bird—she hears every thing. The Mediterranean was not deep enough to drown the story. Last night we were amused with a wild legend. You ran away from our Friday, with a head ache, and you missed the fun.

"The 'Sea' was disappointed; he came to talk it all over with you. You were shut up by disasters by field and fell. I hope 'fell' means water and freshets—or even broken bridges. And he would not have fretted if it had lasted a week.

"But the first night the gallant Howard paddled in a dug out across a creek

4. Any reader of *Mary Chesnut's Civil War* recognizes that it was Chesnut herself who loved farcical nicknames, especially those which alluded to literature or turned on a pun, and who bestowed them liberally.

a mile wide for the nonce, with a coach and four in his wake, and he bore off their heroine with out so much as a 'dam your eyes'—which is a naval salute. But a bit of paper in the hands of the coachman threw light on the mid night flitting. It bore the names of Mr. Newtown and Sydney Howard—with a guarantee for payment—after the unceremonious use of his carriage.

"The darkey had fraternized with your dignified Dick—who answered for Mr. Howard as a responsible man, said he knew all about him—he was 'rich as creases,'⁵ and had been all the winter in your neighbourhood. I dare say they brought you back to stop it. Your old folks could not listen to such nonsense at your age."

"Miss Anne is it true old Sparrow hawk has taken his daughter from you."

"Yes. There is no gratitude in man. Your father is satisfied I hear—but Sparrow hawk says we neglect that dunce of his. Just as I had beaten some geography in her head—she has gone! She was away a month at Christmas and a month at Easter. There must be gaps in her head. The class can't stop when she goes. They were at Texas—and she came back; without so much as crossing the Atlantic, lo! She was in Turkey. Such gaps. She could never know any thing. And grammar! I said, 'Nenaine—the class did verbs— while that dull child was gone.' Nenaine said, 'Anne take her—and make [her] conjugate faithfully all by herself. A girl can not skip verbs.' And I was at it night and day—when Don Pompioso came and said—'she was doing nothing'—but as I was saying of the Howards."

"Come Miss Anne. Take Miss Newtown to see the Seminoles."⁶

With a grateful alacrity I turned to my deliverer. Between us we soon overpowered kind hearted Miss Anne, and we followed her into the court yard of the Planters. There they were—like a monkey show—with a crowd of boys and negroes looking on—The Indian Warriors.

Micanopy who was of Falstaffian proportions, bodily and mentally, sat eating and drinking and laughing.

Not so Osceola. His was the saddest face I ever saw. A rigid, bronze face—from which nothing more might be hoped of good or evil. Under that red skin it seems there was a heart to be broken. The whole effect of

5. Play on Croesus, king of Lydia (560–46 B.C.), legendary for his great wealth.
6. Osceola (1800?-38), Seminole leader, was seized in October 1837 and brought to Charleston in December to be imprisoned in Fort Moultrie. Micanopy (sometimes spelled "Mico-an-opa" or "Mick-e-no-pah"), principal chief of the Seminoles, was captured and imprisoned with Osceola. The chiefs were apparently well treated in Charleston. They were allowed to leave the fort to attend the theater on 6 January 1838, for example. (Mark F. Boyd, "Asi-Yaholo or Osceola," *Florida Historical Quarterly* 33 [January–April, 1955], 249–305, and Edwin C. Bearss, *Osceola at Fort Moultrie* [Washington, D.C., 1968].)

his statue like stillness and immobility was "dignity in defeat." "The Seminole chiefs had been captured under a flag of truce," they said.[7]

I did not feel too proud of my country. And I did not stay there many
minutes. I had seen the Creeks making ready to leave their happy hunting
grounds. And I had seen an ex Chief, just as the Choctaws had gone forever
from theirs.[8] And I had heard him ironically picture the kind welcome of
the savage to the pale face, and the christian virtues of the latter as they prepared to improve him off the land. He was given to compare the exiled savage—and the christian virtues of those who had replaced him. Likewise in
a jeering way he extolled the justice and clemency of the U S A, and its policy of extermination.

Freedom to worship God. If befriending the Indians could with a double barrelled fire subdue and harass a political enemy—how many Philanthropists would arise in an hour.

But for the poor savage—there is no friend. It seemed to me that my
country had not dealt magnanimously with these aborigines of the soil. And
I found the dignified Osceola a sad spectacle.

That night my mother waked us up by shrieking dismally.[9] And she refused to go to sleep again—saying her dreams were too vivid and too horrid. She felt sure something wrong had happened, out west. She was de-
pressed all day Sunday and dreaded the approach of night.

She had not heard from my father for two weeks and her dreams grew
worse and worse.

"Naturally!" said one of her friends, "for you are miserable all day and so
your mind is affected by night, painfully, and it all ends in night mare."

My Mother belonged to the days of superstition. She was far more given
to such terrors than her children. She insisted upon relating an adventure
of mine, which occurred as we were going west. Her facts were correct and
I could not contradict her.

At one of the houses where we stopped to rest for a few days, as I went
up stairs, and heard I was to be the only person on that story I said, "All
right—this house is perfectly new, it can not be haunted."

7. Osceola was summoned for a conference with General Thomas S. Jessup; he arrived
under a flag of truce, and Jessup ordered him seized. At the time Helen would have seen
him (and, of course, Mary Miller did see him) Osceola probably had malaria; he died three
weeks later from influenza of the throat (Bearss, *Osceola*). After Osceola's death, his surgeon,
Frederick Weedon, is reputed to have secretly removed the Seminole's head just prior to bur-
ial and kept it, embalmed, in his home, to be shown as a curiosity (John K. Mahon, *History
of the Second Seminole War, 1835–1842* [Gainesville, Fla., 1985]).

8. Greenwood LeFlore: see chap. 6, n. 4.

9. In "We Called Her Kitty," MBC writes: "for several weeks Mother was haunted with
the night mare & dreams that he was ill—but we laughed at dreams."

"No we have only lived here since the tenth of the month."

As soon as I fell asleep I was waked by Negroes fighting and screaming. Yells; blows; dead bodies dragged about and finally flung down stairs.

I longed for day. This tale I told at breakfast table next day, to account for my pale cheeks. The eyes of the lady of the house were glued to her tea cups. But the oddity of my fancy amused the others highly. Black ghosts were a decided innovation. White as sheets—were the regulation ghosts they said.

I determined to remain below for the next night. And as I rested on Mamma's bed, a quaint little child came in not more than five years old. She crept up to the bed side and watching her opportunity whispered, "You saw Dinah and big Jake last night. They were up there while this house was building." She pointed over head. "Sam got up there too—though they had pulled up the ladder after them. To be sure he could not come. He killed them with his axe. And he flung them down. He was engaged to be married to Dinah. He ran away and hid in the swamp. He came in for fire. Some of Dinah's kin caught him. He is in jail—and they will hang him soon."

Comment is useless. That night I slept by Mamma's side. At breakfast next day, I was asked if I had seen the orthodox article in white.

"Yes—a ghostly assembly—as many as in Tam O'Shanter's ride."[10] This inordinate supply of them, provoked more violent mirth than before. I did not join the peals of laughter which beset me.

My little friend fluttered about me, important and mysterious. She proposed a walk.

I suggested a short cut across those cotton rows.

"Not cotton."

"Then they are corn beds that have not had their rows levelled."

"There was a church here, but it is moved. But they did not move the dead people in the grave yard!" said the little thing mournfully. "This was a grave yard, and mother will not let any body meddle with it."

14[1]

Monday we were sent for. Mrs. Newtown wanted us—and gave no reason for it. Suddenly that great bee hive hum was stilled. The house seemed quiet

---

10. Robert Burns, "Tam O'Shanter" (first published in *Edinburgh Magazine* [March 1791], included in Francis Grose's *Antiquities of Scotland* [Edinburgh, 1791]), in which Tam O'Shanter goes on a drunken ride and encounters witches and warlocks.

1. This chapter (numbered on the MS out of sequence as "15—chap—") is extremely short, begins uncharacteristically in the middle of a MS page, and has no epigraph. This evidence suggests that Chesnut intended to expand the chapter.

and empty. We did not meet any of the girls on the stairs. And the Pianos were dumb. As I stepped towards Nenaine's door to say good b'ye—I heard her hastily lock it inside.

The kind friend who came for us, was so silent and grave, I was sure my mother must be ill.

He reassured me on that point. "Though she is not well, for she is in bed."

So little did I anticipate the blow about to overwhelm us, that I remember my annoyance in the street at one of my usual careless tricks—where dress was concerned. We wore slippers then—even when out on the pavements. Now I had hurriedly changed my dress and put on a blue black silk—forgetting my white stockings. It was scant and short—and I knew my self to be an uncouth figure. With my head running on black silk stockings I entered the Planters.

We saw some of our acquaintances rapidly moving out of our way in the corridor; but we met nobody.

As the door of our room was gently pushed upon—we saw Fanny crying at a window. We hung back frightened. My mother heard us. She started up in bed—and stretched out her hand.

"Children you are fatherless!"[2]

15

Bonheur de se revoir[1]

> She pointed to the title of that book,
> Then gave me one imploring piteous look.
> It was a tale of one, whose fate had been
> Too like her own to make that weeping strange;
> Like her transplanted from a sunnier scene;
> Like her, all dulled and blighted by the change.[2]

2. MBC's father died on 8 March 1838. In "We Called Her Kitty," MBC writes: "—When Kate & I got to the Hotel we saw no body—all was so quiet on that corridor they opened Mothers door & we walked in—I began to be nervous but never for a moment thought of the trouble to come—still nobody said any thing—I noticed one of my Aunts with her handkerchief to her eyes—we went up to the bed—& I said What is it Mother? She sat up—seized me by the shoulder & said—'You poor fatherless children.'"

1. Fr., the happiness of meeting again. Immediately following this epigraph, a note in pen reads "scrappy patchy," indicating that Chesnut intended to expand this section, perhaps by cutting and pasting excerpts from other versions, now lost.

2. Caroline Elizabeth Norton (1808–77), "The Creole Girl; or, The Physician's Story," part 2, stanzas 9–10 in *Poems*, vol. 1 (New York, 1859).

If that long dreary cotton field, ending in a double log house, had caused a sinking of my heart two years ago, when we were all together—bright and hopeful, what was it now? We came in the stage, and at the little town nearest our place we found two saddle horses, for us—and an ox waggon for the luggage. Our poor old Landau had shared the family misfortunes. It had been sent for a thorough repairing, to a carriage maker's; before the bill was paid, the livery stable, horses, carriages, every thing, was burnt up—in a large fire. We lost the Landau—but we had to pay the bill, for its "doing over."

We were met on the plantation by wailings—tears, shrieks—noise and lamentation loud enough to wake the dead. I found it all hard to bear, but my Mother said—it was just such a tribute of respect and sympathy as she had a right to expect from them.

The log house looked as dismal as a prison. And "Banks and Braes"—stood silently wringing her hands.[3]

We had trouble enough. Every thing that could go wrong seemed to have availed itself of that inherent power. We had sent out a lawyer as our forerunner. He took from Dick, to whom his master had entrusted them—with a recommendation to place them in his mistress's hands, and hers only, all of the valuable bonds and papers—and transferred them to the only person who had a motive or wish to injure us. They were made way with—and the person entrusted with them had gone to Texas. We never heard again of either man or papers—or indeed of the nine hundred bales of cotton made that year. It was attached at every wharf—for every small debt any agent of Mr. Newtown had contracted.

Old chief Choctaw came to us, and denounced, "white people's tactics, namely that it was no sin to cheat widows and orphans."

Our friends were as kind as ever; but a sale was inevitable—and we had to lie upon our oars until a certain amount of advertisement prescribed by law was accomplished. The wolves paid their respects to us as before—and the owls down in the Bayou hooted at us without remorse. And my heart was like lead in my bosom.

One day I was sent to a friend's house on business; her husband was a lawyer. On a very dusty corner shelf I captured a few books: Two huge volumes of Waldie's Circulating Library—among other things containing "Japhet in search of a father," Josephus—and a Comstock's Chemistry.[4]

3. Another of MBC's nicknames, from Robert Burns, "The Banks o'Doon," stanza 1, in *Johnson's Musical Museum* (Edinburgh, 1787–97). "Banks and Braes" here is almost certainly a slave who played a minor role in the missing two chapters.

4. *Waldie's Select Circulating Library* (Philadelphia: A. Waldie, published biweekly from 1832 through 1842, and bound semiannually); *Japhet in Search of a Father* (New York, 1835), a novel

Dick wrapped them up in his handkerchief—and tied the bundle behind his saddle. The novels I devoured first. Then the Jewish Chronicle. And a fascinating book I found it. It sent me studying the apocrypha—and the Jewish history of the Bible. Years after—the feeling had not died within me. And I found Merivale's account of those Maccabbes[5] and their unparalleled fight against numbers—good generalship—and training—the most wonderful, and the most eloquent chapter in his history.

When Comstock had been twice conned from cover to cover, I stumbled upon an odd volume of Dufief.[6] So I worked at French once more.

Our faith in humanity had been rather hardly shocked. Every body seemed to enjoy it—when they got the better of us.

A man walked in with his saddle bags on his arm, and gave the customary loud salutation; though standing in a few feet of us.

It was our bedroom—but the door was wide open. Nobody stopped now. The servants—the house gang, they called themselves, whose cabins were very near our house, sent all travellers to the overseer's quarters, which were a mile off.

The man keeping his hat on walked to a table and deposited his saddle bags, and his rifle.

My Mother [was] saying to me all the time, in an undertone, "Why don't you send for Dick?"

To the intruder she humbly apologised, urging him to do as the others did, and take himself off to the overseer's house.

He planted himself squarely in the middle of the room; and in tones as quiet, as he would use in calling the cows, he yelled.

"Answer me one question first. Are you the widow Newtown? There now—."

Mrs. Newtown had never heard herself called so before. And she drew back—as if she had received a blow.

---

by Frederick Marryat, serialized in *Waldie's Select Circulating Library,* July–December, 1835; Flavius Josephus (37–c. 98 A.D.), Greek historian who wrote *History of the Jewish War* and *Antiquities of the Jews;* John Lee Comstock (1789–1858), *Elements of Chemistry* (Hartford, Conn., 1831). Cf. "We Called Her Kitty": "We lived ten miles from the gentleman's house I had been at—& our only means of locomotion was plow horses—Still I contrived to bring away heaps of books—one I remember was Josephus—which I read & reread—Mrs B. & Emily—on Chemistry & Natural Philosophy—I went through over & over again."

5. Charles Merivale (1808–93), *History of the Romans under the Empire* (London, 1850–64). MBC probably refers here to volume 6, chapter 59.

6. Nicolas Gouin Dufief (1776?-1834), author of textbooks for the study of romance languages. MBC here refers to *Nature displayed in her mode of teaching language to man; being a new and infallible method of acquiring languages with unparalleled rapidity* (Philadelphia, 1804).

"Don't you remember the horse your husband sold me on the road two years ago? I have come to pay for him—principal and interest.

"That was a capital bargain for me—but times has been bad, and I have been slow a payin."

He drew out a leather pocket book and began to count out the bills which he laid, upon the table nearest to him.

We desired to cultivate an acquaintance so auspiciously begun. The whole transaction of the sale of the horse, was discussed to its minutest particular. And then we asked him to stay all night.

He enjoyed his visit amazingly. So did we. And he gave Mrs. Newtown a world of practical advice, and information as to plantation matters, which she sadly needed.

He persuaded me to attend a "big meeting" in the neighbourhood.

As we rode up to the Meeting we found it clustered round a half finished house, in a virgin forest. We were asked in the shell of a house. The face of the Earth as far as one could see, was covered by gigs—Jersey wagons— saddle horses—carts.

Inside the family were at breakfast. The man of the house was as new a comer as ourselves. The Choctaws had been gone so short a time.

He was very agreeable, and talked so much as other men do, that I felt inclined to class him with those whom Mamma said "I was sure to find every where." We were gayly recounting our western experiences while discussing a tender venison steak, when some sour individual who thought business should go before pleasure—called out in Methodistically solemn accents, "Brother Samson—you are appointed to lead in prayer."

Without a murmur, down on his knees went my late chatty interlocutor. I listened in amazement if I did not pray.

It was an eloquent appeal to the Almighty to keep his covenant. He had promised. We had his promise; he was a covenant God. There was his bond. We had it in black and white. Those exact followers of Calvin,[7] they like documents legally executed—be the parties who they may.

Some how when he came back, I could not renew the broken strands of our conversation.

Then came sermons and sermons, and hymns to stir the calmest soul.

After breakfast next day our guest prepared to depart.

---

7. John Calvin (1509–64) drew attention to the Hebrew concept that God had voluntarily entered into a covenant or contract with man whereby man is bound to Him by grace. One group of Calvin's followers, known as the Covenanters, were Scottish Presbyterians who subscribed to covenants or bonds pledging to maintain their religious freedom. In the seventeenth century, many of these people immigrated to America; large numbers of them settled in the South.

"What's the damage?" he said with his hat on and his saddle bags on his arm. He took out his pocket book.

"What are you two staring at? You won't take pay. Is that it? You ought. These logs are only daubed with mud. You sat before your chaney cups[8] and saucers—but you sat on a candle box turned upside down. You have only three chairs—and one is in my room." Our faces did not encourage a further inventory of our poverty. So he put up his pocket book.[9]

"Highty tighty! Your foolish fine notions wont suit these parts."

Kitty had told me of the fate of my beautiful white clapboard leanto— it fared black and grimy now. Soon after I left home two years ago Fanny's mother always prolific had proved herself an overbearing woman by producing three children at a birth—and killed her self in so doing. Two of them were born dead. So Fanny fell heir to a baby of a few hours old. She was moved into the shed room—called mine.[10] And then her conscientious mistress gave her little opportunity to shirk this duty. At times Fanny seemed weary of her life, I am sure she loathed her little sister and all the trouble and self denial she entailed.

We had tried to teach Fanny all we knew—but she disliked the preliminary drudgery, and contrived to be out of the way whenever we were ready to hear her lessons. She was not fond of trouble; though very amiable. I dare say when her little sister Chreesia grew serviceable to her, and no longer the plague of her life, that she became devoted to her.

At last she announced the fact that she read better than we did—and scornfully added, "Does you all reckon you is the only ones who kin read— a plenty of 'em knows all about it a sight better than you does.

"I can read every book in this house."

"Then you can do more than I can." And I handed her one.

"I am readin it easy—no use to read loud except in church."

"Do you understand that language?"

"Yes—it is easy as A. B. C. to me."

It was Don Quixote in Spanish.

8. China cups.

9. *Cf.* "We Called Her Kitty": "Sometimes guests of the most distinguished wandered into our swamp—& once a benighted individual asked Mother—'Whats the damage'? He meant to pay—he saw that she gave all the chairs to her unexpected company & sat on a box & we crouched about her."

10. MBC revised this passage about Fanny and the babies completely, writing in pencil between the lines of the ink draft, but without canceling any of her original draft; the passage as it appears in the edited text represents the most probable reading. In chapter 13, Fanny is at the Planters Hotel with Mrs. Newtown, and does not seem to have a child with her. Therefore, this statement that Fanny became the child's guardian "two years ago" constitutes a discrepancy.

A letter came for her now—and she was forced to ask me to read it to her. She acknowledged that she had been to "fountain head."[11] That Miss Stella had written the letter, to which this was an answer, for her, to Mr. Howard's man; "his body servant" she called him. She could only remember that "Miss Stella called her a lone sparrow on the house top—mourning for her mate. She let it go, because it was pretty—but the gentleman's name was Matt—short for Matthew."

Mr. Howard's letter opened finely—and afterwards grew so eloquent in Matt's name that I forget it—. It began:

> Men from England bought and sold me,
>   Paid my price in paltry gold;
> But though slave they have enrolled me
>   Minds are never to be sold.
> Fleecy locks and black complexion
>   Cannot forfeit nature's claim;
> Skins may differ, but affection
>   Dwells in white and black the same.[12]

I belonged to Mrs. Newtown's sewing society—for making negro clothes—but I learned from Fanny the art of not doing more than I liked. I found as soon as I finished one garment another was handed to me. So I inquired how much Fanny was required to do, that is before she was her sister's nurse. That easy task I took upon myself—and no more.

Sunday we had always a black reception. Every creature on the plantation came sometime during the day. I said, "Mamma. You are always reading your bible and prayer book. Why don't you lecture them like the Lady of the Manor?"

"Because I wish above all to set an example of respect for sacred things. From the youngest girl who has just 'got religion' to the oldest crone. They all come here and preach and pray me wild."

"You never show that you are bored."

"If I behave decently it is more than you do—I have seen you shake behind a newspaper, until I feared you'd fall to pieces."

At that time I made my final effort to see something of my white compatriots and then I gave it up forever. I had accepted an invitation to dinner five miles away. I left them all quite well at home—and unusually cheerful.

11. This reference is obscure; it may refer to the fictional town from which the Newtowns moved to Mississippi—as the town's name or, more likely, nickname, apparently introduced at some point in the missing two chapters.

12. William Cowper, "The Negro's Complaint," lines 5–8, 13–16, in *The Poems of William Cowper,* ed. J. C. Barley (London, 1905), 453.

We had a favourite servant called Hannah. She had struck work. The Doctor pronounced her case incurable heart disease. We visited her cabin, and she came very often to see us—with a basket of needle work—she said—"for a witness." This infatuated old African fancied herself in love, and engaged to marry our coachman, who to do him justice was ready to marry every body, a saffron colored Don Juan.

Another woman claimed a similar promise from him. And they rushed in—"to let Missis know."

Missis at first declined to hear of Willis' love affairs in all their complications. This hurt Hannah, too light a view was taken of her wrongs. She began to declaim violently—and to call upon God to sustain her statement. She gave one long howl—and fell down dead at my Mother's feet.[13]

When I came home—Mamma was ill in bed. I blamed myself for leaving her; but she was glad I had escaped so painful a scene. And the Doctor only wondered it had not happened long before.

Of course I did not leave home again.

The mail day was our supreme hour. I had a letter from one of the girls. Pickwick—was now the everlasting topic—it pervaded the air. When Miss Anne condensed her w's, said, "The girls—in *werbs* may now come up," instead of the behind backs grin—and "Double you—double you—I'll trouble you," it now was "Spell it with a we—Samivel."[14]

16[1]

Another most unexpected letter said, the writer had sent me another box of books which I had received some time ago:

13. Cf. "We Called Her Kitty":
one woman who was a great favourite came in to see Mother while I was gone—on my one visit—she sat on the floor by the hearth & began a love story—tho she was middle aged—after telling her tale her own way—& the deluding being Willis—& Mother was to talk to him & shame him for his perfidy—She got up—& courtisied—"good bye my Misses"—& fell in an apoplexy or something before she got to the door—It took Mother some time to get help—& the poor thing with all they could do died there before her eyes. So when I came home I found Mother in bed—ill—& the Negroes enjoying an immense sitting up—singing—shouting—praying—a run mad Africanized *wake*—That ended all visiting.

14. Sam Weller, Pickwick's servant in Charles Dickens' *The Posthumous Papers of the Pickwick Club,* pronounces "v" as "w" and vice versa.

1. The penciled words "scrappy patchy here" on the manuscript are undoubtedly a note to indicate that MBC intended to expand this chapter and add an epigraph.

Who do you think is in this House? "The Arundel!"[2] Thanks to Mrs. Newtown's letter of recommendation—she is here with her pupils. Mrs. Grindstone.

She showed me your letter. I find your life dreary and pathetic—beyond what I can bear for you. You were truly eloquent in depicting your woes. And I am so deeply affected—that I will not wait for the letter of my promise to fulfill itself. I am coming. It was hard enough to wait before—now it is impossible.

I think your father would like me to act at once—I confessed to him the day Dickson was killed. And I was absolved; but a penance was attached of two years' separation; nor was the privilege of writing conceded.

He trusted me. And as you know I have kept faith with him—quand même.[3]

I feel—while things are so uncomfortable for Mrs. Newtown and yourself, that he would not blame me for anticipating the time—somewhat. I will not be long behind this letter.

But I must tell you how I was startled to day. My self control is very great—and I am sure I needed it all. I did not betray myself.

I saw as I thought Mrs. Grindstone in man's clothes, masquerading in the Green Park. She had her mouth concealed under a heavy moustache. She wore her hat tipped slightly over one eye. Her coat was buttoned up to her throat and those huge feet of hers encased in broad bottomed English boots. What could I do? but follow her and stare. She seemed perfectly unconscious.

She had evidently never seen me before, and she coolly gave me look for look. She walked on and I followed her—the more, as she was going my way. The Arundel House was her destination, as it was mine. As I persisted in my parallel movement—she eyed me truculently. Her eye became more savage every moment, but like a fascinated bird, I had no power to draw back.

As we were making our way along a corridor of the Hotel, Dromio

2. The Arundel seems to be both the name of the hotel and another nickname, this time for Mrs. Grindstone, and possibly a reference to Lady Blanche Arundell (1583–1649), who defended her castle against attack by the Parliamentary army for nine days in 1643. "The Arundel" may also be a pun on "hirondelle," sometimes spelled "arundell," a word meaning "swallow" and generally used in connection with the swiftness of the swallow's flight (*Oxford English Dictionary*, 2d ed., s.v. "hirondelle"). Mrs. Grindstone had, in chapter 3, taken swift flight from her would-be pursuers.

3. Fr., all the same.

number two[4]—barred the way: Mrs. Grindstone, in her morning cap, billowy, flounced, and flowing, a mass of every thing feminine, lace and muslin, enveloping her agitated and nervous bulk. She waved her hand imperiously. "Go back! For God Sake! Go back," she cried, standing directly in front of us. "We have not a moment to lose. Take him in your room—I will explain there." She rushed into my room—white—or yellow with fright.

"The Hamlins are here. I saw him in time—his name is on his porte manteau." What would Madelaine have thought! She mistook my servant for Arthur Hamlin.

"I flew to warn you—poor boy!" she cried clinging to her brother. Just then my English servant walked in with a box, Arthur Hamlin's name in full marked upon it. I was to take it, across the Atlantic, to a member of that numerous family. Col. Blueskin pulled out a revolver from some unseen recess in his back, and stood with his face to the door.

"I dont want to do it—No. No more blood on my hands—not if I know it. But I won't be shot down like a mad dog. Do you take me for a sheep?"

Mrs. Grindstone was trembling like a leaf, and wiping her eyes.

I sent the man away and turned the obnoxious package with its face to the wall.

Then I explained. The only Hamlin who had sworn vengeance against them was dead. It would be odious on my part to bring them across my brother in law's path—but he would take any amount of pains to keep out of their way. He was a cultivated, gentle, refined, man of the Period. To connect him with schemes of vengeance, and a savage seeking for any man's blood was an absurdity.

To divert their minds I described the terrible murder of Dickson. She wept spasmodically. And he swore strange oaths—deep and dark—under his beard.

He turned to me, and spoke with great rapidity.

"It was no quarrel of mine. When I came home, I found them at it. Sister tell him. You heard me declare again, and again, that I would not be drawn into it.

"This old man had come since I went away. Before God he gave me no chance. It was kill or be killed. He knew me at first sight. It was only bad luck took me that road. I was going the other; but did not

4. One of twin slaves in Shakespeare's *A Comedy of Errors.*

want to get off my horse and pull down rail fences—enough to cure me of laziness—I should think.

"We are so much alike. He said, riding coolly up, 'And so he has sent one of his cubs.' Even then I did not know who he was. But he began firing away.

"When he fell from his horse I galloped off. How could I leave him there lying across the road? I called a fellow I met to help me. And we went back. By that time his old grey head was soaked in blood. It was a hard sight. And his wide open eyes followed me. They do yet; you may say what you please. There they are now.

"My God! he was heavy. We toted him to the nearest house. And I swore never to kill anybody—if I could help it.

"Life is sweet. He gave me no chance. It was my life or his'n. That is why I run away—I mean that is why I kept out of their reach. I did not want any more blood shedding. And they would have shot me down as a wild cat or a panther or any wild varmint. And I would have defended my life—as long as I had a shot in my pocket—or a grain of powder."

"Oh you poor dear creature," wept his sister. "Go home tomorrow with Mr. Howard. Thank Heavens we are not on the Continent; no need to delay for pass ports here."

"Go home did you say. Do I dare? Wouldn't I like it? I make a poor figure in this grand old world. I was born a frontier man. They call it justice—and bringing me to trial. It is my life they hanker for.

"Don't you think I want to see my own little cotton patch? It rains here forever. I say, 'That shower would be good for the corn.' And then I groan. Who plants cotton or corn on my land now? And all because I turned down the wrong end of the road that morning. God's will be done!

"It's nature for a man to defend his own life. Much as I have suffered, I might do it again."

I persuaded him to begin anew in California. And I even offered to find for him a trust worthy lawyer and an agent to look after his affairs. "You mean," said he bitterly, "to sell me out."

Then he stalked forth in all the majesty of his ugliness—and I meekly followed. In view of the astounding family likeness I inquired what manner of man was the feu Grindstone.

"There warnt none," he said with a grin, and then relapsed into his former forlorn and desolate aspect.

"My father soon died—and she was left alone. She was afraid to stay. Being she is book learned and talented, we thought she could go as a teacher—and get a decent home that way too. I had made our name ring in the country. She wanted to change it; she had no time to pick and choose. As we were bemoaning over hard fate two men were grinding their axes. 'Grindstone,' she said, 'that will suit me down to the ground.' And Grindstone it was.

"A widow is free to come and go. We are all hard featured. My Mother was the first one who told me 'Don't try to run on your face. My little son—your beauty wont take you very far.'

"Sometimes I am glad the poor soul is dead. She was a good soul.

"My sister and me—we are as like as two peas."

My Mother's old maid whom we called Maumer was a privileged character. I said to her with deferential politeness, "Why not keep a bed room in order—some one might drop in suddenly."

"It's a lonesome place. Nobody is likely to come. If they do Missis wont let them stay. Orders is, 'make 'em all go to the overseer's house.'"

"Can't you for once in your life do as you are bidden—and not stop to argue."

"Who is she looking fur? I say—Miss Helen—do you want him to come for true true?"

"Have mercy on us! You are more cantankerous every day. What is the matter with you?"

"Nothing, honey. I wanted to know—to make sho. There is three sho things in this world. If you break a looking glass—seven years trouble. If you cut a frock out Friday, you'll never live to wear it. If you make up a bed—the people won't come to sleep in it. So if you *wants* company don't let any body tetch a bed."

"Some night when I send for you after you are undressed and in bed— you will be sorry you were so lazy and so contrary."

"Oh! If I've gone to sleep—I wont come that's all. Kin always send one of the chillen. Stop Missy. The spine of your back is too stiff. 'Pride comes before a fall.' 'Be ye poor even as I am poor.' You know who says that? 'Out of the mouth of suckling babies and the wayfarers though a fool.'[5]

"Your ma listens to the good book. She is a born angel of goodness.

"How about Jinerwery. He conjured Lorena into fits. And you would never believe it. But your Ma got your pa to sell him. Suppose she'd a listened to you. He'd a had us all—conjured silly by this time."

"Many things happen—and no thanks to the conjuror. January laughs

---

5. "Pride comes before a fall," Prov. 16:18; "Be ye poor even as I am poor," Luke 6:20; "Out of the mouth of . . . a fool," Ps. 8:2, Matt. 21:16.

to split his sides at your foolishness. He is very comfortably situated in town. And he always hated the country. He says 'He only made faces at you'; turning his eye balls—and his mouth inside out. I do not wonder you were scared."

Poor "Braes of Balquedder"—often strayed into the even sadder "Banks and braes of Bonny doon,"[6] as she beat time—on the clothes. But now—though she was eternally washing at the Bayou, she had got religion. And she sung Psalms and Hymns with a deep resounding voice, we had heretofore given her no credit for. At that moment she was pouring forth a terrible Camp Meeting Hymn. "The bending of the mighty trees, before that last blast. The shaking of the Earth as it yawned—and cracked in that fearful day of Judgment."

It was too awful a theme for me. Humbly—I bowed to her—and hurried away.

I had the letter in my pocket still. It was burning there. It was more of life—and not death, that I wanted.

As I slowly returned to our log cabin, I passed Dick's house. In his shirt sleeves, with a hat on his head, and a pipe in his mouth he was sunning himself on a log. So far my efforts to secure a calf for my prodigal's return, had signally failed.

Still with undaunted courage I advanced to the charge.

As I approached, Dick arose—put down his pipe and took off his hat.

"I am glad to see you so comfortable."

He groaned. In the tone of an exhorter at a revival he said, "While the lamp holds out to burn, The vilest sinner may return."[7]

"Ah please Dick! Never mind all that now. Here is a present for you. Somebody is coming—that I want you to take care of."

"He can't take care of himself—you say. That's a pity. My old Master he done me justice—he knowed what I was."

"Sinners turn why will ye die. God your maker asks you why?"[8] sung Dick as he carefully rolled up the bill I had given him—and placed it in his pocket book. He bowed and scraped his foot punctiliously; by way of thanks.

"Missy! Is all that foolishness to begin agin. And sitch a solemn warning as the Lord sent you.

6. "Braes of Balquedder" is a traditional Scottish song. For "Banks and braes of Bonny doon," see chap. 15, n. 3.

7. Isaac Watts (1674–1748), Hymn 88, "Life Is the Time to Serve the Lord," lines 3–4, in *The Works of the Reverend and Learned Isaac Watts* (London, 1810).

8. Hymn by Charles Wesley cited in Katharine Smith Diehl, *Hymns and Tunes: An Index* (New York, 1966).

"I was glad you and yo ma would n't see any body, but they laid it all to your airs. I've wrestled for you many a time—and you gwine on. For says that Holy Volume, 'For every idle word I will hold you in Judgment.'"[9]

This was too bad. I had come out for wool, but it seemed that I was going back shorn. The worst was still to come.

"This is the Land of Sodden and Tomorrow.[10] But my day is done—with this weakness in my head—and this misery in my side.

"I tole your ma—I would never lift a finger agin for you childen—I am ole an porely. I will never lif my house. I am done."

Such a look I gave him then. It was filled to the brim with disgust and disappointment.

"Well then! What you come here giving me money for—as if you could not trust old Dick! You hurted me. You have a heap to larn yet. Is it the one we travelled with? He pays like a lord. I have some of his money yet." I moved off, with all the dignity I could muster, neither looking to the right nor to the left.

"Missy. It's a bad mistake to pay too soon. But you kin make your mind easy."

17

As Weddings Were Fifty Years Ago

Come now, ye damsels, daughters of delight,
Help quickly her to dight:

Now is my love all ready forth to come:
Let all the virgins, therefore well await;
And ye, fresh boys, that tend upon her groom,
Prepare yourselves, for he is coming straight.
Set all your things in seemly good array.
Fit for so joyful day:
The joyfull'st day that ever sun did see.[1]

At that time a church marriage was almost unknown. In the first place the Planters' homes were so far apart, and in the second, so very far from the church. And there was no wedding trip—no honeymoon—so to speak, but

9. Matt. 12:36.
10. Sodom and Gomorrah, Gen. 10:19, 18:20.

1. Edmund Spenser, "Epithalamion," lines 96–97, 110–16.

what could be snatched from a crowd, a gathering of all the families on both sides—and a course of uninterrupted dinner parties and balls.

This bride was married in the old family country seat[2] where her Mother was born and married—and where she had, herself, first seen the light of day.

It was a comfortable country house, large, roomy, airy. It had immense halls, dining rooms and drawing rooms, with chimneys wide enough to warm these rooms in spite of their size, the number of their doors and windows—and their very high ceilings.

In their mode of life there was no wasteful luxury or extravagance; but every comfort known at that time to the wealthy.

The bridegroom furnished his list of friends whom he wished asked to his Wedding. The combined forces—generally made a goodly company.

The Wedding was always at night; and a larger part of the guests remained for several days, to enjoy the Festivities—which were certain to come off on such occasions.

The Chatelaine remarked, that the last marriage—was a tremendous gathering. And the breakfast table stretched from the front door to the back—in that spacious hall, some sixty feet in length.

This was to be a private wedding, and there would not be more than fifty guests staying in the house.

There was a state dinner the day after the wedding. And then a constant succession of balls and parties were given by the bridesmaids in compliment to the bride.

The "Happy Couple" were the centre of a half circle of bridesmaids and groomsmen duly paired—a truly formidable array.

As the clergyman uttered his last word a rush was made and a tumultuous scene of kissing and congratulation ensued. The venerable matrons of the family commended highly this poor little bride's filial piety; when some what blindly she clutched the back of her sole surviving parent's chair. As the ceremony proceeded the room had grown more and more unsteady. When it was over, her only available resource failed, for all hands had hold of the bridegroom and were shaking his arms à merci et à miséricorde.[3] So as things continued to wave and rock madly, she seized what came nearest to hand.

After the ceremony came music and dancing—and a mighty supper. I use this word advisedly—for its proportions were gigantic.

If the officiating clergyman was rigidly righteous, "Too strict," they

2. MBC may here be referring to Mount Pleasant, plantation home of Burwell and Mary Boykin, MBC's maternal grandparents. Mount Pleasant was located about seven miles south of Camden.

3. Fr., with mercy and compassion.

waited for him to go away. Sometimes—the too exuberant gayety of the younger portion of the assembly neglected his restraining influence—and danced him away, which was hard, as the best of men like a good supper. This jollity and feasting lasted the Wedding week generally. Truly to under take a bridal festivity at that time—was to stand up to un ouvrage de longue haleine.[4]

Fortunately the world is given to attend to its own business—and the bride having been settled for life, she was lost sight of, by the gay crowd soon after the ceremony.

The groomsmen took her to dinner and duly danced with her at all the balls; then hastily returned to their own love affairs; which had not reached so successful a termination.

Practically she was supposed to have retired from the world as completely as if she had taken the veil.

Our bride had no veil. At the last moment it was announced to her that she was not to wear one.

It had been forbidden by one in authority, whose age and right, there was none to dispute.

After that her interest in the ceremony as a tableau was very slight. She was saying to herself under her breath, "A barefaced bride!"

The bridal-present Era had hardly dawned. And yet there was a modest pair of china flower pots, a fan—and a tiny pair of smelling bottles—in a mother of pearl box. The bridegroom's present was a diamond cross.[5]

Madelaine entered.

"Her hair is rumpled. Look at her. Somebody might have seen that her hair was smooth!" she said reproachfully.

"It was that bridal wreath—she pulled it off roughly. It stuck up—in the wrong places; without the veil you know."

With a damp brush every hair was soon plastered down, and the bride's rough brown hair, reduced to a satiny smoothness and blackness.

We wore it then straight, and stiff, down over our cheeks and ears. The effect, as it half covered our faces—was called—"walrus ears." What ever is the fashion will soon cease to be ugly or repulsive. If I have not proved this, my story has been told in vain.

4. Fr., a massive undertaking.

5. Almost certainly James Chesnut's wedding present to Mary. In an undated letter of the early 1880s to Jane Williams, wife of her nephew Miller Williams, she wrote, "I am scraping and saving to have my diamond maltese cross set as a ring—I hereby give it to Serena [Jane's daughter and MBC's grandniece]—If I live I will keep it and give it to her myself when she is old enough. . . . If I drop off—the ring is Serena's—I will tell Mr C—and he wants her to have it" (quoted in *MBC*, 194).

So the poor little bride was gently scolded for not having looked in the glass—and for not showing a proper respect for the opinions of the rest of mankind. Then she was smoothed outwardly, and told "that it was time to go."

The rosebud garden of girls rushed by in a whirlwind—crying, "Come! it is time to go." Madelaine put her arm softly around the bride's waist and she found herself out side. Madelaine flew back to give some final touches to her own toilette. Stranded there the bride leaned upon the railing which surrounded this first landing. Seen from below it had somewhat the effect of Juliet's balcony.[6]

Already the bridesmaids were twittering and fluttering at the foot of the stairs—pinning bridal favors upon their own individual groomsmen. The scene was a very gay one and absorbed them quite.

The Bride left alone looked down, utterly without interest, subdued by the numbness, and deadness of mind and body which always overtook her at the supreme moments of her life. She seemed to hear a roar, as of the sound of many waters, and the echoes of faint far away cries; nearer and nearer they were coming.

A man standing near the gay party below, caught sight of this slim figure in white; he gently pushed aside the crowd who were blocking the stair way.

He sprang up three steps at a time.

She saw him coming, as in a dream, for the sound was still in her ear of that far away voice on the Florida shore.[7] She was calmly watching the white gloved hand, as at each upward bound it grasped the railing.

The End

6. Reference to the famous love scene between Romeo and Juliet in Shakespeare's *Romeo and Juliet*, 2.1.

7. Apparently a reference to Sidney Howard's fortuitous arrival in chapter 7.

THE PUBLICATIONS OF THE SOUTHERN TEXTS SOCIETY